Time, Politics, and Policies

STUDIES IN GOVERNMENT
AND PUBLIC POLICY

Time, Politics, and Policies
A Legislative Year

Burdett A. Loomis

 University Press of Kansas

Published by the University Press of Kansas (Lawrence, Kansas 66049), which was organized by
the Kansas Board of Regents and is operated and funded by Emporia State University, Fort Hays
State University, Kansas State University, Pittsburg State University, the University of Kansas, and
Wichita State University

Library of Congress Cataloging-in-Publication Data

Loomis, Burdett A., 1945—
   Time, politics, and policies : a legislative year / Burdett Loomis.
      p. cm — (Studies in government and public policy)
   Includes index.
   ISBN 0-7006-0622-X (pbk. : alk. paper)
   1. Kansas. Legislature. 2. Legislators—Kansas. 3. Pressure groups—Kansas. 4. Political
planning—Kansas. 5. Kansas—Politics and government—1951– 6. Time—Political
aspects—Kansas. I. Title. II. Series.
JK6867 1988
320.9781—dc20   93-29050

British Library Cataloguing in Publication Data is available.

Printed in the United States of America

10 9 8 7 6 5 4 3

To George A. M. Anderson and Donovan J. Thompson, two men who have demonstrated to me how accomplishment and kindness can and should go together

Contents

Tables and Figures

Preface to the Second Printing

When this book was published in 1994, it made the case that policy outcomes could be understood by placing them within the dual cycles of budget-making and electoral politics. Moreover, I argued that close observation of a single year within a single legislature could provide some general insights across most legislatures for any given year. Six years after the publication of *Time, Politics, and Policies,* I think that both the conceptual framework of cycles and the reliance on an intensive case study have proven valuable to understanding the nature of policymaking and political choices at the state level. Although I must rely on the reports of fellow legislative scholars to judge the relevance of the Kansas experience for other states, I can add to my store of evidence by briefly examining Kansas politics and policymaking over the past decade.

All politics and policymaking place long-term trends and immediate issues within the overlapping cycles of budgets and elections. Especially in the (relatively) prosperous years of the late 1990s, the budget cycle dominated Kansas policy development, from agenda-setting to enactment. Simultaneously, legislators and the governor kept their eyes on the electoral cycles of gubernatorial and legislative elections.

Gov. Joan Finney (1991–1995) never mastered the policy and political cycles in Kansas politics, but her successor, centrist Republican Bill Graves, has demonstrated great understanding of these cycles. In particular, Graves has depended on the politics of the budget cycle to make his mark on Kansas policymaking. Although Graves has proven himself an excellent electoral politician — winning two landslide general election victories as well as warding off a potentially strong challenge within his own party — he has never been an especially strong policy leader. That is, with the modest exception of targeted tax cuts, he has never put forth a set of agenda items that would clearly define the nature of his administration. Rather, he has used the budget to set his agenda, even as he has rarely become heavily involved in day-to-day legislative affairs. Then, in the endgame politics that characterizes the last few days of all legislative sessions, Governor Graves has taken full advantage of his position to broker deals with House and Senate leaders.

What benefited the governor most in this setting was his clear understanding that Kansas politics, especially within the legislature, have become a three-party system. That is, throughout his administration there were roughly equal numbers of moderate Republicans, social conservative Republicans, and Democrats in both chambers. Graves could sit back and wait for these groupings of legislators to develop positions on major issues. Then, working with the centrist Republicans in the legislature, who served as his base, he could negotiate with either the social conservatives or the Democrats, and sometimes with both factions, to construct a governing majority. More often than not, he and his legislative supporters chose to work with Democrats on the most important issues facing the state. Frequently, though not always, the social conservatives found themselves having minimal impact on policy outcomes, even though they had experienced substantial success in legislative elections over the 1990s.

In fact, although it was unclear at the time, the 1989 machinations of the so-called Republican rebels (see chapter 3) offered a superb introduction to Kansas politics of the 1990s. The rebels, led by social conservative David Miller, understood that their 10 to 12 members could hold the balance of power between House Republicans and Democrats on closely divided issues. When Democrats held a substantial number of seats in 1989/90, they found occasional alliances with the rebels to be fruitful, especially on procedural issues. At the same time, House Democrats longed for majority status, which they achieved briefly, in 1991/92.

The 1992 elections returned the Democrats to the minority in the House, where their fortunes continued to slide through the 1990s. From 1995 through 2000, Democrats have held just a bit more than a third of all House seats. Although they have sometimes proved important players in legislative politics, it has been the Republicans who have provided the drama in Kansas politics through the 1990s and into the twenty-first century.

At the center of this drama was former "rebel" David Miller, who gave up his House seat in 1990 to run as the lieutenant governor candidate on a ticket that challenged sitting governor Mike Hayden for reelection. Though this pair—real estate broker Nelson Weigand and Miller—narrowly failed to unseat Hayden from the right in 1990 (see chapter 10), Miller did succeed in winning control of the Kansas Republican Party organization in 1994—at the very time that centrist Bill Graves was winning an overwhelming electoral victory over Democratic representative Jim Slattery. This election defined Kansas politics for the remainder of the 1990s, in that the social conservative Republicans could claim to speak for the party organization, which Graves and his allies studiously ignored over the next four years. Only the 1996 nomination of Kansan Bob Dole as the Republican nominee for president produced even the most grudging of temporary truces (for example, during the GOP convention).

Like Miller, most of the original rebels had left the legislature by the mid-1990s, but the 1992 and 1994 elections brought in 40 or so social conservatives (all Republicans, out of a total of 125 seats) in the House and 12 to 13 in the Senate (of 40 seats). For the remainder of the 1990s, social conservatives would continue to roughly balance the moderates within consistently large Republican majorities.

David Miller was scarcely satisfied, however, with inspiring a large, socially conservative, actively pro-life faction in the Kansas legislature. Nor was he satisfied by winning control of the Kansas Republican Party. Rather, he sought to defeat the highly popular Bill Graves in his 1998 reelection bid. With a strong economy and his use of budgetary-cycle politics to cut a series of session-ending deals with moderate Republicans and (often) Democrats, Graves was even more popular in 1998 than he had been when he first won the governor's office in 1994. Taking no chances and seeing an opportunity to regain control of the party, Graves spent $1.6 million (a Kansas record) in the 1998 gubernatorial primary. He far outspent Miller (who spent $400,000), and not only won a smashing 73 percent to 27 percent victory, but his mobilization of the moderates allowed them to win back control of the party organization.

By the end of the 1990s the social conservatives could look back over the decade and find almost no major substantive victories—despite consistently performing well in legislative (and lower-ballot) races.[1]

What the small band of Republican "rebels" began in 1988/89 never generated major substantive victories. Rather, buoyed by a much stronger economy and a more sure touch as chief executive than Mike Hayden, Gov. Bill Graves put forward few imaginative, large-scale proposals as he consistently cut taxes over the first five years of his administration. He could wait to the end of the legislative session and make his deals because, as a rule, he did not have to convince his allies to go out on much of a limb. He negotiated a large, new highway plan, much in the tradition of Mike Hayden, as he used many of the former governor's tactics to win approval of the statewide program. And he cemented this victory by allowing the Democrats to establish a Children's Trust Fund with the money re-

---

1. See, for example, Allan J. Cigler and Burdett A. Loomis, "Kansas: The Christian Right and the New Mainstream of Republican Politics," in Mark Rozell and Clyde Wilcox, eds., *God at the Grass Roots, 1996: The Christian Right in American Elections* (Lanham, Md.: Rowman & Littlefield, 1997), 207–222, and "After the Flood: The Kansas Christian Right in Retreat," in John C. Green, Mark J. Rozell, and Clyde Wilcox, eds., *Prayer in the Precincts* (Washington, D.C.: Georgetown University Press, 2000), 227–242.

ceived from the state's participation in the nationwide tobacco litigation. Again, extra funds helped smooth the way for Graves in 1999, in contrast to Hayden's choice to fund highways rather than property tax relief.

Still, the cyclical nature of politics—annual budgets and biennial elections—has continued to define politics and policymaking in Kansas. And by inference, these cycles play out in all the fifty states. State resources wax and wane and policy challenges differ, but the regular rhythms of budgets and elections offer regularity (if not order) to the political process. So it was in 1988/89; so it will be for decades to come.

Burdett Loomis
Lawrence, Kansas
September 2000

Preface

This book began with a hazy remembrance from an old photo—that of state legislators (perhaps from Louisiana) physically holding back the hands of their chamber's clock. These lawmakers were engaged in the unsubtle charade of pretending that the allotted time of the session had not run out. Journalists who cover legislatures frequently point out the slow pace of progress during much of the legislative session, only to report on a flood of policies that flow out of the capitol in the last days, even hours, before adjournment.

This book provides a base for the analysis of the nature of time as it relates to the policymaking process. Various time-based concepts have been incorporated into political analysis; scholars have identified any number of cycles that relate to presidents, parties, business, legislators and legislatures, and broad notions of economic development. These cycles have proved intriguing but of little relevance to the day-to-day operations of most politicians and policymakers. The cycles these individuals face are more mundane and far more real. The governor must deal with the budget cycle, the election cycle, and the legislative cycle, for example.

We see this all play out at the national level, as long-term trends are interpreted by policymakers (who are often also strategic politicians) in light of relevant cycles. Thus, Bill Clinton must think through health care reforms in terms of extended spending trends as well as specific legislative, budget, and election cycles. And House members who might well vote for tax increases early in their two-year terms may find them difficult to support closer to the general election. In the end, policy actors often face deadlines that are imposed by cycles (need to approve a new budget) or manipulated by leaders (an early vote during a president's "honeymoon" period).

In short, notions of time and timing are important to the policymaking process, yet we have few ways of thinking systematically about the issues

raised by time-based considerations. This book seeks to provide a basic structure for such thinking. It draws on ideas developed by John Kingdon (on
agenda-setting) and Gary Jacobson and Sam Kernell (on strategic politicians)
to flesh out the time-related tensions in the behaviors between the political
and policy-oriented sides of public decision making.[1]

While Kingdon and Jacobson and Kernell have focused their attention on
national politics and policymaking, mine has been turned to state politics,
particularly the politics of Kansas. I wanted to examine the entire range of
state politics and policies over the course of one calendar year.

What did I get for my intense focus on one state? I learned a great deal
about Kansas politics and acquired a depth of knowledge that allowed me
to reach firm conclusions about how policies are made. Second and more
important, because of my tighter focus I could observe the political and
policymaking processes with some hope of obtaining an inclusive perspective. This broad view was crucial, because links between apparently unrelated
policies, actors, and political considerations often proved central to understanding how decisions were made.

This said, I did not strive to make this an "inside baseball" account of Kansas politics in 1988/89; to do so would have narrowed my focus far too much.
Such an arcane approach might have satisfied a handful of Topeka insiders,
but it would have been of little general use. Nor did I undertake much
personality-based analysis, even though many Kansas observers have commented that no complete understanding of the politics of this era is possible
without taking into consideration Gov. Mike Hayden's difficulty in adapting
his behavior or "rebel" Republican Rep. Kerry Patrick's visceral dislike of
many in his party's establishment.

This book has three major audiences: those generally interested in the
policymaking process; those interested in state politics and policymaking,
especially legislative scholars; and those interested in Kansas politics and
government. Probably none of these audiences will be completely satisfied,
but that may be inherent in the nature of this project. My aim is simply to
provide all readers with an enhanced appreciation of how "political time"
operates, a well-developed sense of contemporary politics and policymaking
at the state level, and a set of well-founded explanations of how the historic
1988/89 year of policymaking unfolded in Kansas.

A BRIEF NOTE ON METHOD

The information upon which my narrative is based came from a number of
sources. I conducted about fifty formal interviews with key participants, including Gov. Mike Hayden and various lobbyists and staffers. I surveyed

all members of the legislature and a substantial number of lobbyists in my attempts to pin down the state's policy agenda. I read through a year's worth of relevant articles from sixteen daily newspapers as I patched together the policymaking process on numerous issues. And I conducted running conversations with a substantial number of legislators, bureaucrats, staffers, and journalists as I hung around the legislature between December 1988 and May 1989.

Although I did do some "soaking and poking," to borrow, once again, Fenno's well-used phrase, much of my information came from extended conversations with twenty or so capitol figures. Sometimes these conversations occurred in several short segments during one day, and sometimes they were resumed only after a couple weeks had passed. The important thing was that our discussions were cumulative. As I learned more and more about the process and specific pieces of legislation, I was able to resume a conversation at a more sophisticated level. Because of my wide range of sources, I occasionally came to know more than some of the participants about what was transpiring. From time to time, then, I became a participant, although I never, to my knowledge, disclosed any confidential information. Very quickly I began to identify with the statehouse journalists with whom I shared working space and gossip. But as an academic I could ask legislators and lobbyists questions that they might not have answered had I been a journalist, since they knew they would not see their words in the next morning's newspaper.

Most of the quotations in this book are derived from ongoing conversations, public statements that I personally heard, formal interviews, and the public record (mostly newspaper stories). I have footnoted the latter two sources; all unfootnoted quotations come from informal conversations or public statements (on occasion, my versions differ slightly from published sources). In a very few instances I have footnoted quotations from sources who wished to remain unidentified. I have kept these unattributed quotations to a minimum, but they are often central to my argument or to understanding a particular decision.

Trying to construct a coherent narrative from this confused process has proven a daunting task. Indeed, I have developed a healthy respect for those who write narratives of any kind. Even using the apparently straightforward strategy of exploring events over the course of a calendar year — a common approach for many narratives — I found producing a comprehensible picture a difficult undertaking.

At the same time, I have greatly enjoyed myself over the course of this research. The extended conversations were simply fascinating. For me, the dual role of participant and observer was exhilarating and demanding. As a sometime student of political careers, I was extremely interested in how participants viewed the emerging politics and policies of an exceptional year in the history of Kansas. Their views of their own futures, and of the state's, came together with the end of the session. There was tremendous uncertainty throughout the session, and resolution came only when all the actors looked up to the voting board to see if a key proposal had passed. In the House, at least, no one knew how close votes were going to turn out. There were few good counts, so we all waited to see what the electronic voting board had to say. This waiting was one of many shared experiences for all of us who labored in the statehouse vineyards.

ACKNOWLEDGMENTS

A lot of people helped me with this project. Some have chosen to remain anonymous. Others I fear I have overlooked, given the large number of useful, relevant conversations I've had over the past five years.

My greatest debt goes to the legislative and executive policymakers in the state of Kansas who gave me many hours of their time. In particular, House Speaker Jim Braden and Senate President Bud Burke provided me with press credentials so I could hang around on the floor in both chambers. Nothing was more valuable than this incredible, continuous access to legislators, executive staff, and the statehouse reporting corps.

Sen. Wint Winter, Jr., found ways to sneak me into various closed meetings; I am most grateful. Former students Rep. J. C. Long and Rep. (now Senator) Bill Brady often provided insightful observations, as did Rep. John Solbach from Lawrence. Key staff members Chris Beal and Tom Laing were patient in educating me in the arcane ways of House party leadership. And Michael O'Keefe did his best to explain state budgeting to me. Dozens of other legislators, administration officials, lobbyists, and journalists contributed greatly to my education in the nuances of Kansas politics.

I am especially indebted to those who read earlier versions of this manuscript, including Jeff Cohen, Russ Getter, Paul Light, Jim Maag, Sue Peterson, Tom Sloan, and Bill Wolff. Their comments and insights have greatly improved this work. Even more am I in the debt of John Hanna and Alissa Rubin. A former student of mine, John is now a veteran Associated Press reporter in Topeka. Throughout this project I have talked with him about Kansas politics, personalities, and policies. He delights in the state's politics, and his insights have helped me a lot. Alissa, whom I met in Topeka during the 1988/89 year, has proven a wonderful critic, supporter, sounding board, and friend. Her contributions, both as a reporter and reader of the manuscript, have made this a better book. For whatever shortcomings that remain I take full responsibility.

At the University Press of Kansas, Fred Woodward has been an enthusiastic supporter, and Carol Estes and Susan McRory have provided skillful, helpful editorial assistance. My thanks.

My family—Michel and Dakota—provided the support and space that allowed me to spend a hectic, delightful year in the Kansas statehouse—not everyone's idea of fun, but certainly mine.

1

Introduction: The Beginning
of Political Time

It was just after 11 P.M., May 1, 1988, and the Kansas House of Representatives was lurching toward its final adjournment, much as state legislatures have traditionally raced the clock to complete their end-of-session business. There had been a rush of compromises and deals that produced both long-awaited legislation and shattered hopes. Exhausted lawmakers were more than ready to drag themselves home after almost a hundred days of work and play. The final piece of the legislative puzzle—a modest income tax cut, part of a gubernatorial campaign promise in 1986—was about to be approved. The finish line was in sight.

Enter Republican Rep. Kerry Patrick, who objected to the tax bill. Obtaining recognition, he approached the microphone in the well of the House, toting some notes and a bag of powdered sugar donuts. Awaiting him on the House floor was a cart filled with federal tax code volumes, his ammunition for the next few hours. At the very end of the 1988 legislative session, Patrick began a filibuster, the first such effort recorded in Kansas legislative history. He harbored few hopes of obtaining a larger tax break for his affluent Johnson County (suburban Kansas City) constituents. He recognized that he would make no friends nor exert any positive influence among his 124 colleagues. Rather, he wanted to make a statement, that the issue at hand—the return of the so-called windfall resulting from the 1986 federal tax reforms—would not die with the end of the 1988 session.

Often a thorn in his colleagues' sides, Patrick began to cite relevant portions of the tax code.[1] With no cloture provisions in the legislature's rules, leaders were powerless to halt his monologue. Worse yet, Patrick was amusing, at least to himself. "It was enjoyable," he noted. "I was funny that night. I'm not always, but that night I was."[2] With temperatures rising on all sides—among Republicans and Democrats, leaders and the rank and file—Patrick

1

finally relinquished the floor after three and a half frustrating hours. He had proved no match for Strom Thurmond's U.S. Senate marathon of more than twenty-four hours, but coming as his filibuster did, when exhaustion had set in and tempers had grown short, it burnished his substantial reputation as a maverick and irritant. Indeed, two years earlier his Senate colleagues had offered his name for consideration as "state reptile," in a more than half-serious April Fool's Day joke.[3]

However headstrong and futile, Patrick's filibuster had some real purpose, in that it grew out of legitimate frustrations with the legislative process. The Senate had reworked the original House-passed tax bill, and leaders in the House had denied their colleagues any substantial debate or chance to amend the proposal. In the session's final hours the House could only vote up or down on a conference committee report.

For Patrick and a few other Republican legislators, the income tax episode and the filibuster demonstrated that they could not work with the Republican leadership or Mike Hayden, the Republican governor. Although the filibuster was an impetuous act, it did not come without forethought. Patrick noted that "the filibuster was a seminal event. . . . I had the tax codes rolled in and started doing hypotheticals. It was crystallized over lunch that day, [although] I'd thought about it for a couple weeks. I told [the Speaker] I was going to do it, and I've always done what I'd told those guys I'd do."[4]

The filibuster had virtually no policy effects in the waning hours of the 1988 session, but it was the first salvo in a year-long battle between Republican Speaker Jim Braden and his back-bench colleague. Even before the final gavel had brought the 1988 legislature to an end, battle lines were forming for the session that would begin the next January. Other legislators would neither forget the filibuster nor forgive Patrick for his breach of etiquette. Likewise, Patrick and his allies would seek to affect both policies and process by frequently joining with Democrats in 1989 to frustrate the nominal Republican majority. The filibuster battle of May 1988 might have ended, but the legislative war between Republican factions was just beginning.

A YEAR IN POLITICAL TIME

This book is about politics and policymaking in the year that stretched from the adjournment of the 1988 Kansas legislature to the final moments of the 1989 session. In one sense, it is a story that features Rep. Kerry Patrick, House Speaker Jim Braden, Gov. Mike Hayden, and dozens of other major players in the annual drama of the policy process as it is played out in a single statehouse for a single year. The session-ending filibuster is a convenient starting point, and one that fits with the focus on one legislative cycle, but the politics of 1988/89 were shaped by many other events, trends, and cycles that offered up the specific mix of issues, demands, and actors that paraded across the Kansas stage.

To wit, a massive highway construction package would rise to the top of the state's policy agenda in 1988/89. Although no significant highway legislation was proposed in 1988, the governor was ready to make a major effort in the next session, and a host of interest groups were set to do his bidding. This was an issue with a lot of history, including decades of complaints by southeast Kansans that their roads were inadequate. And the governor had called a special session of the legislature in August 1987, only to have it disintegrate before his very eyes; this absence of legislative action had proved a major defeat in both policy and political terms for Mike Hayden, only eight months into his four-year term.

On another front, although for the rest of the country reapportionment would come after the 1990 federal census, for the Kansas House reapportionment was on the agenda for 1989. The 1990 elections would be contested in the wake of a special 1988 count, the vestigial remains of the Kansas Agricultural Census, the traditional basis for the drawing of legislative districts.

A few blocks from the legislature, Federal District Judge Richard Rogers was busy setting one part of the policy agenda for 1988/89. In responding to a decade-old lawsuit, he ruled that Kansas must guarantee basic civil liberties to its prison inmates.[5] This order would translate into requirements that the state either release substantial numbers of prisoners or build new prison space in the immediate future. Failing those two alternatives, Rogers could turn over Kansas prison policy to a special master, who might well mandate major changes in the state's corrections system.

On the second floor of the statehouse, Governor Hayden was planning to reintroduce death penalty legislation, as the Senate had previously kept him from fulfilling his campaign promise to reinstate capital punishment. Absent the governor's initiative, the legislature would not seriously consider this issue, and few Kansans expressed much interest in the subject. Like presidents, however, governors can move their favored issues onto the agenda, and Hayden was committed to forcing a vote on restoring the death penalty in Kansas. It had been last used in 1965, the same year the state executed Richard Hitchcock and Perry Smith, the murderers who gained notoriety in Truman Capote's *In Cold Blood*.

In addition, the governor recognized that in two years he would be up for reelection and that his record, as of May 1988, scarcely reflected a string of major successes. The next twelve months, he and his advisors reasoned, would be crucial in determining his strength as a candidate in 1990.

Down the street from the statehouse, party activists were seeking to recruit candidates for the upcoming 1988 elections, the last to be held before reapportionment. Democrats sniffed an opportunity to take control of at least one chamber, if they could only unearth worthy challengers. Republicans, conversely, thought they could hold on, but found recruitment difficult, in that Sen. Bob Dole had withdrawn from the race for the Republican presidential nomination. A Dole candidacy would have encouraged increased numbers of talented GOP candidates to enter the fray. Even though Kansas is solidly Republican, without Dole at the top of the ticket, it would not produce the overwhelming landslide that might help elect a few extra GOP lawmakers.[6]

Though other starting points abound for looking at a host of policies and political conflicts, this book will be directed at the 1988/89 year — not because it was especially interesting or important (although by chance it was both), but because examining a single year, a single legislative cycle, can provide any number of insights into the policymaking process in general and how time and timing relate to this process in particular.

The stories that detail what happened in Kansas in 1988/89, while providing the raw material for this study, are not particularly significant unless they illustrate general points. William Muir's *Legislature* has become a classic study of the state legislature not because it teaches us so much about California in the mid-1970s, but because Muir draws general, if idealized, implications about the nature of the legislative process.[7] The goal here is to use a single year's politics and policymaking, in a single state, to raise some questions and illustrate some broad notions about how time and timing influence both process and outcomes and how relevant actors pursue, in tandem, political and policy goals as they react to temporal limitations and seek to manipulate time as a resource.

ONE STATE, ONE YEAR

Examining policymaking for one year, in one medium-sized state, has two particular virtues, aside from the dubious value of allowing readers to become distressingly familiar with the politics and politicians of the Sunflower State. First, the study can be comprehensive. That is, one can obtain a reasonably good grasp of the entire context of politics and policymaking; not only are the major actors identifiable, but the issues are relatively clear. Trying to examine the federal government, or even that of California or New York, with such comprehensiveness would be difficult and perhaps impossible. In a smaller state, however, one can understand most of what is going on, especially if one has patience and access. In 1988/89 I had plenty of both, as I hung around the legislature throughout the spring with press credentials, which allowed me continuous access to the floors of both chambers.

While the legislature is in session, everything filters through these venues.[8] Also in Kansas, as in most smaller states, everyone seems to know everyone else, often since childhood. Fraternity brothers and sorority sisters serve in the legislature together. Former high school opponents in debate and football become legislative allies. Previous 4-H friendships are reborn in Topeka. Once one is plugged into these "friends and neighbors" networks, one can comprehend the subtexts of debates and disputes.[9] All in all, the ability to view small-state politics comprehensively, rather than looking at only a few policies or a single institution, is of great value.

Second, most states go through their budgetary and legislative cycles annually. Although this is the study of a single year, it does reflect many of the rhythms that are repeated, with variations, year in, year out, in state after state. Although a handful of states harbor professional legislatures with full-time legislators, most don't.[10] Most legislative cycles look a lot like the one described here.

In the end, the strengths of comprehensiveness and the typicality of the legislative cycle must be weighed against limits of studying one state for one year.

THE PLAN OF THE BOOK

The next chapter will present an integrated set of perspectives on the nature of political time. After reviewing various ways in which time has been conceptualized in political analysis, the discussion will concentrate on three basic components of political time: trends, cycles, and deadlines.

The following three chapters (3–5) will focus on how the political actors were cast in 1988 and began to draw up the script for the 1989 legislative session. Candidate selection and primary and general elections dominate this section, as prospective and actual officeholders face very clear deadlines and must make a host of timing decisions. Concurrent with the electoral process, however, lawmakers, the governor, administrators, journalists, and interest group representatives seek to set the state's policy agenda through interim legislative committee activity, the budget process, and the public discussion of key issues. Subsequently, the analysis turns to the postelection period in which the legislative leadership is selected, the legislature's rules are set, and the governor's proposals are initially presented. All actors are in their place, ready to act on the state's policy agenda.

The book's second major section consists of several related case studies of the central policy decisions made by the 1989 legislature. These stories emphasize how political time affects the context and results of policymaking. Chapter 6 focuses on the governor's choice to force votes on income tax cuts and restoration of the death penalty early in the process, rather than allowing them to become part of the end-of-session logjam. The next chapter uses several policy decisions to allow for a discussion of the normal flow of issues through the legislative process. In an ordinary year, these items — school finance, reapportionment, higher education funding, and tort reform — would constitute the most important issues on the agenda, yet in 1989 these issues were all settled before the legislature's final days.

Chapters 8 and 9 paint a detailed picture of the "endgames" played at the conclusion of the legislative session. The passage of a massive highway construction package is treated first. The highway issue brought together the central policy and political pressures within the state. A well-funded, well-orchestrated lobbying campaign combined with the governor's great, even desperate, need for a policy success rendered highways the key issue for the four years of the Hayden administration. In this one issue, the components of political time — trends, cycles, and deadlines — are integrated to help explain why policymakers agreed to a highway spending package that was larger than even its most enthusiastic advocates could have predicted.

The second endgame chapter weaves together several apparently unrelated policy issues that were decided in the last few hours, even minutes, of the legislative session. With agreement reached on a highway package, with a potential reapportionment impasse out of the way, the legislators could address discretionary issues like reforming campaign finance and funding a state water plan, as well as the unwanted responsibilities of building a new prison. It is in this chapter that the ability to examine comprehensively one state's policy process becomes the most useful. In the waning moments of a legislative session, endgame decisions are made on disparate issues with mixed political and policy implications, all under tremendous time pressures.

Chapter 10, the first of two concluding chapters, considers Kansas' 1988/89 policymaking from a distance of several years' experience with the most significant decisions. For example, one key issue that was avoided in 1988/89 — ameliorating the effects of property tax changes — came back to help defeat Gov. Mike Hayden in the 1990 election. Also, the legislature's extensive spending commitments in 1989 have contributed to subsequent fiscal stress and calls for increased taxation. The final chapter assesses the usefulness of conceptualizing "political time" as a set of independent variables in analyzing policy decisions and the behavior of political elites. In the end, considerations of time and timing cannot completely explain key policy decisions. The question becomes, rather, how can we take time-related elements into account in useful, systematic ways?

2

The Nature of Political Time

In political life, a sense of time is always present. Presidents seek to act swiftly on some occasions and labor to show patience on others. Judges issue injunctions effective immediately in many instances and allow continuances on other cases that stretch out interminably. Senators filibuster endlessly and then act, often unanimously, with unanticipated speed.

The best politicians possess a well-honed sense of time and timing, but such talent often seems instinctive, not studied. For all the scholarship that uses time, explicitly or implicitly, as a key element of its explanation, there is very little well-developed theory on how time operates to affect political decision making and policy outcomes.

Political time differs from ordinary approaches to time in that it is not linear.[1] Rather, much of political time revolves around deadlines that force action. Filing deadlines, the end of legislative sessions, budget deadlines, and fixed electoral dates, among many others, structure the actions of politicians and policymakers. The ability of a chief executive to set the policy agenda in his or her first year in office differs substantially from the impact of a similar set of fourth-year proposals from a lame duck.[2]

Various other approaches to policy development have emphasized the utility of taking time into account in considering policy choices. Neustadt and May focus on historical cases as teaching devices for contemporary decision makers, while Smith examines the implications of various time horizons in the context of social and economic policymaking.[3]

Turning to specific political institutions, numerous scholars have begun to examine the implications of time within the contemporary Congress; in particular, Bruce Oppenheimer has employed a time-based framework to pull together much of the growing body of work on legislative structure and procedure.[4] A related vein of research emphasizes sequence as central to understanding committee power.[5] Lawrence Dodd and Richard Fenno,[6] among many other students of legislative careers, have recently broached complementary, though distinct, cyclical approaches to understanding congressional career development.

Likewise, time and timing play central roles in many scholarly approaches to the presidency. Paul Light finds time a key resource and important constraint as chief executives proceed through their terms of office.[7] Bert Rockman views the presidency through the lenses of constants, cycles, and contemporary trends—all time-based notions.[8]

More generally, policymaking is often depicted as a cycle of agenda-setting, formulation, adoption, implementation, and evaluation.[9] And cycles play major roles in many theories of electoral politics. What is missing is a comprehensive perspective on how time affects the contexts, processes, and outcomes of the policymaking process. As long as our focus is at the national level—with its scope and complexity—the notion of time must be painted in either the broad brushstrokes of long-term cycles or trends or the more specific contexts of budgetary or legislative sequence.

Although any number of perspectives, such as labor negotiations or the psychology of procrastination, might well be relevant to understanding the linkages between time, politics, and policymaking, two particular political science frameworks inform much of this work. These are Gary Jacobson and Samuel Kernell's organizing concept of "strategic politicians" and John Kingdon's model of agenda-setting, alternative development, and policymaking.[10]

Strategic politicians are by definition concerned with the long-term impacts of their actions, especially as they affect the ways in which their careers play out. Jacobson and Kernell view politicians as entrepreneurial actors who "pursue long-term investment strategies" as they forge their political careers.[11] Although they focus most of their attention on politicians as candidates, the same kinds of calculations affect how officeholders view the selection of agenda items, the construction of a budget, and the choice of which substantive alternatives to support during the heat of a legislative session. In reality, much of the thinking of these politicians is *tactical* rather than strategic. As Jacobson and Kernell note, "key actors . . . systematically anticipate the perceived effects of short-term electoral forces."[12] In Kansas, Governor Hayden would sometimes expect the voters to exact retribution at the polls against his opponents, while in other circumstances he would argue that "people have short memories" and that policy victories would wipe out the electorate's perception of him as an ineffective leader. However inconsistent, Hayden was always thinking in terms of the impacts of current decisions on future actions (often of the electorate).

The time horizons of strategic politicians are structured to an extent by long-term trends, but more often cycles and deadlines are the lenses for their visions. The date of the next election, the filing deadline, the upcoming reapportionment all offer focal points for strategic thinking. At any time, however, fate may force the strategic politician's hand, as occurs when a party leadership position unexpectedly opens up, whether in the wake of Speaker Jim Wright's 1989 resignation in Washington or the 1988 electoral defeat of Rep. Joe Knopp, the House majority leader from Manhattan (Kansas). In short, Jacobson and Kernell sensibly remind us that politicians continually think in the time-based terms of careers and causality — hardly a revelation, but almost impossible to overemphasize. Without a doubt, all of the actors who populate these pages think strategically in terms of their own political careers and their own related policy preferences. This observation is merely a starting point, however, because strategic political and policy thinking will often imply different courses of actions.

Nevertheless, the "policy entrepreneurs" of John Kingdon's agenda-setting research are continually looking for linkages between the politics and policymaking. Likewise, his longitudinal research design explicitly emphasizes time-based concepts such as the persistence of many policy entrepreneurs and the opening of a "window of opportunity"[13] for action. In fact, many of these windows are predictable, in that they open when legislation expires or sunset provisions require reauthorization. Just as some cycles (such as program reauthorization) may demand action, other cycles (such as annual appropriations) may invite it. The differences are subtle but real, and strategic politicians must continually calculate their responses.

More generally the "policy entrepreneur" and "strategic politician" roles often create great tensions for elected officials. Even the most skillful career politicians can encounter great difficulties in maintaining an appropriate balance. Lyndon Johnson, for example, found it impossible to run for reelection while continuing to prosecute the war in Vietnam.

TRENDS, CYCLES, AND DEADLINES: ELEMENTS OF POLITICAL TIME

In day-to-day life, time proceeds in regular and even ways — twenty-four hours to a day, 365 days to a year. Indeed, time can be divided with extreme precision to billionths of seconds. But time is not just the orderly progression of hours and days. There are long-term trends, such as aging, in which we move slowly in a predictable, linear way.[14] We also experience various cycles, ranging from the four seasons to the increasingly unnatural rhythm of sports (the NBA in June?). In addition, we face countless deadlines, such as paying the mortgage or finishing up our Christmas shopping. On occasion, we may use time strategically, as with selecting the credit card that will provide the longest "float" before charges come due. And who has not postponed making a painful decision, hoping that the need to choose may somehow disappear?

All in all, however, for most of us time stretches out, one day at a time, in a life to be lived in an orderly manner. But for political actors, time is a commodity to be used, to be husbanded, to be dealt with, in one fashion or another. In political life, two weeks can stretch out forever, and a year can be a lifetime. Within the policymaking process, time is significant in at least three overlapping ways. First, time becomes important within *long-term trends* that serve as one key contextual element of decision making. For example, population shifts in either state or nation change the nature of representation over time; the aging of the population requires that certain problems be addressed; immigration patterns lead to different considerations; and so on, with an endless series of societal trends.

Second, much of political time is caught up in *cycles*, both regular and irregular and of differing lengths. The prototypical cycle remains that of the budgetary process, and electoral cycles are central to all politicians' calculations.[15] Important too are policy cycles—inherent in program reauthorization or sunset provisions, for example—and the implications of business cycles. In addition, scholars have also noted cyclical elements of executive leadership, especially for the president.[16] Of particular significance is how various cycles interact. An electoral cycle may suggest one set of policies to a governor, while budgetary considerations dictate an alternate course. Indeed, this continuing tension between politics and policymaking is central to time-based analysis.

Finally, political time can be viewed as a *series of deadlines*. Nothing so defines politics and policymaking as deadlines. Most state legislatures can only meet for a limited number of days—often 90 or 120; filing deadlines, primaries, and general elections give formal shape to campaigns. The conventional wisdom is that had Hubert Humphrey been able to postpone the 1968 election for a week he would have won.[17] But the first Tuesday after the first Monday appeared just as the calendar said it would, and Richard Nixon held on. Many deadlines are not immutable, of course. Executives, legislative leaders, and judges can frequently manipulate time limits; that is one of their most notable powers. At other times, policymakers may desire to be held to deadlines as they seek to deflect responsibility for unpopular actions. Finally, time may become more valuable the longer the legislative process runs. Two weeks at the beginning of the session may be worth less than two hours near the end.[18]

Secular Trends: The River of Policymaking

Many of the most significant defining time-based elements in the policymaking process are among those least open to change. These are the powerful, long-term trends that must be confronted, such as population growth and composition, economic transitions, partisan realignment and dealignment, and technological developments. These have been explored at length elsewhere; perhaps the most important general set of policy-related developments are reflected in Lowi's "end of liberalism" arguments. The proliferation of interests and their related claims affect the entire policymaking process, certainly at the national level and increasingly in state capitals.[19]

Still, what lies at the heart of many policymaking activities is how trends are interpreted by key actors, ranging from the governor to the press. As John Kingdon notes, many trends present themselves in terms of "conditions" that are generally accepted as policy and/or political facts of life; only when relevant actors define them as "problems" will these conditions be considered for policy agenda status.[20] For example, the United States tolerated substantial and growing breaches of its immigration laws during the 1960s and 1970s. Only when various policy entrepreneurs and groups depicted the results of this immigration—large numbers of undocumented workers—as a problem did the Congress begin to address the issue in a systematic fashion.

In some instances, there is considerable ambiguity in distinguishing between trends and cycles. Social scientists, given their desire to build models and find regularities, often opt for cyclical interpretations if the data open the door even a crack. In particular, how to depict partisan changes over time is a vexing question. A generation ago, party realignment was generally viewed as a cyclical phenomenon in the United States, given the relative regularity of partisan eras from the early 1800s on. From the vantage point of 1992, however, partisan change since the 1930s looks at least as much like a set of extended, related secular dealigning developments as any kind of conventional realignment.[21]

Embedded in the idea of long-term trends is the possibility that policymakers will come to think about the present in terms of the past. Neustadt and May argue that thinking in time as a stream has

> three components. One is recognition that the future has no place to come from but the past, hence the past has predictive value. . . . [Second], what matters . . . is departures from the past, alterations, changes, which prospectively or actually divert familiar flows from accustomed channels. . . . A third component is continuous comparison, an almost constant oscillation from present to future and back, heedful of prospective change, concerned to expedite, limit, guide, counter, or accept it as the fruits of such comparison suggest.[22]

Although these authors are offering prescriptions for policymakers, the image of time as a stream also proves useful for scholars, who often employ analogies across time. Even more broadly, Kingdon develops much of his agenda/alternative/policy argument in terms of a series of metaphors such as problem streams, policy soups, and windows of opportunity. In addition, Deborah Stone observes that many long-term trends are articulated as central to "causal stories" that imply specific cause-effect relationships and the need for action.[23] All politicians need good stories to explain their actions; frequently these are cautionary tales that warn us not to make the same mistake we made the last time. All in all, trends require interpretation; rarely, in and of themselves, do they mandate action.

Policies and Cycles

Cycles are central to the structure of political life and to its interpretation. From a structural perspective, the regularities of the budgetary cycle, the decennial census, and the staggered terms of office for elected officials (as well as the life terms for judges and Supreme Court justices) all directly affect how politics and policymaking play out. At the same time, there are other, less well-defined cycles, both long and short, that shape policymaking and political thinking. In addition, many policies themselves are crafted for cyclical consideration, as they come due for reauthorization after five- or seven-year periods.

Interpretations of American politics frequently revolve around these cycles, especially as they imply regularities in the opportunity for presidential influence and the impact of social movements. The Arthur Schlesingers (senior and junior) promote the notions of eight- and thirty-year cycles, respectively; the latter Schlesinger sees cyclical patterns in both the "natural life of humanity" and the "psychology of modernity."[24] His cycles are derived from the continuing interplay between public purpose and private interest.

In their analyses of presidential leadership, Stephen Skowronek and Bert Rockman see long-term cycles as defining the nature of the possibilities for individual chief executives. Skowronek proposes that we view the presidency through the lens of extended, predictable regimes, which come together and disintegrate with substantial regularity. Thus Skowronek argues that "thinking in terms of regime sequence rather than linear national development, one can distinguish many different political contexts for presidential leadership *within* a given historical period."[25]

Rockman draws upon Dodd's congressional cycle analysis in positing four "epochs" of congressional-presidential relations that define the possibilities for executive leadership.[26] Although the Rockman-Dodd "epochs" notion would not meet most criteria for repeating cycles, it does place the actions of political actors in a historical perspective. Still, like the Schlesinger and Skowronek formulations, the epochal concept is best seen in the context of this project as one more set of long-term forces that frame decision making.

Indeed, for this research, long-term cycles, even if they do exist beyond the confines of the scholarly imagination, are not especially significant. As they affect a single year's policymaking, such cycles appear more like aspects of extended trends. Moreover, in state-level actions, long-term cycles may express themselves somewhat differently than they do nationally. For example, legislative reapportionment, while causing some modest dislocation in Congress in 1991/92, will have a much larger potential impact nationally from 1992 on; the states, on the other hand, are most affected during the 1991/92 redrawing of the congressional district boundaries. Similarly, business cycles often have differential impacts at the state and national levels.

Of greater significance in the immediate policymaking context are (1) the overlapping electoral cycles that frame actors' political lives and (2) those cycles (budget, revenue estimates, legislative sessions) that dictate the pace of the policy process. Presidents and governors must operate within the intertwined cycles of electoral and budgetary politics. The two archetypal cycles here are paired in observation of declining presidential support and increasing effectiveness.[27] In a similar vein, Neustadt sees the president as most likely to be effective in his third, fifth, and sixth years.[28] As elections approach, in most instances the opportunities for substantive achievements decline as attention is increasingly focused on questions of reelection or succession.

Legislators' electoral cycles differ, both from those of executives and between representatives and senators. The two-year cycle ostensibly leads to short-term thinking in the House of Representatives, although the overwhelming reelection rate of incumbents has led to increasingly long legislative careers. U.S. senators, while becoming increasingly active fund-raisers throughout their six-year terms, do have the luxury of time to move from electoral concerns to policy (or advancement) considerations. Fenno labels these periods "seasons" in his five-book Senate series on Quayle, Glenn, Specter, Domenici, and Andrews.[29] In addition strategic politicians in both the Congress and state legislatures understand how long it takes to build an effective campaign organization and raise the requisite sums to retain one's current seat, to say nothing of running for higher office.[30] And the policy entrepreneurs who are most persistent are often those who ultimately succeed in taking advantage of an open "policy window."[31]

Intertwined with electoral cycles are those within the policy process.[32] The budget cycle, above all, dictates actions, even when everyone involved would prefer delay and avoidance. The budget process of the 1950s and 1960s, as described by Fenno and Aaron Wildavsky, proceeded in predictable, if not always orderly ways, like an annual dance among legislators, the president, and a host of bureaucrats.[33] At the national level, the patterns of the budgetary dance lost definition as reforms were enacted in the 1970s and became even less ordered in the 1980s, an era of huge deficits and attempts to legislate their limits.[34] Still, the budgetary cycle has remained, even as legislative leaders made ad hoc deals on what adjustments could be made and how these were to be enacted.[35]

Finally, policies may develop within their own internal cycles. Social security "reform," for example, reflects a series of reassurances that the system will remain fiscally sound.[36] More generally, Anthony Downs has sketched an "issue-attention cycle" that offers one means for viewing the rise and decline of the public attention accorded various items on the policy agenda.[37]

In the end, many cycles may affect policymaking, but substantial skepticism seems more than justified in assuming direct, clear connections between cycles, especially those put forward by scholars, and the policy process. Rather, the cycles that may well have the most impact are likely to be those mandated by the Constitution (congressional terms), by statute (budget timetables), and by custom and private agreement (many party nomination practices). And that impact often comes with the deadlines these cycles impose upon how policymaking and politics play out, day to day, year to year.

Deadlines

Although trends and cycles affect policymaking in profound ways, frequently their effects are indirect and difficult to specify. Not so with deadlines, which come directly and continually into play. Deadlines affect the policymaking process in at least three distinct, if related, ways. First, many deadlines are imposed by constitutional and legal structures; although such rules of the games are susceptible to change and even manipulation, in the short run they are regarded as fixed by virtually all the relevant actors.

A second set of deadlines reflects institutional practices; the executive and the legislature set many of their own time limits internally. Internal budget deadlines and legislative process strictures provide frameworks for all involved.

Finally, there are strategic and tactical time constraints imposed by those who control the commanding heights of the political process: chief executives, legislative leaders, and judges. For example, in confronting Iraq's Saddam Hussein, President Bush consistently set his own deadlines for compliance with various demands. Although the United Nations officially laid down many of the time limits, Bush effectively controlled how they played out in policy terms.

Perhaps more than any other key policymakers, legislative leaders feel the effects of deadlines. They are increasingly squeezed—in both the Congress and state legislatures—by time limitations. For example, Connor and Oppenheimer conclude that "the tremendous growth in the legislative workload and the corresponding time constraints that have been placed on the House of Representatives have led to a sacrifice of the deliberative functioning of the House floor."[38] Likewise, most state legislatures experience incredible logjams at the end of their short, constitutionally mandated sessions.

We should not infer that the decline of floor deliberation in the Congress and the existence of session-ending scrambles in state legislatures meet with disapproval from legislative leaders. Rather, leaders routinely use time constraints to their advantage in ordering the flow of legislation onto the floor. These powers are especially important in the states, where constitutions, statutes, and norms together produce severe limits on the length of sessions. U.S. senators may grow accustomed to (if less tolerant of) filibusters, but when Rep. Kerry Patrick captured the floor of the Kansas House and began his 1988 end-of-session filibuster, his fellow lawmakers reacted very harshly. It was not in the province of a rank-and-file member to extend the session, even for a few hours.

Still, deadlines do constrain all legislators, even leaders, and executives must submit budgets on time (or at least roughly so), while facing the limits of the legislative schedule. At the same time, chief executives can act tactically to force responses from other policy actors. They may set deadlines in asking for information, drafts, proposals, and so forth. Such requests may be ignored, but most are complied with. In fact, short-term deadlines seem to drive the internal workings of the presidency; one might hypothesize that the more the president can control compliance with these deadlines, the more likely he will be to succeed.

Also of interest are those situations in which policymakers from one branch set deadlines that affect their counterparts in other branches. Whether imposed from the outside or adopted by insiders, deadlines shape the policy process; among other things, the number of players often drops sharply. A dramatic example of this came in the Congress's 1986 conference committee negotiations over the Tax Reform Act, when Ways and Means Chair Rostenkowski and Finance Chair Packwood eventually sat down to work out privately the final differences in the two chambers' bills.[39]

In the end, deadlines force action and tend to concentrate power. In an environment populated by growing numbers of increasingly sophisticated interests, forcing decisions is one antidote to endless study and delay. However, simply observing that deadlines may prompt action (or avoidance) is less interesting or important than analyzing how policymakers use deadlines to further their own political and policy goals while satisfying the constitutional and statutory rules under which they labor.

POLITICAL ENTREPRENEURS, STRATEGIC POLITICIANS, AND POLITICAL TIME

In every policymaking setting, the three elements of political time — trends, cycles, and deadlines — come together to forge a unique situation.[40] No matter how many legislative sessions Sam Rayburn had gone through, he was faced with a new set of conditions in 1961: a Democratic president young enough to be his son; a recently enhanced Democratic majority in the House, perhaps capable of enacting the remainder of the New Deal agenda; an entrenched and powerful Rules Committee chairman; the increasing pressures of the baby boom generation for educational opportunities; and the surging forces of a civil rights movement, which demonstrated a changing set of national political forces.

In this context, Rayburn's strong proclivity to avoid conflict and build consensus fell before the necessity of confronting Congressman Howard Smith's (D-Va.) hold over the Rules Committee in particular and the strength of the conservative coalition in general.[41] The long-term forces of civil rights and population trends combined with the cycles of policy development and party realignment[42] and the deadlines imposed by organizing the House to produce a titanic battle between Rayburn and Smith. Rayburn approached this fight with great reluctance, yet the convergence of long-term trends, cyclical phenomena, including pressures from a new administration, and the requirements of congressional deadlines in organizing the 87th Congress led to his successful attempt to reduce Judge Smith's power as Rules Committee chair.

Most decisions are not as dramatic as the 1961 expansion of the Rules Committee. Still, the interplay among the elements of political time continually shapes the choices confronting legislators, chief executives, and other actors.

Both policy entrepreneurs and strategic politicians must work within the context of long-term trends, various cycles, and impending deadlines. Some entrepreneurs (a lobbyist or a judge, for example) may have no personal stake in the strategic side of political calculations; some political actors (consultants, for instance) may have little stake in the entrepreneurial concerns for policymaking. Most actors, however, and especially elected officials, have both strategic concerns and policy preferences. They operate simultaneously in entrepreneurial and electorally strategic fashions. Time-based considerations are almost always present and often contradictory.

Specifically, in pushing their favorite programs, the policy entrepreneur must take advantage of windows of opportunity, which open and close in both predictable and random ways. These entrepreneurs are frequently very persistent in their backing of an alternative. For the most part, they focus their attention on the legislative and budget cycles, which provide opportunities and deadlines for action.

Strategic politicians, on the other hand, relate most strongly to overlapping electoral cycles. They think in future-oriented career terms, placing themselves within a prospective institutional context. At the same time, as much as any policy entrepreneur, they must take advantage of opportunities

Figure 2.1. Political Time and Policy/Political Actors

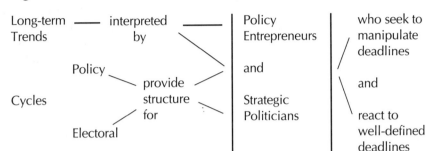

that present themselves on extremely short notice. Their flexibility is enhanced by the fact that they can make a personal political choice much more quickly than entrepreneurs can ordinarily move items through the policy process.

Policy entrepreneurs and strategic politicians (often the same individuals) interpret long-term trends and relate to numerous cycles as they pursue their mix of political and policy goals (see Figure 2.1). It is these individuals who mediate between trends and cycles and the deadlines that force political and policy actions.

Central here is the idea that most policy entrepreneurs, at least in the ranks of the elected, are simultaneously strategic politicians. These identities cannot be untangled, one from the other. And on occasion politicians must make choices between the two roles, as they act in the present with an eye on the future.

POLITICAL TIME IN CONTEXT: KANSAS, 1988/89

This book focuses largely on what happens in the politics and policymaking of one state, Kansas, for a single year, May 1988–May 1989. The time period begins at the end of the 1988 legislative session and ends at the last gavel of the 1989 session. Even more than the budgetary cycle or the fiscal year, the legislative cycle dominates policymaking within Kansas as in most states with part-time legislatures.[43] Thus, although the time and setting here are quite specific, the legislative-based cycle resembles those in many other states.[44]

Likewise, while no single year can be examined in isolation, the discipline imposed by the legislative and budgetary cycles does make one year look very much like the next. The governor makes a speech that helps set the state's agenda. The legislature slowly moves into action, as hearings take place during the day and social events dominate the evenings of the first part of the session. As bills move through committees to the floor, the pace of the session picks up a bit. Finally, in the last few days before adjournment many backbenchers have little to do except vote, as the leaders put together the packages that will constitute the bulk of the legislature's work for the year. Every year has its own idiosyncrasies, but the notion of legislative cycle is generalizable across time as well as among the states.

Trends and Cycles

How policy was made and politics played out in Kansas during 1988/89 derived in large part from long-term trends and assorted cycles that affected the choices available to strategic politicians and policymakers.

Trends. There are no real surprises among the trends affecting Kansas (see Table 2.1). The state's population has risen steadily since 1890, from 1.4 million to 2.5 million, but it has declined just as steadily as a percentage of the U.S. population, from 2.27 percent in 1890 to 1.00 percent a century later. Reflecting this change, Kansas has consistently lost seats in the U.S. House of Representatives (from a high of eight between 1890 and 1930); barely avoiding such a fate in 1980, it was all but preordained that one of the state's five House seats would be lost after the 1990 count. This in turn affected the thinking of the Kansas delegation to the U.S. House as these legislators viewed their options for 1988 and beyond.

More immediately, Kansas House members faced redistricting in the 1988/89 period based upon the results of a special state census—a vestigial remnant of the Kansas Agricultural Census that had historically served as the basis for legislative apportionment. After 1991, the state would use the national census figures, and thus the state senate, not up for election until 1992, did not have to reapportion itself. Nevertheless, historical trends in Kansas population shifts continued as many rural areas experienced sharp declines; of the state's 125 counties, 37 lost more than 10 percent of their population in the 1980/90 decade.[45] With suburban Kansas City (Johnson County) and Wichita gaining population, the 1988 election was viewed as the last time rural areas would be so favorably represented within the legislature. This perception had an impact on a wide range of policies, since rural legislators saw the 1989 and 1990 sessions as their best chances to make deals favorable to their constituents. For example, such perceptions made a real difference in the last-minute compromise over funding the state's water plan.

Like its population changes, the development of two-party competition in Kansas, a traditional bastion of Republican strength, has been gradual but consistent, at least since the 1950s.[46] The governor's office and potentially

Table 2.1.   Long-term Trends in Kansas Politics, 1988/89

- Low population growth (13.6 percent, 1960–1990)
- Population shifts
    West to east
    Rural to urban/suburban (78 percent rural, 1900; 33 percent rural, 1980)
    Aging population (median age, 30.2 in 1980; 32.8 in 1989)
- Growth of two-party competition for governor, state legislature, House of Representatives
- Rising prison populations
- Decline of active railroad track miles
- Large, aging intrastate highway system
- Increasing federal mandates (e.g., Medicaid)
- Decreasing number of farms (135,000 in 1950; 69,000 in 1989)
- Increasing General Fund revenues ($301 million in 1970; $2.24 billion in 1989)
- Declining unemployment (6.3 percent in 1982; 4.0 percent in 1989)

Source: Thelma Helyar, ed., Kansas Statistical Abstract, 1989–90 (Lawrence, Kans.: Institute for Public Policy and Business Research, 1989).

both legislative chambers have moved within the Democrats' grasp. In fact, a series of moderate-to-conservative Democrats have controlled the governorship over much of the past thirty-five years. And in 1990, Democrats would capture the House by a single seat; aside from 1977/78, Democrats had not controlled even one house since 1915. In 1988/89, Republicans had every right to be concerned about the increasingly competitive nature of Kansas politics.

Some specific trends also required the attention of state policymakers. A rising inmate population presented legislators and administration officials with little choice but to release prisoners or build more prisons. As a geographically large state with substantial highway mileage, Kansas needed to confront growing maintenance requirements, to say nothing of building new roads. A declining rail industry also contributed to the need to deal with highway infrastructure issues. In higher education, the state sought to increase funding levels that had fallen behind those of similar states. And the drought in 1988/89 provided evidence that Kansas water policies, which depended heavily on tapping the declining reserves of the Ogallala aquifer, needed substantial revision.

Finally, Kansas, like its sister states, faced the dual trends of increasing numbers of federal mandates and decreasing levels of federal support for many continuing programs. Thus, in 1988/89, Kansas policymakers had to wrestle with requirements for increased funding of welfare and come to terms with standards on underground gasoline storage tanks, among other items placed on the state agenda by federal initiatives.

Cycles. Various cycles defined the nature of Kansas politics and policymaking in 1988/89. These included electoral cycles, legislative organization cycles

Table 2.2.   Cycles in Kansas Politics, 1988/89

• Electoral (date of next election)
    Presidential (1988)
    U.S. Senate (1990, 1992)
    U.S. House (1988)
    Governor (1990)
    State Senate (1992)
    State House (1990)
• Legislative reorganization
    House (biennial)
    Senate (quadrennial)
	• Census
	    State, 1989
	    Federal, 1990
	• Fiscal
	    Budget (annual)
	    Revenue estimates (semiannual)
	• Property tax reassessment
	    1988 and every four years thereafter
	• Depletion of highway maintenance
	    fund

for both houses, two decennial censuses, the cycles of taxing and spending, and at least one policy area (highways) in which a multi-year cycle of funding helped to define the key policy alternatives. These cycles (see Table 2.2) are relatively straightforward; that is, they resemble the cycles in virtually all other states, with the exception of the Kansas census, a holdover from a bygone era.

What roles the cycles play in a given year, however, is not necessarily obvious. For example, the 1988 presidential election would seem to bear only the most modest relationship to state policymaking. But Kansas Sen. Bob Dole was a major competitor for the Republican presidential nomination until his campaign's Waterloo in the Super Tuesday balloting of March 1988. State Republicans held high hopes that Dole would win the nomination; with the senator at the head of the ticket, state party officials expressed confidence that they could recruit a strong set of candidates for both the House and Senate. A successful Dole candidacy also would have generated more enthusiasm and effort in some tight legislative races.

After the 1988 legislative election, Governor Hayden felt great political pressure for a productive legislative session. Even though he did receive credit for the 1989 results, he still had to face the 1989/90 cycle, a period dominated by the property tax issues that would prove his electoral undoing.

More directly, the property tax sequence interacted with the gubernatorial election cycle to affect the candidacy of one strong challenger to incumbent Republican Hayden. Congressman Jim Slattery seriously considered pursuing the 1990 nomination for governor, and observers generally regarded him as the strongest potential Democratic candidate. As Slattery was pondering a challenge, a lengthy process of reappraisal and classification of property was nearing completion. Although it was clear that protests were sure to be mounted, in the summer and early fall of 1989 they had not yet materialized. Only when property tax notices were mailed in November 1989 did the scope of the problem become apparent, and Governor Hayden was the major target of growing outcries. By then Slattery had passed up the opportunity to seek the nomination, leaving the field to other candidates (including State Treasurer Joan Finney, who would win both the Democratic nomination and the governorship). With its annual November notices, the property tax cycle had come too late to provide the cautious congressman with enough timely information that would have prompted him to throw his hat into the ring.[47]

The plethora of political and policy cycles combine in ways that produce almost limitless combinations, even without considering the multiple problems and policy alternatives that rattle around within the "garbage can" of decision making.[48] But trends and cycles do not interact automatically. Rather, specific situations are defined by political actors who interpret and seek to take advantage of the myriad cycles, which may have only limited impact in and of themselves. In the end, however, cycles do structure policy decisions and the choices of strategic politicians. And cycles often impose their own deadlines, which make up the most immediate element of political time.

Deadlines

The day-to-day manifestation of political time does not come with trends or cycles. Rather, it is expressed in a continuing series of deadlines — filing for office, submitting a budget, producing a set of revenue estimates, moving bills out of legislative committee, and so forth. There may be countless reasons for items to appear on the policy agenda (or agendas, as the case may be), but most issues are resolved as they run up against one deadline or another. Further delay is often a possibility, but deadlines force choices that may make explicit the costs on putting off a decision.

In the year following May 1988, Kansas political actors faced the predictable deadlines inherent within the electoral and budgetary cycles and the legislative process as well as various deadlines imposed by strategic politicians who sought particular policy outcomes (see Table 2.3). As with cycles, three major types of deadlines affect state policymaking. First are those that reflect statutory or constitutional requirements, both state and federal. Second, the administration and the legislature set many of their own deadlines, on the budget and in the adoption of rules, for example. Third, key policymakers often establish time limits, ranging from the routine (amount of time provided for legislative debates) to the strategic (prison population goals set by a federal district judge). In addition, key policymakers can make many deadlines contingent, while other deadlines reflect linkage between policies. For example, Governor Hayden threatened not to sign any appropriation bills until the legislature had passed legislation that returned the so-called income tax windfall derived from 1986 federal tax reform. Conversely,

Table 2.3. Selected Deadlines in Kansas Politics and Policymaking, May 1988–May 1989

MAY (1988)	JUNE	JULY	AUGUST
Legislature adjourns (6-day wrap-up session) Governor signs/ vetoes bills Various legislative retirements in anticipation of June filing deadline Lobbyists file spending reports	Filing deadline for legislature Interim legislative committees appointed	$301 million ending balance reported in state General Fund Legislative campaign finance reports due	Primaries held

SEPTEMBER	OCTOBER	NOVEMBER
Prison population limit to be set Census figures released	Judge Rogers' deadline for plan for further prison population limits	Campaign spending reports due General election Revenue estimates reported, $166 million higher than previous estimate Agencies make requests in budget cycle

DECEMBER	JANUARY (1989)	FEBRUARY
Leadership contests, House and Senate Year-end campaign finance reports due Internal budget deadlines	Gov. Hayden sets Feb. 1 deadline for legislature to pass return of income tax "windfall" Budget presented; Gov. Hayden delivers "State of State" message Committees/chairs appointed Rules adopted, both chambers	Hayden pledges not to sign any spending bills until windfall return is passed Judge Rogers calls for end to all prison overcrowding by July 1991

MARCH	APRIL	MAY
Deadlines on bills to pass first house County deadlines for distribution of new appraisal figures	End of regular session (4/4); wrap-up session begins (4/26) Lansing prison population is cut, falls below limit set by Judge Rogers for April 1 Democratic legislators vow no end to session unless reapportionment settled	End of wrap-up session Governor signs/vetoes bills

although no public deadline was ever articulated, House Democrats held that they would refuse to permit action on numerous late-session policy decisions unless a satisfactory reapportionment plan was worked out. Such a plan was adopted, which cleared the way for various important policy initiatives in the session's waning days.

Table 2.3 includes a number of deadlines, but does not come close to detailing all the limits that compose this component of political time. Indeed, many deadlines may never be made public, especially in the last few days of a legislative session. Some are imposed by the governor and top legislative leaders; others may simply arise as the policy endgame is played out in the concluding days of the session.

In the end, political time emerges as a central element of policymaking, even as it appears in multiple forms—in particular, long-term trends, different kinds of cycles, and countless deadlines. Policymakers and politicians must frequently respond to time dimensions while attempting to use deadlines strategically to achieve their goals. The broad rivers of long-term trends combine with the eddies of cycles and flow into the dams of deadlines.

Although most studies of policymaking have focused on national actors and institutions, the implications of political time seem most amenable to sorting out within the states. In such contexts, one can hope to examine virtually all the myriad strands of politics and policymaking. This is especially true when one seeks to examine the relationships between multiple policy arenas and between political and policy considerations. Time pressures may well forge linkages that individual case studies would miss and that broader gauge analysis—especially at the national level—would overlook. Thus, looking at the effects of political time in a single state over the course of a single year may well allow us to analyze how strategic politicians and policy entrepreneurs react to time pressures and seek to manipulate the timing of various actions, all the while employing multiple visions of the future for themselves and their audiences.

3

Casting the Drama:
March–November 1988

As the curtain fell on the 1988 session of the Kansas legislature in early May, the casting was already under way for its next performance, which would commence the following January. All legislative seats — 125 in the House and 40 in the Senate — would be filled in November, and Democrats harbored realistic hopes of reducing the Republican majorities and even winning control of one or both houses. The 1988 election would be the last before redistricting took place in 1989; the long-term urbanization and suburbanization of Kansas had continued during the 1980s, and Kansas City's Johnson County suburbs would certainly gain seats in the post-1989 alignment. The 1988 elections would thus reflect the most favorable alignment that Kansas' rural interests would enjoy for the foreseeable future.

Even before the 1988 session had ended, however, Sen. Bob Dole's promising bid for the Republican presidential nomination had crashed (in February's New Hampshire primary) and burned (with a series of March 15 Super Tuesday defeats). George Bush, not Dole, would head the party's 1988 ticket. Despite the near certainty that Kansas would vote Republican in November, prospective GOP candidates foresaw less enthusiasm and lower turnout levels for Bush than for native son Dole.[1]

Beyond those state legislators to be elected in 1988, many key players were already in place: Gov. Mike Hayden, elected in 1986; Federal District Judge Richard Rogers, a former state Senate president who had served on the bench since 1975; department heads Roger Endell (Corrections) and Horace Edwards (Transportation), two independent policy advocates with strong personalities; Budget Director Michael O'Keefe, a Hayden loyalist; as well as the important group of academics and administrators who issued semiannual revenue estimates — predictions that traditionally served to frame the debates over taxing and spending.

RECRUITING THE LEGISLATIVE CAST

Looking toward the forthcoming state legislative elections, Republican leaders were guardedly optimistic in early 1988. After all, Sen. Bob Dole was one of the frontrunners for the Republican presidential nomination. Dole at the top of the ticket would probably mean an especially large GOP turnout at the polls, a showing that would aid all the party's candidates in this normally Republican state. Early on, the prospect of Dole's presidential candidacy served to entice would-be legislative candidates—especially for the state Senate. As one Republican recruiter noted, "Dole's presidential candidacy was one of our biggest selling points. . . . One candidate said that she never wanted to run [for the state Senate] in the first place, [but that] 'I sure wanted Bob to run. He would have helped me in my race.'"

But by March 1988, Bob Dole's hopes of topping the ticket had been dashed. After winning the caucuses in neighboring Iowa, Dole lost the New Hampshire primary, failed to provide coherent direction to a campaign in disarray, and ended his efforts in the wake of an across-the-board defeat in the southern-oriented Super Tuesday primaries of March 15. The electoral deadlines of presidential politics worked to shape internal Kansas decisions well before the state's filing deadlines on June 10. Although Dole's early departure was a blow to GOP activists, it was not a complete negative. As Governor Hayden pointed out, Dole's absence "is a two-edged sword, really," in that "if a Kansan had been on the ticket, it would have had a beneficial coattail effect on legislative candidates. But, without a Kansan [either Dole or the immensely popular Sen. Nancy Kassebaum as a vice-presidential nominee] on the ticket, it makes it easier for local candidates to raise money . . . within the state."[2]

Likewise, state Republican chair Fred Logan noted that the party would have had "people beating down doors" to work in a Dole campaign, but that "we'd be a lot better off if we got them to work for the Dave Crockett . . . [Wichita] Senate race."[3] Still, Dave Crockett was no Bob Dole, and volunteer work in campaigns has become increasingly oriented toward individual candidates rather than toward the political party as a whole.[4] The legions of Dole supporters simply were not available to Republican candidates for other offices, regardless of their chances to win. Like his famous namesake at the Alamo, Dave Crockett was on his own, and the results, while not so dramatic, were similar.

Absent Dole atop the ticket, GOP recruiters had to convince candidates to come aboard one at a time, on a district by district basis. With anticipated retirements, a 24–16 Senate GOP margin, and a relatively unimpressive legislative record over the first two years of the Hayden governorship, Republican leaders faced the possibility of losing their control of the state

Senate. Although a wider (74–51) GOP advantage in the Kansas House made the chances of a Democratic victory there appear somewhat less likely, Republican legislative recruitment for the lower chamber became increasingly important in the wake of the Dole withdrawal.

Controlling neither the governorship nor either legislative chamber, Democrats could concentrate their attention on cutting Republican majorities in both the House and Senate. As top Democratic legislative aide Tom Laing points out, the recruitment of strong candidates is always central to greater Democratic electoral success, in that the party must overcome the natural Republican advantages in the state. The Democratic recruitment strategy emphasized both quality and quantity of candidates. Besides seeking well-qualified aspirants for potentially winnable races, the Democrats also sought to pin down the opposition by fielding as full a slate as they possibly could.

Facing the June 10 filing deadline, Laing, Democratic staffer Bob Wootton, and Minority Leader Marvin Barkis spent long hours in cajoling as many strong candidates as possible into the race. Perhaps the most notable Democratic success was Barkis's last-minute entreaty that helped convince Manhattan attorney Sheila Hochhauser to oppose House Majority Leader Joe Knopp. Hochhauser filed for the seat on the last possible day, after a previously declared candidate agreed to withdraw.[5] Equally significant was the Democrats' ability to offer a nearly complete roster for state legislative seats. Though some nominees offered only the most nominal opposition, Democrats did slate primary candidates in all 40 Senate seats and 119 of 125 House districts. Republicans failed to nominate candidates in 6 Senate and 20 House seats; especially noteworthy was their failure to find an opponent for Senate Minority Leader Mike Johnston, an effective campaigner who was able to devote time and direct funds to a number of other legislative races during the summer and fall. To the extent that a campaign represents a series of deadlines, the Democrats had responded to this initial test more effectively than had their GOP counterparts.

THE 1988 CAMPAIGNS

Despite a handful of hotly contested races, the August primaries did little to define the nature of the 1988 state legislative campaigns. Subsequently, two major themes and a minor but significant issue came to dominate the campaigns that began in earnest after Labor Day. The related themes turned on the following questions: Who would control the legislative chambers, now that Democrats were within shouting distance of winning both? To what extent could or should the 1988 election be considered a referendum on Governor Hayden's record? The most important campaign issue focused on the

1988 enactment of a generous retirement package for state legislators, which was folded into a broad state employee compensation package.

Missing from the campaign were substantial debates over the key policy problems facing the state of Kansas. By and large, the major issues of the 1989 legislative session—highways, prisons, school finance, higher education, and tort reform—were not central to the candidates' discourse, since many candidates in competitive races agreed on the key issues. Divisions over highways, for example, were established on geographic grounds, rather than partisan ones. Thus, virtually all southeast Kansas candidates were enthusiastic about a large-scale highway package, while most Johnson County candidates were skeptical.

Local issues and traditional one-on-one contact dominated 1988 campaigning. As Republicans sought to retain their legislative control, they often maintained a substantial distance from their fellow partisan in the governor's office. Indeed, to the extent that important issues were raised in the campaign, it was the Johnson County Republicans who brought them to the fore as they often campaigned against Hayden's 1987/88 record on income tax reductions.

The Democratic Challenge

With a single exception (the House in 1977/78), Republicans have controlled both chambers of the Kansas legislature since 1915; there has been no Democratic U.S. senator from Kansas since 1934. And Kansas is among the most reliable of Republican states in presidential elections. Still, Republicans can scarcely rest easy. Since Democrat George Docking's election as governor in 1956, the Democrats had controlled that office for sixteen of thirty-two years. In 1988, before redistricting would give Republican Johnson County four more representatives (for the 1990 elections), Democrats held at least modest hopes of capturing the lower chamber, despite a 74–51 deficit. The state Senate provided at least as attractive a target, in that a shift of five seats would produce a Democratic majority. With that in mind, legislative Democrats forced a number of politically motivated roll call votes in both chambers during the 1988 session; such votes often required Republicans to defeat attempts to bolster politically popular programs in order to protect overall levels of state spending, even though they might alienate various specific interests that sought more funding (education advocates, children's groups, state employee organizations). These votes provoked the wrath of the legislative Republicans, who saw the opposition's tactics as political posturing. Democrats understandably viewed these votes in more benign terms. Rep. Joan Wagnon (D-Topeka) observed that such tactics "made things rough. Accountability was inferred as dirty campaigning."[6]

The Democratic challenge proceeded on a district by district basis; there was no strong statewide issue, save the questionable popularity and effectiveness of Governor Hayden, to provide the party's candidates with broad-based campaign fodder. Ironically, the most vociferous opposition to Hayden came not from the Democrats' strongest bases of support, but from the GOP bastion of Johnson County, where suburban Republican legislators and voters found much fault with Hayden's record. When the dust settled, the only Johnson County incumbent to lose a seat was a Hayden loyalist, defeated in the Republican primary by a fellow partisan who subsequently prevailed in November.

A Hayden Referendum?

In the week before the general election, Kansas City radio listeners woke up to Democratic advertisements that attacked Mike Hayden's record as governor. Throughout the state, Democratic candidates sought to use the relatively modest Hayden record of accomplishment as a major campaign issue. As Democratic House aide Laing put it, "People won't have a chance to vote on [the] governor this year to tell him how they feel, so they'll do the next best thing and vote for the legislative candidate they believe will let the governor know how they feel."[7] This was easier to project than to accomplish; there is no evidence that voters viewed the 1988 legislative elections in these terms.

Despite Hayden's perceived lack of popularity, especially in Johnson County, there were few clear Hayden-based issues that candidates could grasp in the 1988 campaign. The one that did begin to play, however, was the governor's apparent waffling over cutting state income taxes in the wake of federal tax reform in 1986.[8] Hayden commented that "a whole lot of people out there thought they were *due* money back," and that the issue "took off in the legislative campaigns of 1988, even though we'd made a significant tax cut in the 1988 legislative session."[9] For Democrats, however, the issue of a state income tax windfall was difficult to exploit. First, the most ardent advocates of a tax cut were those Johnson County Republicans who represented the affluent constituencies that would benefit most from further reductions. Second, many Democratic lawmakers preferred retaining income tax revenue to fund their own favored programs.

Hayden sought to avoid becoming an issue in Johnson County by not appearing there during much of the campaign.[10] At the same time, he did intervene in a few close Senate races. In five such contests the Republicans won three seats, but all these races took place in small-town or rural districts, where Hayden's western Kansas background played better than in urban and suburban areas.

In the end, Democrats failed to make Hayden the central issue of their campaigns; rather, some of the toughest anti-governor rhetoric came from those Johnson County Republican incumbents, such as Reps. Kerry Patrick and Robert Vancrum, who would oppose Hayden vigorously during the 1989 legislative session. Although Patrick's animosity was well known by the time of the campaign, it was a surprise when Vancrum, a prominent House Republican, began his reelection brochure by listing his "opposition to the governor's tax plan."[11] In many ways the campaigns against Hayden presaged the frequently cooperative arrangements between House Democrats and a core of dissident Republicans, including Patrick and Vancrum, that would dominate legislative politics in 1989.

Legislative Pensions

Many challengers did have one effective issue to use in 1988: in the last days of the legislative session the lawmakers had voted themselves a 43 percent increase in their pensions. Buried within a broader state employee compensation package that did not require a separate vote on its legislative retirement provisions, the pension issue was slow to surface. By a month after the end of the session, however, the state's editorial writers had worked themselves into a lather of righteous indignation. They named names of those who had voted for the increase; the *Hutchinson News* even included pictures in its editorial blast. The *Emporia Gazette*, the paper made famous by William Allen White, editorialized in sharply partisan terms: "This pension fiasco was engineered by a Republican Governor and Republican leaders in the Legislature. All of the legislators who voted for this bill should be replaced. Because they are mostly Republican, this would give control of the Legislature to the Democratic party."[12]

Although most Democratic lawmakers had voted for the pension bill, it was Republican incumbents who were hurt most by the issue, in large part because the skids for the increase had been greased by GOP leaders and Governor Hayden. Still, there was no wholesale impact on those who voted for higher pensions. Nor was there any effective action taken in 1989 to roll back the pension increases.

Hayden's lack of popularity and the legislative pensions notwithstanding, the 1988 campaign broke down into a series of 165 local contests that only infrequently related to broad patterns in state politics. Neither newly elected legislators nor editorialists could move the pension issue past a preliminary stage of consideration in the 1989 legislature. Rather, the policy agenda was set outside the electoral process, although the November results greatly affected how the legislature would address its agenda in the months to come.

THE 1988 ELECTION: THE PARTISAN GAP NARROWS

When is a victory not a victory? That was the question that Republicans faced November 9, 1988, the day after the general election. GOP party chair Fred Logan expressed relief: "The main thing is that we avoided losing either chamber and maintained our majorities."[13] Although Logan and other Republicans argued that in historical terms Republicans had lost relatively few seats, both legislative chambers would be reconstituted in January with significantly reduced GOP majorities. The Senate margin declined from 24–16 to 22–18, while the House numbers fell from 74–51 to 67–58. One top Republican aide noted ruefully that his party's candidates "got the shit kicked out of them." However expressed, similar sentiments prevailed among most Republicans.

Democrats reacted with predictably congratulatory statements. House Minority Leader Barkis concluded, "I think we are poised on [sic] a two-party system," and Senate Minority Leader Johnston observed that "we are very nearly a full partner, arithmetically."[14] Nevertheless, it was dissident Republicans who stood to gain the most politically. Johnson County's Vancrum observed: "I look for it to be a real acrimonious session. The Democrats are not going to give [Hayden] too much. They smell blood in 1990."[15] Unstated in Vancrum's observation was that a group of shark-like disaffected Republicans also sniffed blood, not for 1990, but for the upcoming legislative session, when they would often constitute the balance of power in the House.[16]

Mike Johnston would soon be reminded that close only counts in horseshoes. The narrow partisan margins led to very different outcomes in the House and Senate settings, respectively. The Republican Senate, as it turned out, would not even allow the Democrats to function effectively, let alone act like full partners. In the House, however, Democrats would join with dissident Republicans to affect both the pace and substance of the forthcoming session (see Chapter 5).

Much as the Democrats' attempt to win control of the legislature fell short, so too did their efforts to make the election a referendum on the governor. Hayden was simply not a major issue in most campaigns outside Johnson County, and there Republicans continued their dominance. At the same time, the election did nothing to make Hayden a more formidable figure, and he continued to appear potentially vulnerable for a 1990 reelection bid.

Although there were several notable individual races and incumbent defeats, the most significant loss of a sitting legislator was that of House Majority Leader Joe Knopp, who represented Manhattan (the "Little Apple," home of Kansas State University). Aside from guaranteeing a leadership shake-up, Knopp's defeat was significant for several, more general reasons. First, as an ambitious party leader and a strong Hayden loyalist, Knopp was pictured as having lost touch with his own constituents. Second, his opponent was an articulate, aggressive attorney, Sheila Hochhauser, who reflected the ability of House Democrats to attract strong women candidates to their ranks. Third, Knopp's defeat, coupled with that of his chief adversary and potential opponent for majority leader,[17] produced a wide-open contest for this office that allowed an independent, reform-oriented legislator, Rep. Robert H. Miller, to win a narrow victory.

Knopp's defeat stood as a lesson to those who might serve as party leaders. He had been perceived as carrying the governor's water and acting against the best interests of the district, especially in an important, if arcane, census debate. That perception hurt Knopp, whose post-election comments demonstrated a continuing insensitivity to his constituents. Stunned by the loss, Knopp reacted dismissively, "I thought that the people understood the political system."[18] If the ambitious Knopp had been cut down because he chose to pursue statewide goals and side with the governor, his successor as majority leader might well think twice before making sacrifices for Hayden or the legislative party.

OPPORTUNITY KNOCKS:
THE HOUSE MAJORITY LEADER'S RACE

The electoral careers of strategic politicians are long-term undertakings that unfold in dozens of choices they make during decades of effort and planning.[19] Nevertheless, many key career decisions must be made very quickly, given the juxtaposition of unexpected events and electoral deadlines. For example, in 1941 Congressman Lyndon Johnson reacted almost instantaneously to the news that Sen. Morris Sheppard had died.[20] Within two days he had begun to plan with a group of key advisors to campaign for Sheppard's seat; the special election was only ten weeks away, and every moment counted once this electoral window of opportunity had opened.

Even the regular election cycle and its well-advertised deadlines can produce great indecision among career politicians;[21] indeed, much of Kansas politics in 1988/89 revolved around the question of whether or not Democratic Congressman Jim Slattery would challenge Governor Hayden in 1990. For would-be House majority leaders, however, there was no time to waste in pondering a race for the office. This could be the political break of a lifetime. The Republican majority leader would be in line to become Speaker in 1991, and the last two chief executives (Democrat John Carlin and Hayden) had used the speakership as a steppingstone to the governorship.

Since party caucuses would be held the first week of December, the prospective candidates needed to act quickly. Rep. Robert H. Miller, the eventual winner, recounts:

> On the night of the election, we were having a party at our house and I got a call at about 10:30 saying that Joe Knopp had been defeated. About a half hour later the call came that Bob Ott [who had planned to challenge Knopp] had lost. That left the majority leadership wide open. Well, I had all my wheat planted and had planned a family vacation. That night I made a few phone calls and stayed up most of the night talking with my wife about whether I should do it or not.[22]

Miller decided to make the race, and "the next three and a half weeks I traveled around the state meeting with all the House Republicans."

In many ways, Miller was an unlikely candidate for a top party leadership position. A long-time advocate of good government policies and campaign reform, Miller had made a point of not accepting any political action committee funds; although generally respected, he "also had a reputation for being personally aloof and distant in his relations with House members."[23] Opposing Miller was ten-term veteran David Heinemann, who gave up the position of speaker pro tem to run for majority leader, and Robert Vancrum, the Johnson County legislator who had often differed with the governor and had lost the 1986 majority leader contest to Knopp by a single vote.

The race and its outcome foreshadowed the problems House Republicans would have throughout the 1989 session in holding their legislative majority together. None of the candidates could easily command support from enough of their colleagues to win the position. Despite his status as a veteran party loyalist, Heinemann was generally viewed as less politically forceful than either Miller or Vancrum.[24] And Vancrum was suspect on two grounds: first, he represented those who had vociferously opposed the governor on various issues; and second, he had business connections to a large number of interests that dealt extensively with the state government. In short, although one of these candidates would have to win, all were seriously flawed, and none would have an easy time riding herd on a House majority that was becoming increasingly fractious even as it lost members.

After a whirlwind campaign, the House Republicans voted for Miller by the slimmest of margins. The initial caucus vote went Vancrum 24, Heinemann 21, Miller 21 (34 votes—a majority of the 67 Republicans—were required for victory). A second ballot eliminated Heinemann (20 votes); Miller received 24 and Vancrum 22. The Republicans had rejected the candidate who occupied the party's center. They were faced with a contest between those who, in Representative Knopp's words, "occupy the opposite extremes of the pendulum," at least in terms of their relations with special interests. The Republicans would elect either an independent outsider or a well-connected representative of various special interests, including a racetrack enterprise. In the end, Miller received 34 votes, the minimum number required for victory. Thus, a legislator noted for his independence and aloofness had won the majority leadership position, which would require that he convince fellow partisans to hang together and support their Republican governor.

In retrospect, the Republicans may have paid dearly for this choice; Miller remained a highly independent legislator on such issues as highways and campaign reform. One key to his victory, ironically, was his support by Speaker Jim Braden, who opted for Miller over Heinemann, fearing that Heinemann, while a party loyalist, would not be a strong enough advocate in rounding up Republican votes. In addition, Vancrum's second consecutive one-vote defeat added to the animosity between a core of his supporters and the party leadership. A Vancrum victory at least could have led to a more integrated Republican majority to the extent that it would have opened doors to dissident legislators. In any event, the whirlwind majority leader's race left the House Republicans fractured and without strong, coordinated leadership. Speaker Jim Braden did remain in place, but he was viewed as firmly allied to Governor Hayden, which did nothing to solidify his hold on the Patrick-Vancrum faction.

THE SENATE LEADERSHIP: DISCORD WITHOUT DIVISION

As the December 5 Republican caucuses approached, the contests for Senate president and majority leader heated to the boiling point. Senate President Robert Talkington had announced his retirement soon after the 1988 legislative session, and the Senate Republicans had had five months to position themselves for their leadership races. At the same time, they were in much the same situation as House members, in that they had only a little over three weeks after the election to build their final coalitions. With a reduced GOP contingent of senators and just four newcomers, these races were much more intimate than those in the House, but no less intense. Indeed, the potential for fracture was at least as great among Senate Republicans as among their House counterparts, precisely because the politicking was so personal. A single vote could mean everything.

The Senate leadership races were clearly defined in one sense, yet more murky in another. The clarity came in the head-to-head contest between sitting Majority Leader Bud Burke (Johnson County) and Fred Kerr (Pratt, a rural district); this face-off was a rematch of a very close 1984 majority leader's race, and there was little love lost between these two ambitious legislators. The results of the presidency race would shape the subsequent contest for the majority leader position, in that the loser of the first might well become the frontrunner in the second. Although Sen. Wint Winter had declared for the majority leadership, he was not a serious candidate. Rather, he was serving, more or less, as a stand-in for Kerr. Otherwise, Sen. Jim Allen, who was a most serious candidate, might have wrapped up enough commitments to win the position against either Kerr or Burke. In fact, Allen went into the Republican caucus thinking he had enough support to prevail.

After weeks of intense lobbying, the leadership was shaped by a last-minute deal. With the caucus deadline at hand, Kerr withdrew from the presidency contest, leaving Burke as the sole candidate. Kerr then turned his attention to the majority leadership, where he confronted a confident Allen, who reported a few days before the caucus that he had twelve "solidly committed votes, plus a spare."[25] In such a contest, however, many is the slip between the cup and the lip, and Allen's support fell short of a majority. Kerr won, 12-10, with some votes swinging to him as part of his withdrawal from the race for the Senate presidency. A large man and a savvy politician, Allen was both surprised and irate at the fatal defections of two votes from his base. Given a narrow majority and within the highly personal Senate context, Allen's disaffection represented a serious challenge to the Burke/Kerr leadership — at least as serious as the discontent among House Republicans. Although the major differences between the chambers would play out in the January's votes on rules, Burke and the Republican leadership immediately acted to bring Allen and his supporters back into the party fold.[26]

Reflecting the small size of the Senate and the intensely personal nature of small-state politics, Burke observed:

> Jim Allen and I had double dated when we were at KU. He's a close friend, a confidant. He has great rapport with the rural community. . . . I never played games with him, . . . and Jim believed to his core that he had it in the bag. When Organization, Calendar, and Rules Committee met, I recommended him for Agriculture Chair and for Ways and Means, which had been lobbied heavily by others, but not by him.[27]

Allen remained upset, especially with defectors from his candidacy, but Burke had immediately begun the process of bringing him and his supporters back into the GOP fold. Although there would be some rough times, Allen would prove a most valuable asset to the Senate Republicans and to Governor Hayden as the Senate wound up its business in May (see Chapter 9 on the water plan).

These three-week leadership contests within the Republican majorities of both chambers were fascinating to behold; they were simultaneously vicious and intimate, as friends, allies, opponents, and enemies jockeyed for position in close quarters. The key venues here were a pair of meetings in two separate manifestations of that quintessentially heartland institution, the Holidome. (Holidomes are gussied-up Holiday Inns that have popped up across the Midwest since the 1970s. They are Hyatt Hotels on the cheap, with the standard rooms surrounding an indoor swimming pool and a modest recreation area. In the winter the humidity of Holidomes contrasts sharply to the frigid, windy weather outside, leading one to expect to find a crop of mushrooms being cultivated amidst the coffee shop's flowers.)

First in Topeka, then in Lawrence, legislative leaders conducted their campaigns in Holidome hospitality rooms and in the corridors outside a presession "legislative institute." The musty, moist atmosphere of these settings is fertile both for cultivating fungi and hatching political plots, and prospective leaders would ease freshmen legislators aside, whisper in their ears, make their promises. Small groups of veteran senators would form and reform. Almost palpably, one could see Fred Kerr's chances for the Senate presidency slip away inside the glorified Topeka motel, only to have his supporters regroup to push him into the majority leader's position. The deadlines of time—the caucuses would be held the next day—were immutable, and the senators wanted to avoid surprises. The House candidates faced too many imponderables, too many new faces, but the Senate Republicans could focus on their few undecided peers, all in the hothouse humidity of Holidome politics.

THE PLOT THICKENS:
THE GOVERNOR MOVES CENTER STAGE

Various legislators, staff, administrators, and private sector individuals were already in place, waiting for the legislative chambers to organize. The governor was the most important player, of course, but many other actors were set to play major roles in the making of policy between December 1988 and the legislature's final act in May 1989. Rather than catalog them all here, I will allow them to make their entrances as the year's politicking and policymaking unfold.

The 1988 elections could not be read as a renunciation of Gov. Mike Hayden and his policies. Nor did the results afford him much comfort. After all, both houses harbored narrow, uncertain Republican majorities, and many of the key GOP lawmakers had campaigned against much of his record, especially on taxes. More importantly, Hayden had won precious few substantial policy battles over the course of his first two years in office. In fact, his most noteworthy initiative—a highways package proposed in a 1987 special session —had suffered total defeat. The 1989 legislative session offered him one last chance to compile a record of accomplishments that he could take to the voters. As he put together his FY 1990 budget, Hayden knew that he would be judged in large part on what the legislature did in the next few months.

Longtime Hayden advisor Ed Flentje speculated that the performance in the third year of a governor's term was crucial to his reelection chances. The fourth year would allow too much politics to creep into the process. But the third year offered substantial possibilities. This was especially true in 1988, because Kansas' coffers were full to the brim with revenues that had been consistently underestimated. As Sen. Wint Winter, Jr., put it rhetorically: "How hard can this year be? We can cut taxes and increase spending. Lots better than the reverse."

Still, there were clouds on Hayden's horizon. First, Congressman Jim Slattery, an attractive moderate-to-conservative Democrat from Topeka, won an overwhelming 1988 victory (72 percent of the vote) in a district that had been in Republican hands as recently as 1982. Slattery was seriously considering a 1990 gubernatorial race; as an effective campaigner with no state politics baggage, he would make a very strong opponent.[28] Second, Hayden would be judged on several major items from his own agenda. Highways represented a key issue for many Kansas interests, but he alone would be responsible for pushing a reinstatement of the death penalty. Johnson County voters waited to see how much of the income tax windfall would be returned. Lurking in the wings was another major tax issue—the property tax reappraisal and classification process, which would be completed in late 1989. Hayden, both as Speaker and governor, had supported reappraisal and classification, and an increasing number of signs indicated that this issue would become extremely dangerous for anyone associated with it.

Aside from a host of substantive issues (see Chapter 4), Hayden was faced with the question of how far he should get out in front with his own legislative program. In 1987 his leadership had proven inadequate to win acceptance of a major highway overhaul. Indeed, the governor had ignored advice from Senate President Talkington and Speaker Braden, both of whom had counseled him not to call a special session.

In the wake of the 1987 highway debacle and the results of the 1988 elections, it became clear that a highly partisan or personal set of appeals would not be successful. The Republican legislative margins were simply too slim, and Hayden recognized that, regardless of his public role in the 1989 legislative process, he would be judged on the overall results, whether his involvement was visible or not. On highways, in particular, his best chance for success might be to withdraw almost totally from the policy debate. More generally, such a decision to remain in the background reflected the need for many key actors simultaneously to pursue political and policy goals. As a policy entrepreneur on highways, Hayden's activist nature pushed him to battle for a large-scale program, given the 1989 window of opportunity. At the same time, as a strategic politician with an eye on reelection in 1990, the governor had to weigh the risks of his personal involvement in the legislative process. The coupling of policy and political streams that Kingdon observes within the agenda-setting process also occurs in the thinking of career politicians.

As Mike Hayden worked late in November and early December building his budget, he knew that the 1989 legislative session represented a great opportunity for him and his administration. At the same time, failure to win a series of policy victories could fatally injure his reelection chances and permanently derail his political career.

4

Setting the State's Policy Agenda

As the political process unfolded through candidate selection and elections, policymaking went forward on a separate track, often engaging the attention of the same actors who figured prominently in the electoral arena. Given a part-time legislature that meets each spring for ninety days (or so), most agenda-setting in Kansas politics takes place between May and early January. As soon as the 1988 legislative session adjourned, policy activists in and out of government sought to affect the 1989 legislative agenda.

Although the 1988 legislature generally received high marks for its work, few major issues were resolved. In the wake of the defeat of the highway package in the 1987 special session, neither the governor nor the legislature sought to consider a major construction plan in 1988. The legislature also left hanging the ultimate resolution of the so-called income tax windfall resulting from 1986 federal reforms; nor did it act on building the new prison a federal judge had virtually mandated. For Gov. Mike Hayden there had been no series of key legislative victories that might propel him to a second term in 1990. In fact, his reluctance to reduce income taxes and his continuing inability to pass a large highway package placed him at odds with both suburban Johnson County Republicans and many rural Republicans outside the Kansas City metropolitan area.

This chapter will explore how the Kansas policy agenda was set in 1988/89. After a brief look at policy formulation at the state level, the focus will shift toward the ways in which long-term trends and cyclical forces flow together in setting the legislative agenda.

AGENDAS

How do policies get considered by decision makers? Why do certain issues make it onto the agenda, while others languish? Who sets the agenda? These are difficult questions. There are so many potential issues, so many ways an issue can creep, stroll, or jump onto the agenda, and so many people willing to take credit (or sometimes avoid the blame) for pushing an item forward, that knowledge about agenda-setting has been slow to accumulate. In examining agenda formation at the state level, there are even fewer general conclusions. Despite some useful case studies[1] and findings on innovations,[2] little attention has been accorded agenda-setting processes at the state level.

In an early formulation, Cobb and Elder distinguish between the systemic and formal agendas.[3] They define the systemic agenda as the broad list of issues commonly perceived by members of the political community as worthy of attention and within the legitimate jurisdiction of existing governmental authority. In contrast, the shorter formal agenda consists of issues actively under consideration by authoritative decision makers.

This distinction is preserved in most subsequent studies of agenda setting. Although she leaves the concept of the formal agenda intact, Barbara Nelson gradates the systemic agenda as she distinguishes between a broad popular agenda and much narrower professional agendas.[4] Nelson's differentiation of the systemic agenda is significant, since Cobb and Elder ignore the fact that many of the issues reaching the formal (or governmental) agenda may lack popular appeal.

In a system of separated powers and federalism there are numerous governmental agendas. Robert Eyestone introduces the notion of an operational agenda, to give more shape to the formal agenda.[5] For example, a legislature's operational agenda consists of issues (in bill form) that are reported out of committee. A chief executive's operational agenda comprises legislative proposals as well as items mentioned in public statements. Kingdon points out that it is also possible to identify the specialized agendas of bureaucrats, interest groups, and other political actors by identifying the issues they are currently addressing.[6]

Locating the actual governmental agenda requires a prolonged look at the broad arenas of political action, policy formulation, and problem definition. Kingdon examines two policy areas (health and transportation) at the national level over a four-year period. My strategy is to investigate *all* major policy domains, but for a single state in a single year. By examining the operational agendas of numerous political actors (the governor, the legislature, interest groups, the media) I am able to specify Kansas' entire policy agenda as the legislature began its 90-day 1989 session.[7] The data suggest that overlapping operational agendas may converge to form a consensus on which issues compose the formal agenda.

Problems, solutions, and politics are all key elements in agenda-setting. Kingdon modifies the garbage-can model of organizational choice to describe a process in which separate streams of problems, policies, and politics converge to move an issue onto the agenda and toward potential action.[8] This notion of convergence, which he labels "coupling," emphasizes the chaotic and unpredictable nature of agenda-setting. Kingdon notes that

> there comes a time when the three streams are joined. A pressing problem demands attention, for instance, and a policy proposal is coupled to the problem as its solution. Or an event in the political stream, such as a change of administration, calls for different directions. At that point proposals that fit with that political event, such as initiatives that fit with a new administration's philosophy, come to the fore and are coupled with the ripe political climate. Similarly, problems that fit are highlighted, and others are neglected.[9]

The coupling of these three streams does not happen automatically. Policy entrepreneurs often seek to pull together diverse forces, but success is not guaranteed. Alternatively, many policy items, such as annual budgets, require resolution, even if channeling the problem, policy, and politics streams into a single set of proposals appears impossible. Indeed, the cyclical nature of much policymaking creates deadlines that political actors must react to, therby forcing the three streams to merge. Jack Walker, among others, distinguishes between required and discretionary agenda items.[10] Where there is substantial discretion, policymakers have more room for time-based maneuvers, and interminable delay can emerge as a real option, as it frequently has in the U.S. Senate. Conversely, required decisions produce a different strategic environment. If budgets must be balanced and public education funded, all within the time limits of a legislative session, tremendous pressures build for resolution, even if large cuts must be made or tax increases enacted (California and Connecticut, respectively, in the early 1990s).

Ordinarily, those with formal authority—particularly the governor and party leaders—exercise more leverage than the rank-and-file in the waning days of the legislative session because of their ability to manage the flow of specific alternatives onto the agenda. In state after state, however, legislative leaders and executives have experienced growing difficulties in maintaining control over their majorities.[11] In these instances the tables are sometimes turned; dissident lawmakers may be able to use the deadlines of required policymaking to exact concessions from those political elites who have traditionally controlled the flow of policies in the last few days of the legislative session.

SETTING THE AGENDA:
MAY 1988 TO JANUARY 1989

When the 1988 Kansas legislature adjourned in early May, the FY 1990 budget cycle was already moving ahead, as agencies drew up their budget requests to present to Governor Hayden. Although the budget cycle dictated the pace of policy formulation, it was the electoral cycle that drove many items onto the state's agenda. Results from the 1989 legislative session would go a long way toward defining the success or failure of the Hayden administration when the governor sought reelection in 1990.

At the same time, all political actors faced real restrictions on what they could legitimately hope to push onto the state's operational agenda before the legislature returned in January 1989.[12] Many important issues, including highways and the windfall's return, remained on the agenda, held over from previous years. Other items, like school finance, were perennial sticking points, battled over year in, year out. Still other issues required legislative attention in light of past decisions; thus the 1989 legislature would be faced with reapportioning the House in the wake of the 1988 census. Finally, various decisions surrounding the construction of a new prison had been placed on the agenda by Judge Richard Rogers, who had become the driving force in corrections policy.

In the months outside the legislative session, policy formulation develops both in regular, ordered ways and along unique, idiosyncratic lines. The executive branch constructs a budget, while numerous joint and interim special legislative committees meet to consider a wide range of proposals mostly drawn from rank-and-file suggestions. Still, the governor can continue to play a major role, as he did in relying heavily on an interim body to piece together a highway construction plan.[13] At the same time, policymakers track both actual revenues and projected receipts, which serve as constraints on future expenditures.[14] Although budgeting, committee activity, and revenue tracking take place through the summer and early fall, all overlap in November. It is then that committee reports filter in, the governor begins to make final budget decisions, and the six-month revenue estimates are announced. In 1988, of course, these processes took place as the legislative parties were reacting to the results of the general election.

Finally, various groups and actors operate outside the normal cycles of budgeting, interim committees, and revenue estimates. In 1988, the Governor's Children's Commission, the Democratic legislative caucus (see Chapter 5), and federal Judge Rogers all sought to move items onto the legislative agenda. At the same time, Kansas experienced a serious drought, which focused attention on the largely unfunded state water plan. In addition, the House struggled to reapportion itself in the wake of census figures that were announced in the fall of 1988.

Interim Committees

In discussing agenda-setting, Kingdon notes that the separate streams of problems, policies, and politics usually come together near the end of the process, when the appropriate "window" opens.[15] Interim committees, appointed at the end of the previous legislative session, comport with Kingdon's notion; at the same time, however, they reflect the beginning of the agenda-setting process for the next session.

More prosaically, interim committees are often appointed to provide some extra days of work for various legislators, along with the symbolic assurance that an issue is being considered. The efforts of interim committees often duplicate those of the standing committees, since their memberships do not necessarily coincide with those of the standing committees. As one veteran reporter observed, "We plow the same ground again during the session. Interim studies are not worthless, but . . . everyone's had their say in the summer."[16]

Still, interim committees do address some major issues outside the glare of publicity that marks the regular session; at the same time, the reporting deadlines of the late fall (for December printing) mean that the committees must move along if they are to make meaningful recommendations. In addition, party leaders control the appointment of interim committee members and select the topics to be considered (and ignored); thus, in 1988 they could appoint an interim transportation committee that would almost certainly put forward a major new highway bill for the 1989 session.

By December 1988, twelve interim committees had made a total of fifty-four specific proposals for the 1989 legislature; these ranged from revising city franchise fees to improving firefighter training to spending more than $3 billion for highway construction. Although the legislature had not dealt with all its most nettlesome issues through its interim committees, it did have a comprehensive highway bill on the table and ready for immediate consideration in January 1989.

Estimating Revenues

More than anything else, revenue estimates both drive the agenda-setting process and place constraints upon it. This essentially nonpolitical activity is fraught with political implications, since estimates shape all subsequent spending proposals.

The estimating committee is composed of representatives of the Budget Office, the Department of Revenue, and the Legislative Research Department, along with three academic economists (from the University of Kansas, Kansas State University, and Wichita State University, respectively) and two consultants, who provide employment and agricultural economy forecasts, respectively.[17] Meeting in the fall, the group makes its estimates public in mid-November. The governor then shapes his budget to these estimates, which recast the preliminary figures that agencies have used to construct their initial requests. The committee also meets in March, during the legislative session, to provide a midcourse correction in its fall estimates.

The formal description of the revenue-estimating process masks the political implications of revenue levels in the summer and fall of 1988. In fact, the November report, which raised the FY 1989 estimates by $166 million, followed several months in which revenues routinely outpaced earlier estimates. Previously, the state took in $149 million more in FY 1988 than had been predicted in November 1987. Although the process of estimating revenues was depoliticized, the resulting numbers immediately changed the nature of the policy debate: there was more money on the table.

The Governor's Agenda: The Budget and the "State of the State" Address

While interim committees address a select number of specific topics, the governor has a broader responsibility in building a budget that encompasses all governmental agencies. At the same time, the governor can emphasize only a modest number of major policy initiatives, most of which will be highlighted in the annual January State of the State address.

Building a budget begins with revenue estimates. Working from baseline estimates in June, Hayden's Budget Director Michael O'Keefe noted that "we ask the governor what kind of balance he wants at the end of the year. So you take the revenue, subtract the balance at the end of '90, and that's what you've got to work with."[18] Adding in capital expenditures and social spending commitments, O'Keefe argued that despite substantial budget balances, the surplus would only amount to 2 percent.

Under Hayden, capital budgets were due July 1 and agency requests September 15; after that the Budget Office provided help to the governor in constructing his own set of priorities. O'Keefe states: "Mike Hayden builds the budget. Groups come in and see him, so do agency heads, but it's his budget. Budget gives him scorecards on the A, B, C level budgets, but the choices are his."[19] The timing here was crucial, because the governor would review each agency request and personally heard appeals in November and December, just before the final budget figures were decided upon.

As Hayden constructed the budget, he simultaneously crafted his State of the State message, which would highlight his agenda for the 1989 legislative session. Although the budget and the speech-writing processes were complementary, they were not at all identical. While budget building revolves around a series of incremental decisions with nonobvious consequences, choosing the emphases for the State of the State address affords the governor his most important opportunity to focus the state's attention on the few issues he deems most important. He can also allow various nonfiscal proposals (such as the death penalty) to surface in the speech.

In 1989, with substantial revenues and a host of key issues, the State of the

State address assumed special significance, largely because Hayden's political circumstances would virtually require him to have a successful legislative session. On the eve of the governor's speech and budget presentation, Senate President Bud Burke observed that "Hayden's situation right now [is] like halftime of a football game. If he does well in the second half, I think he will win in 1990."[20]

Numerous cycles would come together to shape the political and policy agendas for Kansas in 1989. The interim committees delivered their reports in December, and agencies made their final appeals as the governor put the final touches on the FY 1990 budget. As legislators struggled with leadership races and committee assignments in the wake of the 1988 elections, Mike Hayden was looking toward 1990, when the voters would judge his record. As he prepared his State of the State address, opposition Democrats, fresh from a fall caucus, stood ready to put forward a host of proposals that would draw down the budget surpluses to the point that Hayden would have little room to maneuver in the final year before his reelection bid. Budget, legislative, and election cycles all dictated the pace, if not the substance, of agenda-setting; at the same time, several other diverse forces helped move specific items onto the 1989 agenda.

Other Forces

Although any number of actors sought to move particular items onto the agenda, four developments merit brief attention here (and more in subsequent discussions of policymaking). These include children's issues and the governor's commission on this subject, the drought, the actions of federal judge Richard Rogers to force Kansas to comply with his standards in a prison overcrowding case, and the census and reapportionment issue.

In May 1988, Governor Hayden appointed an eleven-member commission to make recommendations on children's and family issues by December 1. Hayden's wife, Patti, was named co-chair, along with Wint Winter, Sr., a former legislator and father of sitting senator Wint Winter, Jr. The commission also included several prominent child advocacy figures and Lisa Donnini Miller, the wife of Rep. Robert H. Miller, who would win the majority leadership in December. This group possessed the expertise, energy, and connections to have their recommendations taken seriously. Indeed, their proposals had the potential to be very expensive, thus placing the governor in an awkward position when responding to them (see Chapter 6 for further details).

During the summer of 1988, Kansas experienced another in a series of relatively dry summers. The drought had little direct connection to the state's overall water plan, which had received only partial funding since its adoption in 1984, but the arid conditions did focus attention on the water issue. Both the governor and an interim committee recommended funding the plan, but, as in the past, funding was not guaranteed.[21] The specter of low water levels and inadequate supplies hung over the policy formulation process, and this issue became increasingly salient for growing numbers of legislators.

Like the water plan, prison overcrowding had long been on the Kansas agenda without occasioning much action. The 1989 session would be different, however, largely because of the aggressive stance taken by Judge Rogers. After a ten-year-old prison overcrowding suit was reopened in 1987, Rogers had consistently pressured Department of Corrections (DOC) officials to correct the problem by setting deadlines for reductions in prison populations. In September he expanded the original lawsuit to include inmates beyond the original complainants at the Lansing facility. The governor and his DOC secretary, Roger Endell, were committed to increasing the number of beds in the prison system to forestall Rogers's orders to ease overcrowding. At the same time, many legislators looked to alternate means, such as sentencing reform and expanding the role of community corrections, to hold down prison populations.

Although Hayden, Endell, and the legislators would debate prison size and incarceration policy until the final hours of the 1989 session, there was no question that a new prison would be built to comply with the judge's order. Otherwise, hundreds of prisoners would be freed, scarcely an attractive prospect for any of the political actors. Judge Rogers's order essentially imposed a deadline on the legislators: either they solve the overcrowding problem by the session's end or face the real possibility that the state would lose control of its prison system to a federally appointed master. There was little doubt that the legislature would act, although the shape of that action was hotly debated throughout the 1989 session.

One final issue was brought before the legislature by its own actions in mandating a census for 1988 and subsequent reapportionment in 1989 (for the 1990 election). Historically, Kansas had used its own agricultural census to redraw its political boundaries. This practice would come to an end in 1991, when Kansas would join the rest of the nation in using the federal census figures as the basis for reapportionment. Under the state's constitution, however, a census was mandated, along with reapportionment, for 1988/89. The elimination of this census was thoroughly considered, but the legislature decided to have the census done, even though it would serve as the basis of only one election—for the state House of Representatives in 1990. As in any reapportionment, the stakes would be high, but the single-election nature of the decision made it more transitory and less complex, since it would not affect the makeup of the state Senate or the U.S. House. This may have contributed to a process that never generated the partisan rancor so typical in redrawing district lines. Chapter 7 will provide an extended consideration of the census and reapportionment issues.

THE KANSAS AGENDA(S), 1988/89

Much of the literature on agenda-setting emphasizes, for theory-building purposes, *an* agenda, be it one carried in the minds of citizens or policymakers, or one that reaches some stage of formal legislative or executive consideration.[22] This conventional view should not obscure the fact that agenda items, and even whole agendas, are often in competition with each other. Indeed, participants in the policy process may well view "the governmental agenda" in very different ways. At the national level, these diverse perspectives reflect the normal politics of agenda formation, the fragmentation of policymaking, and the vast number of items that compete for position on a long and varied agenda. Particular members of policy communities frequently focus almost entirely on their own agendas, even within a general policy area. For example, Kingdon reports little overlap between the various transportation subspecialties, as railroads, aviation, highways, and mass transportation generate their own policy communities.[23]

Within the context of state policymaking, such specialization also occurs, but policy communities, to the extent they exist, are smaller and less insular. In most states, a number of key actors — especially those on the governor's staff, within the legislature, and among the corps of lobbyists — operate simultaneously in several policy arenas. Thus individual networks and interests overlap, so that there may be an emergent consensus on some single, overarching set of agenda items.

In addition, agenda-setting at the state level tends to be more constrained than in national policymaking. Most notably (and obviously), states do not conduct their own foreign or defense policies, save for some international trade initiatives. More significantly, states often operate under restrictions that reduce the entrepreneurial activities of individual actors. Budgets must be balanced, federal mandates must be complied with, and judicial orders must be addressed.

Nevertheless, the struggle over agenda items in the states roughly resembles that at the national level. The players are essentially the same, at least in name: the chief executive, his/her staff, administrators with political appointments, civil servants, legislators, their staffs, interest groups, researchers and consultants, the media, and on occasion, election-related participants.[24] Public opinion can also play a role, although it is often less well-defined in the states than at the national level, where polls abound on almost all subjects.

In 1988/89, Kansas policymakers of various stripes had their own preferences for agenda items. At the same time, all the major political actors roughly agreed on the items that constituted the operational agenda for the state at the beginning of the 1989 legislative session. Specifically, I have identified five agendas, one each for the governor, the legislature, lobbyists, print media, and the general public. Despite some differences, the political elites basically agreed on the major elements of the state's agenda:

- highway construction
- the return of the income tax windfall
- prison construction
- school finance
- tort reform

Even with the addition of issues mentioned less frequently (reapportionment, a state water plan), the list of important issues was relatively short. Kansas' operational agenda was firmly in place before the general election, and the election did nothing to change the thinking of political elites.

There were a few important disparities in the elite agendas. Though the governor (Table 4.1) and the legislature (Table 4.2) agreed on most issues, Governor Hayden did emphasize one issue that did not appear prominently on other elite agendas: the death penalty. The governor resolutely supported the death penalty and essentially forced otherwise reluctant legislators to address the issue. In the minds of lobbyists, legislators, and journalists, the death penalty was not a pressing concern. As the 1989 legislative session got under way, however, awareness of the issue increased, and in February the death penalty was viewed as an important issue by 20 percent of the public (Table 4.5). The legislature acted quickly on this agenda item in dealing the governor a narrow, but convincing, defeat. In this instance, the governor could set the agenda and force a decision, but he was unable to produce a favorable outcome (see Chapter 6).

The issue consensus among elites did not completely foreclose agenda-setting opportuntities. Prior to the session, for example, lawmakers were asked if there was a "sleeper" issue that the 1989 legislature might address. Of 110 respondents, none suggested campaign finance reform, which did prove an important issue (Chapter 9) in 1989 and one that reflected the efforts of a key entrepreneur.

The media's agenda ran parallel to those put forward by governmental elites and lobbyists (see Tables 4.3 and 4.4). In editorials published between May and early January, sixteen daily newspapers emphasized the same issues as did the other major actors. Especially noteworthy was the media's focus on highways, often in the form of highly supportive, even pleading, editorials.[25]

Table 4.1. The Governor's Agenda: Issues

Return income tax windfall
Enactment of death penalty
Highway program
School finance
Prisons
Tort reform

Washburn University inclusion in state university system
Water plan
Libraries
Taxpayer bill of rights
Children and families
Reapportionment

Source: The first six issues were clearly featured in the governor's State of the State address (and emphasized afterward). Six additional issues were mentioned sporadically, but stood out from others. The governor expressed no priority ordering among the top six issues or among the remaining six.

Table 4.2. The Legislative Agenda: Issues

Question: "What are the most important issues facing the legislature this session?" Up to five responses were possible. (% of respondents mentioning)

School finance/reappraisal	102[a]	Tort reform	31
Highways	74	Higher education funding	11
Prisons	65	Adoption of state water plan	10
Tax windfall return	49	Various social issues	18
Reapportionment	35	Economic development	9

[a]Multiple responses may be coded in the same category.
N = 110 (of possible 165)

Table 4.3. The Lobbyists' Agenda: Issues

Question: "What are the most important issues facing Kansas in the upcoming legislative session?" Up to five responses were possible. (% of respondents mentioning)

Highways	88	Enactment of state water plan	21
Return of tax windfall	88	Death penalty	15
School finance	73	Higher education	15
Tort reform	48	Washburn University entry	
Prisons	45	into state system	12
Reapportionment	24		

N = 33

Table 4.4. The Media Agenda: Issues

	Number of editorials (May–January)		Number of editorials (May–January)
Highways	42	Revenue balances	14
Prisons	25	Reapportionment	12
Windfall	20	Property tax/school	
Tort reform	16	finance	9
Legislative pension	15	Campaign reform	7
Washburn	14	Death penalty	5

Numbers of pre–legislative session editorials emphasizing important issues facing Kansas government that were published in fifteen Kansas daily newspapers, plus the *Kansas City Times*, which offers extensive Kansas coverage.

Table 4.5. The Public Agenda: Issues

Question: "In your view what are the most important policy issues facing Kansas this year? You can name up to five." (% of respondents mentioning)

Highways	29.6	Primary/secondary	
State economy	24.9	education	10.1
Taxes (general)	21.7	Reappraisal	9.8
Social programs	20.3	Higher education	
Death penalty	20.1	funding	9.6
Education	18.7	Water	8.9
Rural issues	18.4	Health issues	8.0
Jobs	14.1	Prisons	6.4
Crime	12.2	Malpractice (tort	
Taxes (windfall)	11.5	reform)	3.1
Environmental issues	10.8	Savings and loans	1.7

Source: 1989 Legislative Issues Survey (Institute for Public Policy and Business Research, University of Kansas, February 1989).

Table 4.6. The Cumulative Operational Agenda

Highways (1.875)
Return of income tax windfall (2.875)
Prisons (3.5)
School finance/property tax (3.5)
Tort reform (4.25)
Death penalty (7.75)
Reapportionment (7.75)
Water plan (8.75)
Washburn University inclusion in Regents system (9)

Figures are averages of issue ranking for governor, legislature, lobbyists, and media. Governor's ranking = 3 for top six issues, 9 for remaining six issues. Any issues not considered by an actor is rated at 11 for that source (beyond the "top ten" issues for the session).

The media did play up two issues that none of the other actors addressed: legislative pensions and a presidential primary. The pension issue was especially significant, and it did affect the 1988 campaigns in a handful of specific races. Editorialists railed at the legislators' greed in increasing their pensions by 43 percent, and some reelection campaigns did turn on this issue. Once the legislature met, however, the issue was effectively buried, even though a few members did introduce bills to roll back the increments. Likewise, editorial calls for a presidential primary fell on deaf ears, at least in 1989. In short, the media's attention simply could not move either the pension or primary issue onto the operational agenda. Although the legislature gave these subjects pro forma hearings, neither received serious consideration.

There was one major exception to the general ineffectiveness of the media in affecting agenda-setting and policymaking. The *Wichita Eagle-Beacon* consistently sought to influence legislative actions as it planned coverage of the 1989 session and commissioned a special study on campaign finance (see Chapter 9). In turn, legislative leaders often reacted, privately at least, to *Eagle-Beacon* stories and editorials.

The agendas outlined by legislators and lobbyists are almost identical; although the orderings are different, the top six issues were the same. Legislators placed a bit more importance on traditionally difficult property tax and school finance issues as well as reapportionment, which affected them directly. Lobbyists saw the more discretionary items of highway construction and tax cuts as more significant. In essence, however, those who sat on the floor of the legislative chamber and those who observed from the balcony agreed on the state's operational agenda.

To the extent there was disagreement over the nature of the agenda, it came from the public at large. The public's agenda (Table 4.5) did diverge considerably from the generally similar views of elites.[26] Central to the public agenda was the existence of very broad issue categories. Active participants in the law-making process were much more likely to break up general issue categories than were citizens. For example, most public respondents answered that "education" was an important agenda item, while legislators, lobbyists, and the governor ordinarily made distinctions between primary, secondary, and various elements of higher education. Similarly, elite respondents commonly distinguished between sales taxes, property taxes, and income taxes, while many citizen respondents simply mentioned "taxes" as an important issue. These differences are not surprising, given the more specific and detailed information that elites have at their disposal.

This generality in citizen responses can account for many differences between the public agenda and the others. The five "consensus" issues appear lower on the public agenda than on the others. Many "reappraisal" and "windfall" responses are probably subsumed by the more general category of taxes, while school finance is most likely included under both taxes and education. Crime is high on the public agenda and prisons are low. Combining the two categories demonstrates that the crime/prison response is the seventh most common. The low ranking of tort reform on the public agenda is probably the result of its complexity and relatively low visibility. Most Kansans view tort reform in large part as a rural health care issue. Other responses that top the public agenda cannot really be considered issues at all. The responses "state economy" and "rural issues" are so general as to lack substantive, if not political, meaning. In fact, almost all major spending and tax issues were cast in terms of economic development and the health of the state economy.

In the end, there are relatively few issues high on the public agenda that do not appear near the top of the other agendas. The key exception is the concern with social programs; the public expressed many more concerns about increased social service spending than did political elites.

Overall, however, the data demonstrate considerable agreement. Save for the generality of public preferences, the agendas tend to converge. Few issues—the death penalty and social service spending are exceptions—engender much disagreement among respondents. The legislative survey showed negligible differences between Democrats and Republicans, and with the exception of the death penalty, the Republican governor's agenda contained no issues that legislators of both parties did not place near the top of their lists.

The most significant finding here is the great consensus on the agenda (see Table 4.6). In 1988/89, Kansas policymakers stood ready to address numerous issues that had been on or around the agenda for several years. Highways, the windfall, prisons, reappraisal and school finance, and tort reform were all "old" issues, with multi-year histories in obtaining agenda status. Even the death penalty issue was a well-ridden hobbyhorse in the governor's stable of concerns. And because the state's revenue picture was far rosier in 1989 than at any other time in the 1980s, policymakers saw a real window of opportunity for addressing a series of chronic problems rather than pushing new items forward.

ACT I, FINAL SCENE

Thirty-five reporters are crammed into the executive reception room, awaiting the details of Governor Hayden's budget, as presented by his press secretary, Kathy Peterson, and his budget director, Michael O'Keefe, neither of whom are renowned for their comfortable relations with the press. Given a huge budget surplus and a proposal to cut income taxes, Peterson and O'Keefe scarcely provide an image of confidence; rather, there is a distinctly frantic element to Peterson's fifteen-minute run-through of the budget. O'Keefe follows with a series of graphics, but little analysis of the budget choices being outlined.

Governor Hayden finally shows up, essentially to respond to questions; this puts an end to speculation that he would not appear at all. The session lasts a half hour or so, and many of the queries focus on school finance, the movement of revenue from one category to another, and some apparent inconsistencies in the budget. Even though legislators and lobbyists agree that the 1989 session could be historic in terms of accomplishments of substance, the initial budget unveiling remains focused on relatively minor issues. The governor and the press relate to each other by sparring, which may not be the best way to introduce a set of sweeping tax, highway, and prison initiatives. The governor and his staff do not seize the moment to place his initiatives in the historical context of a great opportunity for the state. Rather, it's business as usual, which includes a substantial gubernatorial antipathy toward the press.

That evening Governor Hayden presents his State of the State message to the legislature. There are few surprises, in that virtually everyone agrees with the composition of the state's policy agenda. Agreement on the nature of the agenda does not, however, imply consensus on solutions or even agreement on how the problems should be addressed. Moreover, within forty-eight hours the legislature will become so fractured that the governor's proposals will be immediately placed at risk.

The 1989 stakes were unusually high, and although the governor could formally set the agenda, he could only hope for favorable outcomes once the legislative session began. In fact, on the issue of highways, the governor's public support for any given proposal might have meant its demise. In 1989 the distance would increase between the governor's office on the second floor of the state house and the legislative chambers on the third. If the governor had set the agenda, the legislature would define the policy alternatives.

5

Rules of the Game

It did not take the Legislature long to make a monkey out of me. On Tuesday [Jan. 10], I ran a glowing editorial about the tranquil start of the 1989 session. It started . . . : "As the troops gathered in Topeka this week to make law, they left their bayonets at home. Both camps at the annual bivouac seemed quiet, unwilling to do battle." Before the ink was dry on those words, the lawmakers were tearing each other to shreds.

Editorial, *Emporia Gazette*, January 12, 1989

January 9, 1989. Kansas's coffers were bulging. A large income tax cut seemed a certainty. Republicans held the governor's office and both legislative chambers. Virtually everyone agreed that a large-scale highway program was in the cards and that a host of difficult, expensive, persistent problems could be addressed and resolved.

Then, without warning, both legislative chambers were rocked by major rules changes that would affect all significant actions of the next four months. In the Senate, President Bud Burke and the Republican leadership severely restricted the abilities of minorities (read Democrats) to obtain roll call votes and move bills onto the floor. In the House, Speaker Jim Braden lost on a series of votes that seriously compromised his ability to function as an effective leader. The large Democratic minority and a solid set of dissident Republicans demonstrated that they would be forces to be reckoned with throughout the legislative session. And Gov. Mike Hayden would have to confront a tremendous schism in his party that would haunt him both during the 1989 legislature and through the 1990 elections.

The Kansas experience echoes what was happening in many state legislatures during the late 1980s. Exercising effective party leadership was becoming an increasingly difficult task, and in various other states legislative leaders were deposed, either by their own party or by a bipartisan coalition.[1] Thus, as the 1989 session began, both Senate President Burke and Speaker Braden faced formidable tasks in holding their modest Republican majorities together.

From the perspective of political time, the legislative upheavals—especially the continuing stress in the House—demonstrate how the random and the unexpected can influence policymaking in ways that are different from the effects of long-term trends, identifiable cycles, and specific deadlines. The very nature of policymaking in a democracy is disorderly; the Republican "rebellion" in the House would be only the first of several major shocks to the system absorbed during the 1989 legislative session. In the Senate, however, the party leadership prevailed in mandating order. Indeed, Senate Majority Leader Fred Kerr and Vice-President Eric Yost argued, however disingenuously, that the rules changes would simply make the legislative process run more smoothly. With a straight face, legislative veteran Kerr stated: "We've got to deal with the logjam at the end of the session. The process has the potential for bogging down."[2] In this case, the notion of time simply became a tactical talking point to buttress a purely political case for limiting the power of the minority. In any event, Burke's initial aggressive action as Senate president did serve its purpose: the large Democratic minority found itself at a tremendous procedural disadvantage from the very first day of the 1989 legislative session.

THE SENATE: THE REPUBLICAN LEADERSHIP ASCENDANT

With their narrow (22–18) margin in the Senate, Republicans appeared to have little room for maneuver as the legislature convened. Moreover, Democrats were viewed as campaigning in 1988 on issues that they had forced to a vote in the previous session—not for legislative purposes, but to embarrass the majority party. In particular, a highly publicized Topeka race between GOP incumbent Jeanne Hoferer and Democratic challenger Marge Petty became extremely contentious, with Petty, the eventual winner, making detailed attacks on Hoferer's legislative record. "The campaign left some of our people very angry," Burke stated. "They want to retaliate, but we must be very careful because this could be very divisive and detrimental."[3] Democrats responded that the Republicans, long the Senate majority, simply had grown unaccustomed to being held accountable for their positions. Democratic Sen. Jim Francisco put it bluntly in the opening day's debate: "What we are seeing here today is that Democrats gained two seats and scared the hell out of [the] Republicans."[4]

Burke, with the cooperation of the completely Republican Committee on Organization, Calendar, and Rules (OCR), ultimately opted to put forward a pair of rules changes that would strengthen the majority's position throughout the session and beyond. Democrats viewed the changes as direct attacks, but there was nothing they could do to stop the determined majority. The Republicans not on the OCR received two or three days' notice of the rules changes; indeed, Burke talked to them personally only immediately prior to the January 9 vote. Democrats literally got no warning, in that Burke explained the rules changes in the minority caucus immediately after the Senate convened on the opening day.

Aside from various minor alterations, two major changes stood out. First and most importantly, the Senate president proposed that twenty-one votes be required to force a roll call vote on amendments. Thus, although a plurality vote could pass an amendment, at least twenty-one senators (an absolute majority) would have to request a recorded tally. Second, a supermajority of twenty-seven senators would be needed to pull a bill out of committee, as opposed to the twenty-one votes previously required.

In sum, as long as it could retain the loyalty of its fellow partisans, the Republican leadership effectively precluded the Democrats from mandating roll calls on politically sensitive amendments. The leaders also retained near total control over the substance and order of bills that could reach the floor. Burke could depend on these procedural straitjackets to allow him to control the pace and content of Senate actions. This proved a great boon to Governor Hayden, who could usually rely on Senate support for his initiatives. Democrats could seek to defeat legislation on final passage, but they could not seriously affect the agenda nor could they gain political advantage through the amending process. Amendments could still be offered, but they would be voted up or down on nonrecorded divisions of the body.[5]

The minority was stunned by the proposed modifications in the rules. The Senate Democrats immediately caucused, delaying the rules vote, but they had little recourse. They could only watch as the Republicans rolled over them. Democratic senators reacted bitterly to the procedural limitations. Assistant Minority Leader Paul Feliciano of Wichita stated that "it is the first time in 16 years I've seen such a blatant abuse of power." Minority Leader Mike Johnston, a close personal friend of Senate President Burke, reacted with anger tempered by understanding, noting that "I deeply resented it . . . as totally unnecessary. It diminished the democratic nature of the institution. It didn't have much impact on my relationship with Burke, but I still resented it. He did what he needed to do to keep the support for his leadership."[6]

Although senators on both sides of the aisle predicted continuing problems as the session proceeded, in part due to ill will over the rules revision, Burke had done exactly what was required to maintain control over the Senate. With a four-vote margin and tremendous rural-urban differences on a host of substantive issues, the Senate president needed all the procedural advantages he could muster. Republicans might wander on particular policy matters, but Burke retained strong control over the legislative process. Despite angering the Democrats and upsetting some of his own senators, the president accomplished his major goal of eliminating high-profile partisan bickering on the chamber's floor.

In an ordinary year, the Senate rules coup would have dominated legislative news at the beginning of the session. In terms of procedural wrangles, however, 1989 was no ordinary year. No sooner had the Republican leadership asserted its dominance over the Senate than the House GOP leadership lost virtually all control over both its own caucus and the chamber as a whole.

THE HOUSE: REPUBLICAN LEADERSHIP IN TATTERS

On January 10, 1989, Rep. Kerry Patrick finished what he had begun seven months earlier with his filibuster in the waning moments of the 1988 legislative session. On seven consecutive roll call votes, a combination of ten to twelve dissident Republicans joined a disciplined Democratic minority (fifty-eight votes) to rewrite the permanent rules of the Kansas House and greatly diminish the Republican leadership's ability to dominate the legislative process. Speaker Jim Braden was left reeling, never to recover control of his majority during the remainder of his tenure. The House, hardly the epitome of decorum in the most tranquil times, became even more unruly as mainstream Republicans, "rebel" Republicans, and Democrats all struggled to gain temporary advantage through the 90-plus days remaining in the 1989 session.

In the end, major agenda items were resolved, as coalitions did form, but the process was rarely pretty and often incoherent. Vote counts were tenuous at best, and often the leaders of the minority-rebel coalition had the most accurate numbers. On controversial issues, all heads simply turned toward the electronic display of legislators' votes to see what the results were.

Upon adjournment in May, all factions could claim a string of victories — substantive, procedural, or symbolic. But the legislative process suffered mightily, as the emotions of the rules debate bubbled under the surface throughout the session. The one continuity in the session was the great uncertainty over what bills would pass the House and which way the rebel Republicans would jump on any given issue.

The Rebels

The hard-core group of ten-plus Republican dissidents that emerged had two primary roots—the traditional urban-rural split in Kansas politics and the alleged discrimination against some Johnson County representatives in the House. At the same time, almost all the rebels harbored some personal animosity against Speaker Braden over committee assignments or procedural arrangements.[7] Three factors added to the divisiveness: first, most of the rebels thought they were smarter than the Speaker; second, they generally professed a purity of conservatism that set them apart from the governing clique of more pragmatic Republicans, which included Hayden and the legislative leadership; and finally, the rebels counted in their ranks some older legislators as well as a substantial number of young veterans—those in their late twenties and thirties who had served for several terms. All in all, a mixed bag.

The rebels traced their lineage to the mid-1980s, when Mike Hayden served as House Speaker. However, the immediate causes of their defections emanated from the 1988 legislative session, when they were denied the opportunity to debate Hayden's proposal to return a part of the income tax windfall.[8] The Senate had included a tax cut in a substitute bill for a previously passed House measure; the Speaker subsequently ruled that as an amended version of a House bill it could proceed directly to conference, thus bypassing both the committee and floor stages in the lower chamber. The conference committee issued its nonamendable report, which contained the governor's tax provisions and did not address the issue of the deductibility of federal taxes, an item of great importance to the Johnson County representatives and their wealthy constituents. This situation had led directly to Patrick's filibuster and the disarray of the last few hours of the 1988 session.

Both the leadership and the rebels had set their sights on changing the House rules in 1989. Seeking to paper over intraparty divisions, the leadership wanted to close its daily party caucus to the public and the press, and it also crafted a rule to provide a mechanism for ending filibusters. However, these proposals never saw the light of day, for it was the rebels who succeeded in rewriting the rules.

After the 1988 session, Representative Patrick held several conversations with Minority Leader Marvin Barkis in the context of some business deals as well as their mutual political interests. Well before the 1988 elections, these two legislators had developed a sense of trust and some strong personal ties. The 1988 elections provided a clear opening for this relationship to produce significant results. If the fifty-eight Democrats (of 125 total seats) could stick together, a handful of Republican votes would hold the balance of power in the House. For Patrick and his cohorts, the opportunity could scarcely have been more appealing.

In the two months following the elections, Reps. Patrick, David Miller, and Robert Vancrum, all with districts in or adjacent to Johnson County, began to forge an alliance among a few dissatisfied Republicans. Rep. J. C. Long, one of the original activists, had talked frequently with Patrick over the summer about developing a small, unified group of dissidents that could add other members on specific issues.[9]

Their initial goal was not to weaken the Republican leadership but to capture a part of it. Long noted that "we supported Vancrum for Majority Leader not because he was so superior to R. H. Miller, but we thought there should be some geographic balance in the leadership, to get Johnson County involved. When Vancrum was defeated, [it was] not because of merit. Rather, word came down, from Hayden, Braden."[10]

After Vancrum's one-vote defeat in early December, the rebels turned their attention to revising the chamber's rules. Combing through the list of Vancrum supporters, Patrick, Long, and others came up with a ten-member core group that would hold together, with some exceptions, throughout the session. Their resolve to proceed with rules changes was steeled by the committee assignments they received from the Speaker in the days before the legislature convened.

The initial committee assignment issue revolved around David Miller's bid to head the Appropriations Committee. Miller wanted to replace Rep. Bill Bunten, a leadership loyalist, who had served as chair for an unprecedented three terms. To obtain this post, Miller would have had to jump past Vice-Chair Rochelle Chronister, a veteran mainstream Republican legislator. The leadership did not seriously consider Miller's bid to head Appropriations, but he was slated to become chair of the Post-Audit Committee. Indeed, four of the ten core rebels did become committee chairs, and three served as vice-chairs. Dissatisfied nevertheless, four rebels voluntarily gave up seats on the Appropriations Committee to protest the rejection of Miller's bid for the chairmanship. Braden, who considered his committee assignments for the rebels to be generous, never did completely understand what he had done to earn their ire. Regardless, the rebels, as well as the Democrats, felt they had been slighted in the committee assignment process.

In particular, the dissidents grumbled that Braden had passed over Vancrum to chair the State and Federal Affairs Committee. Although Vancrum's private business and legal affairs produced many situations in which he might have had a conflict of interest, the rebels saw the Speaker's failure to name him chair as unfair and punitive.[11] David Miller concluded that when Braden "passed over Vancrum . . . it was clear that [the leaders] were still practicing the politics of exclusion," especially since Vancrum "was a guy who came within one vote of becoming the floor leader."[12]

As the session approached (with its requirement that permanent rules be adopted at the very beginning), the rebels entered into serious discussions with Barkis and two of his lieutenants — Reps. Bill Roy and Donna Whiteman. Reps. Miller and Vern Williams represented the rebels in the ensuing discussions on procedural changes. On the night before the opening of the session, in a lengthy set of meetings held in the participants' homes, the rebels and the Democrats finally agreed to an agenda of reforms to loosen the Speaker's control of the chamber.

At the same time, various trial balloons were floated to elect either Barkis or a defecting Republican (though probably not a rebel) to the speakership. Both the rebels and Barkis recognized the dangers here, in that their budding relationship depended not on running the chamber jointly, but on limiting the capacity of the Republican leadership to dominate the process. Substantively, the Democrats and the rebels shared almost no issue positions, and Barkis expressed little interest in obtaining the speakership, since he would be unable to exercise real power. Rather, his major goal was to encourage as deep and permanent a split within the Republican ranks as possible. "What's the best thing to do if you're in the minority?" he asked rhetorically. "Divide the majority."[13] Barkis thus became an active and enthusiastic participant in continuing conversations with the rebels about rules changes that would end in an agreed-upon set of proposals as well as a relationship that would continue throughout the session. Still, given the policy differences between the rebels and the Democrats, their cooperation meant only a short-term victory for the dissident Republicans, not a long-term shifting of overall legislative priorities.

The chance to produce a substantial Republican cleavage came with the adoption of permanent rules for the 1989 legislature. As the Senate was clamping down on dissent, the House was moving in precisely the opposite direction. The requirement for adopting rules provided a singular opportunity, in that the legislature simply could not proceed without meeting this immediate deadline. Moreover, the rules vote advantaged the rebels and the Democrats in that the two groups did not need to agree on anything substantive; even a momentary alliance would be devastating for the regular Republican leadership.

Their initial alliance with the Democrats forged, the rebels announced their independence by refusing to participate in the early-session Republican caucuses. Instead of joining their peers off the floor, the rebels remained seated in the House chamber. In part this maneuver was designed to minimize public conflict, but it also served as a clever tactic to hold the rebel group together by making it difficult for the leadership to pick off one or two wavering members. For the first three days of the session, until rules were agreed upon, the rebels avoided their party's caucuses.

Although temporary rules had been adopted, the leadership was obligated to offer a permanent set. The rebel-Democrat coalition had its amendments ready, with an array of fundamental changes. These included:

- Requiring only 70 votes, rather than 84, to pull a bill out of committee[14]
- Decreasing the number of votes needed to force a roll call from 25 to 15
- Allowing the full House, by a simple majority (63 votes), to change the rules
- Prohibiting in most instances debate on a bill unless it has been placed on the debate calendar by 4 P.M. or at the end of the previous day's session
- Providing members with the opportunity to debate and change the entire budget when debating any particular appropriations bill

Initially offered by the rebels as a single set of amendments to the permanent rules, the Speaker ruled that the proposals could and would be voted upon separately. Representative Long, who served as the rebel whip throughout the session, noted:

> We offered the rules change as a package. It was all go or no go with the Democrats. Braden came to the microphone and divided the question. . . . Once we knew the first [change] would go, we knew they all would. Braden got beat on each one, individually. The Democrats were nervous. Our proposals were first on the list. The series of votes was probably the worst thing that could happen to Jim Braden. *The Democrats found out that they could trust us, and we found out that we could trust them.*[15] [emphasis added]

After the succession of votes, Braden acknowledged that he had lost control of his majority and the House as a whole. Adjourning the chamber, a dazed Speaker observed that he knew what it felt like to lead the minority party. In fact, "I certainly was [the Minority Leader] today."[16] Despite their denial of any personal ramifications in the defeat, both Braden and the leadership Republicans were dealt a tremendous blow. As the Speaker put it, "It's very serious to the majority party and to the Legislature as an institution. I don't know what to do now."[17] Indeed, for several weeks, the Speaker struggled with his leadership role. One Republican aide reflected a consensus view in noting that "it took Braden three or four weeks to regain his [nominal] control after the first days of the session. It was definitely not fun."[18] In fact, for the remainder of the session, no single individual or faction would dominate the floor.

This situation meant that Minority Leader Barkis, with a well-disciplined group of Democrats, or rebel leaders Miller and Patrick, with a well-crafted amendment, could seize control of the floor at a moment's notice. Speaker Jim Braden was essentially deprived of his control of legislative time. Uncertainty reigned into the last hours of the session, when Democrats and rebels dictated the terms and process of prison decision making (see Chapter 9).

After the Flood

Despite his rules defeat, Jim Braden continued to occupy the speakership. Both rebels and Democrats agreed that had Braden been the target, he could have been removed or his powers completely emasculated. Braden's response was relatively muted. He offered no public rebukes, although privately and individually he did excoriate some of the defectors. Most importantly, none of the rebels lost their committee positions.[19] In the end, the Speaker remained somewhat befuddled by the rebels' intentions. Reflecting on their actions after his 1991 retirement from the legislature, Braden noted that the bloc voting by the dissidents was disconcerting.

> In making up the committee assignments, I spent gut-wrenching weeks to do everything I could not to ignore them. Of the twelve rebels, six were committee chairs, and two were vice-chairs[20] But with these guys it didn't matter what I did. . . . David Miller envisioned secret meetings going on, things they didn't even know about. They got paranoid and nothing we could say or do could convince them otherwise. That's why I worked so hard on committee assignments.[21]

In the end, Braden's work was to no avail. The rebels had scored a direct hit on the Speaker and indirect, if no less telling, hits on Governor Hayden and the Republican party as a whole. Reactions were quick in coming.

Although the Speaker did talk with the rebels, little was resolved in the aftermath of the rules rebellion. Speaker Braden was withdrawn for several weeks, often allowing his chief aide, Mark Skinner, to dominate the daily legislative leadership agenda meetings. But Braden did not go public in his criticism of the rebels. This task was left to Fred Logan, chair of the state Republican party. Writing to four hundred leading Republican officials three days after the rules vote, his criticism was unambiguous.

> Make no mistake. This was no argument over public policy. The story is this: Ten House Republicans consistently voted with the Democrats to amend the rules *to favor the minority party.* . . .
>
> There is, and always should be, room for debate in a political party on public policy issues. However, in my view, a political party can govern only when it acts in concert on organizational matters. In my view, these changes were spiteful and affect the integrity of the party.
>
> *I solicit your support and help in restoring the integrity of the Republican Party.* [emphasis added][22]

Coming from outside the legislature, with an implicit threat of primary election challenges, Logan's letter did nothing to bridge gaps within the legislative party. Indeed, questioning the rebels' conservative motives only hardened their opposition to the GOP establishment.

The most notable critic of the rebels was their ultimate target. Governor Hayden stewed about the rebels' actions for more than a month, then went semipublic with his criticism in the wake of the windfall votes (see Chapter 6). Before an audience of high school students and teachers, with no reporters present, the governor lambasted the rebels for not doing their jobs and added that several of them had been removed from committees, which was simply not true. In general, Hayden "became aggressive" when asked about the dissident House Republicans.[23] Gleefully, reporters interviewed the students and reconstructed the governor's attack.

The rebels shot back that the governor knew perfectly well that four of them had requested to be taken off the Appropriations Committee. David Miller, renowned for his long legislative hours, stated that the leadership "may not have liked the result, but none of us were slackers."[24] Although Hayden's barbs did sting, by midsession the rebels had won enough victories and weathered enough criticisms to ignore them. In fact, the rebels found they could pressure the governor. Arguing that they had not gone public with their criticisms of him, the rebels called for an end to his attacks. Amazingly, they succeeded in prompting Hayden to write individual letters to them, in which he observed "what fine fellows we were." Thus, observed Rep. Miller, "if my opponent picked up on [the governor's public] comments, I could pull out a letter saying what a great guy I was."[25]

Inside the legislature, however, David Miller's role as a rebel leader began to produce repercussions. Although Speaker Braden had not moved to oust any dissidents from their committee positions in the immediate aftermath of the rules fight, he and other party leaders did seek to keep David Miller from assuming the chairmanship of the Legislative Post-Audit Committee, which was composed of five representatives and five senators.

By early March, past the midpoint of the legislative session, the committee had still not convened; its vote was potentially split 5-5, which pitted five regular Republicans against Miller and four Democrats. The committee rules required that the first meeting take place no later than the fifteenth day of the session (January 23), but the House leaders did not interpret that date as an absolute.

With the legislative session rapidly slipping away, at least two Democratic senators were urged not to support Miller, possibly in exchange for being named vice-chair.[26] Ultimately, as the press played up the story and as a sixth vote could not be found, the Republican legislative leadership reached a compromise with Miller, who agreed to a pair of committee rules changes in exchange for his election as chairman. Ironically, the tough-minded and fiscally conservative Miller was especially well suited to head the Post-Audit Committee, but his ability to function effectively was reduced by the long delay in his election. Finally, on March 6, almost two months into the legislative session, Miller won the chairmanship, which lasted only through 1989, since rules dictated an annual rotation between the House and Senate. He would remain an energetic and quick-witted adversary for the governor and the legislative leadership for the rest of the session and well beyond.[27] His transformation from an Appropriations Committee insider to a rebel was complete.

Squelching the Rebellion? A Consensus of Sorts

Could the Republican rebels have been coopted or coerced into becoming partners with the leadership in 1989? Former legislative leaders Pete McGill, Pat Hurley, and Jim Maag (all lobbyists in 1989) argued that some combination of compromise and tough-minded reprisal might have worked. Maag noted that "the Speaker didn't yank all the rebels' chairs. A lot of people have questioned that."[28] Ex-Speaker McGill, who presided over the House in its path-breaking 1973 session, contended that as a result of Braden's ineffectiveness in dealing with the would-be rebels in his first term as Speaker, he "had no control in his second term (1989–90)." More bluntly, Hurley stated that "you could have dealt with six of them and buried the rest."[29]

While the Republican House leaders and their aides remained divided over reconciliation and retribution, the rebels themselves argued that the leadership could have done much more to placate and manage the dissidents, especially by treating Vancrum better in the wake of his narrow loss to Rep. R. H. Miller. Representative Long argued that "Braden wouldn't talk to us . . . [and] never made an effort to compromise or reason."[30] The Speaker clearly thought that he had gone far enough to placate the rebels, especially in not stripping them of their chairmanships.

In the end, however, the gulf between Hayden/Braden and the rebels, which had grown steadily since 1987, had broadened with Kerry Patrick's 1988 filibuster and had widened even further before the legislative session. Finally, it may simply have grown so wide that there was no possibility for reconciliation. Nor was coercion a realistic possibility, given the small Republican majority. The rebels knew when to stay together (on procedural matters, on prison financing, on matters that embarrassed the governor) and when not to force the issue (highways, for example, where their interests diverged). In short, the governor and the legislative leadership chose not to address the Republican split directly; it would fester for the rest of the 1989/90 legislative cycle and beyond.

GOVERNOR HAYDEN:
A LOWERED PROFILE ON THE SECOND FLOOR

In the Kansas state house, the governor's office sits one floor beneath the legislative chambers on the third floor. Although attention was focused on the legislature in the early days of January 1989, changes were afoot on the second floor as well. By early 1989 Mike Hayden had altered his style of governing. Rather than seeking to intervene actively in the legislative process, Hayden worked hard at setting the policy agenda and then, with some notable exceptions, withdrew from public visibility on many significant items. On some key issues he was simply not a major force, even as the legislative session entered its final days.

Ironically, Hayden's decision to pull back from a public role derived directly from his understanding that the legislature's performance in 1989 was absolutely central to his reputation as an effective governor and would be crucial to his reelection chances in 1990. Perversely, the House's disarray in the early days of its session contributed substantially to his decision to remain aloof from the legislature. The House looked almost totally out of control—a dangerous place to try to exert one's influence, given its weakened Republican leadership. With a large revenue balance and a major income tax cut on the table, Hayden's best chance to compile a strong record of accomplishment was to allow the legislature its own head. After all, he could use his veto power to shape legislation to his liking, he could make late-session deals that would suit his preferences, and above all, Hayden knew that as governor he would ultimately receive credit or blame for whatever the legislature produced.

In explaining his strategic decision to distance himself from the legislature, Mike Hayden commented that in his first two years as governor he might well have viewed the process a bit too much like a Speaker, and too little like a chief executive. In 1989, however,

> before the session we sat down and looked at the situation. We wanted to be successful with the tax cut, highways, prisons. . . . We tried to take care to make people aware of the issues, to work with interest groups. We wanted to bring pressure from the outside, not from the second floor. There was a conscious decision to operate in a different mode. It proved very successful.[31]

Close observers—the media, legislators, bureaucrats, and lobbyists—agreed that Hayden did remain personally outside the legislative fray for most of the 1989 session. But most saw Hayden's actions in terms of tactical adjustment rather than strategic planning. Indeed, for the first few weeks of the legislative session, on the tax cut and death penalty issues, Hayden was front and center within the policymaking process. From their vantage points, various reporters and legislators argued that only after the raucous debate on the return of the income tax windfall in the House and the defeat of his death penalty bill in the Senate did Hayden retreat to his second-floor office, as much in frustration as in reasoned reconsideration of his own position.

In the end, both Hayden and his critics may be partially correct in assessing his reversal of form. The governor may well have decided before the session to take a less active role in the proceedings. When the legislature opened, however, the veteran legislator could not keep from throwing himself into the fray, especially in the wake of the leadership's setbacks in the House. After his tax plan was amended and his death penalty defeated by votes from his own party's senators, the governor saw that his chances for a successful record—crucial to his reelection chances—were jeopardized by his visibility. According to Jim Maag, the senior vice-president of the Kansas Bankers Association and a former legislative leader,

> Mike knew that it was counterproductive to be so active legislatively, but you've got to understand Mike Hayden. It takes every governor some time [to reach this conclusion]. The governor is much better off to let his lieutenants do the negotiations or compromise on the issues. Just by becoming involved, it becomes his issue. You need to lead without the perception of leading. No legislator wants to be perceived as being told how to vote, yet they covet being on the inside. There's a fine line that the governor—and the legislature—have to walk.[32]

Whatever Hayden's intent, he did continue as a legislative activist in the early days of the 1989 session, first pressing for a tax cut, then pushing for a vote on his death penalty bill and criticizing the House rebels. By midsession, however, the governor had retreated to his office, leaving the bulk of the policy agenda in the hands of a legislature that remained, in the House at least, in continuing disarray. Hayden's approach did prove largely successful, given that the legislature would eventually pass a number of major initiatives. At the same time, legislators would empty the state's coffers and leave unresolved an impending property tax crisis, which, in concert, would lead to the governor's electoral vulnerability in 1990.

THE DEMOCRATS: WAITING IN THE WINGS

If Governor Hayden had to balance his strategic political goals and his desires for major policy changes, the Democrats could relish a general congruence between their policy and political goals. Likewise, while Mike Hayden retreated from the daily grind of legislative politics, the Democrats — especially in the House — enjoyed both substantial numbers of opportunities and the capacity to take advantage of them.

Minority leader Marvin Barkis had little talent for nailing down every detail of a policy proposal. Here was a guy who listened to *Les Miserables* as he made the two-hour drive to Topeka from his Louisburg home. In some ways he seemed as headstrong as the French schoolboys who sacrificed themselves in the Victor Hugo classic. But Barkis was smart enough to make a virtue of necessity. He delegated responsibility to a group of talented younger members, many of whom headed task forces (on corrections, children's issues, mental heath, the water plan) that would provide the party with unified positions as these issues came before the House. Barkis stated: "I've got so many race horses. The task forces [organized in the fall] developed from my own inadequacies. You have to be able to take a lot of shit in an open leadership."[33] At the same time, Barkis contended that the rules vote shifted power to the Democrats as much as any other group. He stated that "control of the House rests with 63 votes on a given issue," and that in the end it was the House itself, expressed through whatever majority could be mustered, that could force the formal leadership's hand.

In that context the Democrats' goals were simple: to pursue various social spending ends and increase the governor's vulnerability by spending down the state's fund balances as much as possible. "And we wanted to keep [David] Miller and the rebels in the game," Barkis pointed out. With the notable exception of highways, where the Democratic coalition split apart, the minority could effectively pursue its policy and political interests, which were congruent. In addition, their immediate, short-term goal of embarrassing the leadership and the governor meshed seamlessly with their long-term goal of capturing the House and the governorship. For Barkis, as for the rebels, the session passed in the twinkling of an eye. For Braden, it dragged on unmercifully.

TIME AND STRATEGIC POLITICIANS

Facing future deadlines and current opportunities, elected officials seek to shape both present policies and the context of future political events, especially elections. In early 1989 Governor Hayden and House members could see windows of opportunity for tax cuts, a highway program, and a series of other major policy enactments. At the same time, they understood that the upcoming session would provide most of the context for the 1990 gubernatorial election as well as the 1990 House races, which would be fought in districts redrawn in 1989. House Democrats sought to spend down the state's balances and place the governor in a difficult situation in 1990; Hayden desperately needed a successful legislative session in 1989 to demonstrate that he could win acceptance of his legislative agenda. The disarray in the House prevented anyone from making firm predictions about what legislation would or would not pass.

As the legislative session progressed, the participants' time horizons appeared to shorten; they focused on the opportunities afforded by full coffers and the possibilities of passing a series of historically significant laws. The governor and the legislators alike moved from strategic planning to tactical maneuvering. When the dust cleared, however, the *short-term policy success* of passing legislation did not necessarily prove congruent with *long-term strategic political interests*, especially for Mike Hayden and the House Republicans.

6

Death and Taxes:
The Governor's Agenda

A tax cut was built this week on the shaky foundation laid by Governor Hayden. Although it could have collapsed at any moment like a house of cards, the tax cut survived and was sent to the Governor yesterday. The Governor may sign the bill any moment now because he is already taking credit for the big cuts. . . .

Although the 1989 session began amid bitter bickering, there are signs that the lawmakers at last are ready to get down to business. . . . If the trend continues, the people of Kansas may have reason to be proud of their Legislature, come spring.
—Editorial, *Emporia Gazette*, February 16, 1989

Legislative sessions rarely get off the mark quickly. Ordinarily there is a lot of posturing as committee hearings move forward and the legislature establishes its agenda. Gov. Mike Hayden had other ideas in 1989, however, as he pushed two of his key issues — return of the income tax windfall and the death penalty — to legislative resolution in the early days of the session. Still reeling from their tumultuous battles over rules, both the House and the Senate were immediately faced with proposed tax cuts that would reduce state balances by $100 million. Such a reduction would virtually guarantee that other taxes would be raised to pay for a comprehensive highway package, to say nothing of funding for additional elements of the governor's agenda.

Hayden also pressed energetically for a death penalty vote early in the session. The governor alone was responsible for moving capital punishment onto the policy agenda, leaving the legislature a choice between delaying an emotional, difficult decision or resolving the issue quickly.

On both the windfall and death penalty issues Mike Hayden put his own preferences and political capital on the line; by mid-February, with a partial victory on the tax issue and a stinging defeat on the death penalty, he had retreated into his office for the remainder of the session. The House remained a dangerous, unpredictable place, and the Senate had reacted badly to his pressures. For the governor to emerge in May with a record of legislative triumphs, he would have to let the House and Senate leaders do most of the heavy lifting. Such a prospect, especially for the House, guaranteed him more than one sleepless night.

THE WINDFALL

It is difficult to poinpoint exactly how most discretionary items move onto the short list that represents the operational agenda. Occasionally, however, an issue will arise at a specific time and place and not pass from the agenda until it is resolved. Such was the case with the so-called income tax windfall that Kansas reaped from the 1986 federal tax reform legislation.

In the waning days of the 1986 gubernatorial campaign, Democratic candidate Tom Docking had closed Hayden's margin in the polls to a few percentage points. At a campaign forum in Johnson County, where income tax rates were taken very seriously, Docking answered a question on returning the windfall with a positive, if somewhat ambiguous, response. Hayden then stood up and categorically agreed to return the windfall. This is what John Kingdon labels a "focusing event," in which a condition (the consequences of the 1986 tax reforms) emerged almost full blown as a problem (a "windfall" for Kansas tax collection).[1] Although no dollar amount had yet been attached to a tax cut, Hayden and Docking had both adopted a powerful term — the windfall — which virtually assured that a substantial state income tax reduction would be proposed and passed.

From that moment in October 1986 until March 1989, when Hayden signed his second income tax reduction bill in ten months, "returning the windfall" remained at the top of the Kansas policy agenda. Strangely enough, for all its power as a political issue, the windfall was subject to tremendous debate over how much revenue was actually represented and how it should or could be returned to the taxpayers of Kansas. Even more strangely, this major tax cut provided almost no 1990 political boost for Mike Hayden in the strongly Republican Johnson County suburbs. Given its emergence from the 1986 campaign, the windfall issue was rooted in a past promise, not a vision of the future.

Defining the Windfall: Words and Numbers

For more than two years, a cut in the Kansas income tax had retained its status as a key agenda item. Although the budget did not allow any action in 1987, the issue simply would not go away, given the specificity of Hayden's promise and the growing balances in the state's treasury in 1988/89. What became increasingly clear was that establishing the existence of a windfall was simpler than agreeing on how much the windfall amounted to and how it would be distributed back to the taxpayers.

Words

Deborah Stone argues that "policy stories" form the context of decision making; she sees strategic politicians as seeking to establish control over the policy process by "represent[ing] the world in such a way as to make themselves, their skills, and their favorite course of action necessary."[2] Stone's observation is acute and, in most instances, correct. But Governor Hayden and his fellow strategic politicians in the legislature could not represent the world as completely as they might have wished. Instead, they were stuck with the definition imposed on the tax issue by the 1986 campaign: any extra funds that flowed into the Kansas treasury in the wake of federal tax reform were labeled as a windfall.

The formal definition of windfall, "an unexpected or sudden gift, gain, or advantage,"[3] was only marginally relevant to how the issue was framed in 1988/89. More powerful was the assumption that changes in the federal tax code had dumped a pile of money into the state's coffers. As *Kansas City Star* business columnist Jerry Heaster put it, "the windfall . . . is that massive lode of extra tax money that is now cascading into the state treasury as result of changes in the federal tax law."[4] In Johnson County, Heaster's characterization certainly held sway; Hayden had virtually no political choice but to cut taxes so as to "return the windfall," even though all players acknowledged that there was no way to write a law so that those most affected were relieved, on a dollar-for-dollar basis, of their additional tax burdens.

The windfall appellation was powerful beyond its impact on regional politics. With their affluent constituents, Johnson County legislators campaigned hard for its return, while most rural lawmakers had little stake in the issue, given the modest incomes of their districts' residents. The windfall label obscured the fact that no new state tax law had increased the state's revenues. Tax rates remained precisely the same before and after the 1986 federal reforms, which simply raised the base amount that was touched by the state income levy. Indeed, one impact of the federal laws was to recapture some of the monies lost to the repeal of the "booster" tax on incomes that had been in force during the early 1980s. In addition, the windfall notion, especially as presented in Hayden's promise, preempted any attempt to retain the additional tax revenues in order to fund programs or serve as the basis for substantial property tax relief.

Still, beyond the politics of Hayden's reelection efforts for 1990, there were strong reasons to reduce income taxes in 1989. With a substantial amount of the state's revenues off the table, lawmakers could then assess state needs in light of available resources. As the *Topeka Capital-Journal* editorialized, "For two years Kansans have lived with an unlegislated tax increase. Hayden now says the state can afford to return it. So the state should do it. Then, if it needs to take some of it back for new projects it can do so by levying new taxes."[5]

Numbers

Policy stories are not exclusively told in words. As Stone notes, "In policy debates, numbers are commonly used to tell a story" and thus set the agenda. In particular, she observes that "to count something is to assert that it is an identifiable entity with clear boundaries."[6] Even if the very definition of the extra tax revenues as a windfall made it certain that an income tax reduction would be forthcoming, there was no immediate agreement on either the amount of the windfall or how it should be returned. All sides eventually agreed on a $135 million figure as an estimate of the annual increment of state taxes derived from the 1986 federal reforms, although they simultaneously agreed that no completely accurate accounting of the figure was possible. As Secretary of Revenue Ed Rolfs concluded, "The only safe statement is that no one really knows what the windfall is." In addition to the problem of not being able to estimate the tax consequences for a single year (1988), Rolfs observed that this inability would affect subsequent baseline estimates for economic growth. Still, the $135 million figure remained intact and provided a tangible target for all sides to shoot at.

The Hayden administration had two important reasons to underestimate the size of the windfall: (1) to retain as much revenue as possible to pursue its own policy initiatives; and (2) to claim that the bulk of skyrocketing tax receipts were coming from the state's economic growth, not the vagaries of the tax code. To this end, Budget Director Michael O'Keefe accepted the initial estimate of $135 million, which was probably somewhat low,[7] and proceeded to enumerate a laundry list of ways in which the windfall had already been returned in 1988. O'Keefe argued that $36 million in income tax cuts had been made, along with $21 million in income tax revenues automatically returned to school districts. Coupled with those changes, O'Keefe noted that $13 million of the windfall was paid by out-of-state residents and that the 1988 legislature passed measures that reduced Kansas business taxes by $24 million.[8] Throughout the fall of 1988, O'Keefe and Hayden contended that only $41 million of the windfall remained to be distributed to the Kansas taxpayers.

The O'Keefe-Hayden position simply could not stand up to a barrage of criticism from editorialists and legislators. In a typical editorial, the

McPherson Sentinel laid out Hayden's figures and concluded: "Sorry, governor, it won't sell any better than the other shell games you have played with the voters so far. The only approach that will work is an honest one."[9] Indeed, by sticking to a demonstrably unrealistic figure, even as he promised to reduce taxes, Hayden continued to be at odds with many of his own partisans, including the Johnson County Republicans, who generally put the remaining windfall increment at approximately $100 million.

As the 1989 legislative session approached, the governor was committed to "returning the windfall" and was unable to set the amount to be returned as low as he desired. Backing away from his original estimate and seeking to wring from the predicament as much credit as he could, Hayden made arrangements to announce his proposed tax cut in Johnson County on January 5, four days before the legislature was to convene.

Sweeping the Money off the Table: Timing and the Windfall

With the unveiling of the FY 1990 budget, which included a proposed $79 million income tax cut and almost $15 million in income tax rebates to school districts, Mike Hayden set the stage for resolving the windfall issue. The governor set the agenda on both the size of the tax cut (twice his previous estimate) and the timing of its enactment; he called for final passage by February 1, a mere three weeks after the legislative session opened.

John Kingdon observes that in setting the policy agenda, there is frequently a "window of opportunity," when the three streams of problems, policies, and politics can combine to produce a tenable alternative that addresses a particular issue.[10] As a strategic politician and policy formulator, Mike Hayden recognized the advantage of resolving the windfall issue early in the legislative session. He hoped to win substantial credit from the Johnson County Republicans, who would then be in his debt as he sought to patch together support for an extensive highway package that would appeal largely to areas beyond the Kansas City suburbs. From a political vantage point, an income tax cut for the affluent Johnson County voters and a highway program directed at much of the rest of the state would help create a winning coalition for the 1990 election.

To achieve this particular pair of victories, however, Hayden calculated that he would need to remove the possibility of using windfall monies ($80–90 million per year) for funding highways or other programs. The longer those funds stayed on the table, the less likely the legislature would be to reduce taxes in line with Hayden's proposal. "To lessen the temptation [to spend the money for new programs] I am asking that the return of the windfall be made your first priority," the governor requested in his State of the State Address.[11]

Concurrently, both legislative chambers were engaged in their rules battles. Hayden had to face the fact that rebel Republicans in the House had initially been drawn together in 1988 by their opposition to his tax cut package, which had not included the deductability of federal income taxes in computing state taxes. Again, this was essentially an issue put forward by Johnson County legislators, but it also represented a procedural sore point, in that the House had been prevented from debating or voting on deductability the previous May, thus precipitating Rep. Kerry Patrick's filibuster.

In January 1989, fresh from their House rules victory, the rebels could turn their attention to the issue that had fomented their initial insurrection. By holding up Hayden's legislative initiatives, they could embarrass him as well as force consideration of their pet tax provision. The governor might desire to act strategically, looking ahead to the 1990 election, but the rebels could afford to take a more short-term approach that emphasized their tactical advantage in a chamber where they held the balance of voting power.

After pro forma Taxation Committee hearings and a narrow (6–5) favorable vote, the Hayden windfall bill passed the Senate on January 24 by a 29–11 margin; the February 1 deadline might not be met, but the proposal was on a fast track. As Senate Minority Leader Mike Johnston put it, the windfall "has taken on a life of its own . . . [in that] the governor thinks he has to have a victory here today or he's going to be in real trouble in 1990."[12] Indeed, several Republican senators were upset that other taxation issues, most notably property tax relief, were not considered concurrently.

The House, with its weakened Republican leadership, would pose a much more difficult test for the governor. The rebels were waiting to attack the tax bill. Furthermore, the minority Democrats had also been denied any voice in constructing the windfall package of 1988, and looking at the Senate actions and the governor's timetable, they saw the potential for being shunted aside once again. Rep. Joan Wagnon, a veteran Taxation Committee member, observed that "you can't push real big decisions without people feeling they were rolled over by a truck."[13]

At the same time, House Democrats were legitimately divided over the prospect of a large income tax cut. Many of their favored programs—children's issues and education, among others—were in need of additional funding, and most had not committed themselves to return the windfall. Still, it was difficult to oppose a substantial tax reduction, and returning the windfall would be an important initial political step in reducing the state's revenues to the point that the governor would lose spending flexibility in 1990. To some extent then, the strategic goals of both legislative Democrats and the Republican governor might be served by returning the windfall. Hayden would get credit for fulfilling his campaign promise, and the Democrats would take a first step toward creating a tight budget situation in 1990, which they thought would hamper the governor's flexibility in running for reelection. Conversely, if state budget balances remained high enough, Hayden would be in the driver's seat, as the *Wichita Eagle-Beacon* observed.

> Thanks to the current financial surplus, the state can probably get by the next two or three years without a tax increase. That time frame runs through the 1990 election, giving the governor an incredible campaign boost. Thus, when the imbalance between revenue and spending hits in the early 1990s, Mr. Hayden could be well into his second, final term, leaving legislators to explain things to voters.[14]

As the legislative session moved forward, however, long-term strategies almost immediately gave way to tactical maneuvering related to Hayden's February 1 deadline for passing the tax cut bill. The House Taxation Committee approved the Hayden package on January 27, after defeating two attempts to amend the bill, including one proposal that would have restored the deductability of federal taxes. Floor debate was scheduled for January 31.

By the end of business on January 31, the governor's set of proposals had been placed in jeopardy and his timetable set back by virtually the same forces that had changed the House rules three weeks earlier. The Democrat-rebel coalition lowered the Hayden income tax cuts from $79 million to $53 million, while offering property tax reductions of $50 million. Most importantly for dissident Republicans, federal taxes could be deducted on state returns if the taxpayer was willing to choose a somewhat higher set of rates. At the same time, the property tax cuts in the House version were tied to the school finance formula and would not benefit the wealthy school districts of Johnson County at all.

The House actions, taken during a chaotic session, demonstrated conclusively that neither the party leadership nor the governor could count on solid Republican majorities in the chamber, even on an issue as popular as a $79-million income tax reduction. In the Democrats' January 31 morning caucus, Minority Leader Marvin Barkis concluded that "the main goal is to have delayed this for a while," and Rep. Donna Whiteman argued that the "bottom line is that we want an amendment, so it will go to conference." In the end, forty-two Democrats joined twenty-nine Republicans in adopting GOP rebel Vancrum's amendment in favor of federal deductability.

For the second time in three weeks, the House leadership was stunned, as was the governor. After the vote, the governor's press secretary, Kathy Peterson, and the leadership's top aide, Mark Skinner, stood in the well of the House and identified the twenty-nine Republican defectors—almost half the party's contingent in the chamber. Meanwhile, the Speaker could do little more than shrug, responding to reporters' queries with his own rhetorical question, "Do you expect me to explain what happened?"[15] The leadership had done the governor's bidding but had failed to test the levels of support for his bill; instead they had sought to keep to Hayden's initial timetable, a tactic that reminded many of the dissident Republicans of how they had been steamrollered in the waning hours of the 1988 session. After eight months, they got their vote on deductability of federal taxes.

In tactical terms, the House actions meant that a conference committee would meet to review the differences between the chambers' bills. In fact, it was the House and the governor who were on the opposite sides of the table, although there were real questions as to how long the governor could hold the Senate in line. Sen. Fred Kerr, the majority leader, observed that the governor's bill, a "straightforward step to collecting the windfall, [now] contains a lot of different questions." He wondered "whether this bill can be revived at all" and concluded that "we're not going to be able to work things out very quickly."[16]

Strategically, the governor's defeat meant that the windfall issue might not be decided until the end of the session. Such a delay could endanger Hayden's highway package and open up the tax cut to reductions from Democrats (and some Republicans) who wanted to increase spending. Both the legislative leadership and the governor redoubled their efforts to get the income tax monies off the table. From February 1 until the tax bill was passed two weeks later, their central theme was that expressed by Senate President Burke: "We have a window of opportunity this session, but it is closing fast."[17]

Hayden's response to the House's actions on the windfall was the rough equivalent of a two-year-old's promise to hold his breath until he gets his way. The governor immediately vowed that "I will sign no spending bill until the windfall is returned to the taxpayers of Kansas."[18] As House-Senate conferees began to meet, the governor's threat helped frame the issue, but more significant was the fact that the two houses had both passed substantial tax relief measures and that, as Johnson County Republican Sen. Audrey Langworthy put it, "the people want their money back. They don't want us to spend all session fighting over it."[19] Most legislators agreed that some resolution would be forthcoming, but as conference committee negotiations started to drag, their optimism for a quick solution became less marked.

The House-Senate conference exhibited two patterns that would be repeated later in the session on other major pieces of legislation (highways, prisons). First, the House Republican leaders appointed conferees who did not faithfully support the chamber's position; Senate conferees, conversely, strongly backed the chamber's bill.[20] These circumstances led directly to a repeating game in which the Senate's version served as the major legislative vehicle. Subsequently, the original Senate legislation would be changed slightly and sent back to the House, with hopes that the necessary votes could be rounded up to support a version as close to the first Senate version as possible. The House's voting majority—the coalition between Democrats and dissident Republicans—was left without effective representation in the conferences because leadership-appointed Republicans (two of three from both houses) could dominate the proceedings.[21] Kerry Patrick observed that this pattern had been evolving for some time and that "for two or three years the House conferees didn't support the House position on lots of legislation."[22] Again, a long-term problem was translated into an immediate confrontation, given Hayden's imposition of a deadline.

To increase the pressure to support the governor's position, mainstream Republicans argued each time the windfall came up that it might well be the last chance the legislators would have to vote on a tax cut. Rep. Rochelle Chronister, a Republican leader, argued that

> I'm getting short of patience in supporting a $79 million income tax return. Like most rural legislators, the income tax refund is not a major concern in my district. The longer it goes, the less likely it is to happen. . . . *This may be your last opportunity to see that that $79 million goes back. I say that in all sincerity.* [emphasis added]

Other rural legislators joined the chorus with similar arguments. Finally, the Speaker came to the floor, stating that "if you seriously want a $79 million tax cut, you should vote against sending this bill back to conference. *I am firmly convinced that this will be the last opportunity to vote on an income tax cut* [emphasis added]." As a rule legislators gave little weight to such threats, yet unquestionably there was some truth in the claim that rural districts were impatient with the windfall issue.

As the House took its first vote on the conference proposal, the governor carried his case to the public in a series of speeches around the state. Beyond the tax cut itself, Hayden personally was becoming the central issue, as he set deadlines and encouraged a conference process that discouraged compromise between the two chambers' versions of windfall legislation.

The House played its accustomed role February 9 by again defeating the original $79 million Hayden package by a 67–56 margin, with the core rebel-Democratic alliance (ten Republicans joining fifty-seven Democrats) voting to send the bill back to conference. While the press played up public debates between Hayden and House Minority Leader Barkis, even more serious divisions remained between leadership Republicans and their dozen or so dissident party colleagues. More important, a second solid defeat of the Hayden package demonstrated that some significant modifications would be essential if the governor was to obtain an early resolution of the windfall issue. One Republican House conferee, Taxation Committee Chair Keith Roe, stated: "I am not going down there [to the House floor] with an $80 million bill."[23]

What the conference did produce was a "grab bag of programs . . . put together in hopes of luring enough House votes to move the measure to the Senate,"[24] where support remained reasonably strong. The compromise package included: (1) $69 million in income tax cuts; (2) an option that allowed for deducting federal taxes in calculating state obligations; (3) substantial short-term property tax relief for those most affected by the state's impending reappraisal; and (4) significant increases in state income tax rebates to school districts, a provision that also addressed the property tax issue, especially for wealthy areas. The tax bill sailed through the House, 99–25, and the Senate, 38–1. Returning $100 million or so of tax money is scarcely an unpopular action.

All sides could claim a victory, another pattern that would be repeated during the session. The governor got the bulk of his windfall proposal; the rebel Republicans obtained deductability and more funds for their school districts; and Democrats provided higher levels of property tax relief for those most seriously affected by reappraisal.

Hayden immediately sought the lion's share of credit for the legislation, observing that "we kept the Legislature's shoulder to the wheel by standing firm in vowing not to sign any spending bills until taxes were cut first."[25] At the same time, he claimed no active involvement in constructing the final compromise; rather, he waited to see what the legislature would produce, only then deciding to sign the bill into law.

Ironically, Hayden ultimately received little electoral credit for his efforts to return the windfall. Although Johnson County residents gained the most from this action, the wrangling over the amount of the windfall and the issue of federal deductability undercut Hayden's ability to benefit from the tax cuts. Moreover, removing the income tax money from the table early in the session meant that funding Hayden's programmatic priorities would require tax increases in the months to come. Hayden later argued, in a different context, that voters have "short memories." That may not always be the case, but in the instance of credit for the return of the windfall, both the 1990 primary and general elections demonstrated that the voters gave him little long-term credit for the largest tax cut in Kansas history.

In addition, Hayden's other agenda items began to receive legislative attention. The day after Hayden signed the tax cut legislation (March 2), the House Transportation Committee reported a bill that would raise taxes $169 million annually. As House Majority Leader Robert H. Miller observed, "There's no doubt that the public is going to view this as inconsistent."[26] The delay in passing the windfall legislation cut meant that it received relatively little play before new tax issues came to the fore. Hayden's inability to control the timing of multiple issues weakened his capacity to act effectively as a strategic politician. The legislative session was moving on, and the 1990 election remained almost two years away — an eternity in political time.

DEBATING DEATH: THE GOVERNOR SETS THE AGENDA

The Kansas policy agenda for 1989 included the death penalty only because Governor Hayden placed it there. Although the death penalty produced much emotional testimony and demanded serious debate, the legislature would not have raised the issue on its own. The governor had made the death penalty a key 1986 campaign issue, and he had already pushed for its passage, only to be defeated in the previous legislature. With a handful of new faces in the Senate, however, victory seemed at least a possibility in 1989.

The death penalty did not play a major role in any legislative race; in fact, it was rarely mentioned, and then only in the context of the governor's active advocacy. At the same time Kansas public opinion strongly supported the idea of reestablishing capital punishment. As of the November 1988 election, 69 percent of the population supported the death penalty; Hayden's personal commitment seemed mirrored in public attitudes.[27] Legislators and especially state senators (who had opposed capital punishment, 18–22, in 1987) thus found themselves in a difficult position if they chose to oppose the death penalty.

A postelection head count showed that once again the Senate would probably defeat a bill reinstituting capital punishment. However, the governor's personal commitment drove him to place the legislature on the record in 1989, especially since survey results showed that "the people of Kansas overwhelmingly want the death penalty restored."[28] Hayden not only placed capital punishment on the state's agenda, he formulated the specific alternative to be considered by the legislature. For 1989, Hayden's proposal called for the death penalty in a relatively small number of instances, rather than reflecting his prior commitment to capital punishment in all cases of felony murder.[29] This issue was completely shaped by Hayden, from start to finish, as he placed his own political capital at risk. In seeking legislation that the public overwhelmingly supported, Hayden's risk seemed minimal, but a defeat would illustrate real political weakness.

As he had done with the windfall, the governor sought an early vote, and the Senate was willing to oblige him. In late December newspaper stories depicted the Senate as close to supporting the death penalty, at least in principle. Hayden saw himself as having a tactical advantage, given indications that support was evenly split. "If it fails by one vote," he reasoned, "then all twenty of the people who voted 'no' could be held accountable by their constituents as 'the' vote that caused it to fail."[30]

Hayden's reasoning was open to question, since constituents would have to wait almost four years to hold their state senators accountable for their death penalty vote. But if the governor's long-term strategy was problematic, its flaws paled before the problems with his immediate approach to the issue in January 1989. His first major news conference on the death penalty was held January 16, the date of the Martin Luther King, Jr., holiday. Across the state, critical editorials burst into print, including one in the *Hutchinson News:*

> Timing is important.
> In politics, sometimes it's all that matters.
> Kansas Gov. Mike Hayden's timing of his death march through the state to drum up support for a Sunflower State death penalty couldn't have been planned at a worse time. . . .
> The governor is entitled to his views, but his timing proves he may well be insensitive to the concerns of many of his constituents, . . .
> Perhaps Monday was just another day off for the state's chief executive, but he should have realized his proselytizing for death . . . could easily have been conducted on a different day.
> . . . it wouldn't surprise us if he planned his next death march on the next inappropriate holiday, say Valentine's Day.[31]

The governor had taken a politically popular stance (in favor of capital punishment) but had actually injured himself with his timing.

Once the governor moved capital punishment onto the legislative agenda, discourse on the issue proceeded quickly in an emotional yet routine manner. Like abortion, debates on the death penalty take on a ritualistic cast, with proponents and opponents offering a mix of rational arguments and heart-tugging personal cases. Although television coverage of the legislature had fallen sharply over the 1980s, six cameras were on hand to record the drama of the death penalty hearings. After years of conflict, everyone knew their lines, and the issue moved through the legislative process with remarkable speed. Senate committee hearings were held Janaury 24–25, and the bill was advanced to the floor without a committee recommendation on January 30, although some opponents complained that the chair, Sen. Ed Reilly, had "unnecessarily rushed" the legislation.[32]

At the same time, a bipartisan group of eighteen senators provided the chamber with a legitimate alternative to the death penalty in their proposal to require a forty-year sentence for premeditated murder.[33] This so-called Hard 40 alternative provided a way of demonstrating toughness on crime without opting for the death penalty.

On February 1, just one week after the initial committee hearings, and one day after the House defeated his original windfall proposal, the Kansas Senate voted 22–18 to reject Hayden's death penalty bill on a procedural motion. Although the governor tried to complain that he had not received an up-or-down vote on the issue itself, David Mills, his legislative liaison, had in fact agreed that the procedural motion reflected a substantive decision. "It won't come back at the behest of the governor this year," he stated. "There are a number of important things to be done."[34] Senate Judiciary Committee Chair Wint Winter, Jr., concluded that the vote was "the parliamentary equivalent of driving a stake through the heart of the vampire."[35] The death penalty was thus swiftly swept off the agenda. Both the governor's aides and key legislators interpreted the vote as the chamber's final say on capital punishment for 1989. Republican Sen. Dick Bond concluded that "the leadership clearly wanted a roll call vote to put some finality to the question and not just keep it hanging, so we can move on to the significant issues of the session — taxes, highways, prisons, reapportionment."[36]

For Hayden, the capital punishment rejection coupled with the initial defeat of his tax bill the previous day represented a major political setback. It also marked the beginning of a new gubernatorial style, in which the chief executive maintained a much lower profile for the remainder of the session. With the two defeats of January 31 and February 1, Hayden got the message that a high-visibility, confrontational style would not be productive in a legislature where Republican majorities were razor thin and partisanship was often a secondary consideration in sorting out votes.

Still, Hayden lost relatively little with the early death penalty vote. He had supported a popular measure, lost narrowly, and did not have to revisit the difficult issue during the remainder of the session. Indeed, the death penalty's resolution allowed for the legislature and the governor to address other major criminal justice issues — especially sentencing guidelines and prison construction — in an environment less charged with the high emotion of capital punishment. In addition, the legislature passed and the governor signed a measure requiring forty years of imprisonment without the possibility of parole for a murder conviction. This did not satisfy the most avid of the death penalty advocates, but it put the issue to rest for the remainder of the Hayden administration.

SEQUENCE AND THE POLICY AGENDA

Chief executives can place items on the operational agenda but cannot necessarily control the subsequent decision-making process, either by structuring alternatives or obtaining favorable results. In 1988/89 Gov. Mike Hayden faced a particularly promising legislative session, since the state's coffers were full, as well as tremendous political danger, since he needed significant policy victories to demonstrate his gubernatorial leadership abilities. As a former Speaker and committee chair, Hayden understood as well as anyone the dynamics of the legislative session, with its tendency toward delay and endgame politics. Indeed, the governor had proven himself a formidable practitioner of these politics. In the waning hours of the 1986 session Speaker (and gubernatorial candidate) Hayden had agreed to a sales tax increase that ended a revenue-based policy stalemate that he had helped to create.

In 1989 Hayden would again prove adept at playing the political endgame in the legislature's last days and hours, when top leaders can often cut deals that would be impossible at any other time. Nevertheless, with several major spending items on the agenda (highways, prisons, and social programs, among others), as well as the politically difficult problem of reapportionment, Hayden did not want too much on his platter at the end of the session. Rather, he sought to demonstrate his political clout early on by resolving two major issues during the legislature's first month of activity. With the dollars of the tax cut and the emotion of the death penalty behind it, the legislature would be free to focus on the central issues of the session — a prison demanded by a federal judge, a highway program lusted after by the governor and others, and a reapportionment map required by the constitution.

As of mid-February Hayden had been pummeled on the death penalty and had won at best a mixed victory on the tax cut. He had also abandoned any attempt to lead publicly during the session. Despite these setbacks, his sense of sequence was apt. Delay on the death penalty and, especially, on the windfall's return would have provided the legislature with too many issues and too many resources to sort out easily in the waning days of the session. Absent these issues, the legislature could at least hope to resolve the other major agenda items by May's adjournment.

7

Dogs That Don't Bark,
Those That Won't Hunt

If the state's highest priority issues were to be ripe for settlement in the final days of the legislative session, many other important items had to be resolved. The operational agenda must be of roughly manageable proportions; if not, major issues may simply be ignored or handled in slipshod ways. Moreover, too many items may reduce the capacity for coherent bargaining among a relatively small number of key actors.[1]

As February 1989 gave way to March and the Kansas legislature entered the homestretch, a host of significant issues remained unaddressed. By April 26, however, when the legislature returned to Topeka for the final few days of its wrap-up (or veto) session, many of these potentially divisive agenda items had been resolved.

Some issues could be categorized as "dogs that won't hunt"—political vernacular for agenda items that simply did not have enough support to move through the legislative process. More significant were these "dogs that didn't bark"—thorny issues that ordinarily elude resolution until the last days of the legislative session. These included such difficult problems as reapportionment, tort reform, and the annual battles over school finance funding and social welfare spending. Through a combination of luck, a strong financial position, and the pressure of other concerns, these issues were settled early so the legislature could turn its attention to the most intractable issues—highways and prisons—in its final days.

DOGS THAT WON'T HUNT

Problems will frequently reach the agenda stage only to go no further. No compelling conditions or energetic policy entrepreneur will force the coupling of a problem to a politically palatable solution. In such an instance, the problem will be dismissed, perhaps to resurface another year. Not every agenda item is ripe for policymaking. In 1989 two major issues fit this category: Washburn University's proposed entrance into the state university system and the legislative pensions question, which had been crucial in several 1988 election races.

Higher Education: The Politics of Linkage

> *The Board of Regents . . . has compounded its past practices in groveling to get money at all costs. The board has told Gov. Mike Hayden that it will go along with adding Washburn to the state system if the governor throws enough money the Regents' way.*
> —Editorial, *Hutchinson News*, February 27, 1989

May 1988 brought good news to the higher education community in Kansas. The first installment of a three-year salary enhancement package—labeled the Margin of Excellence (MOE)—passed the legislature, and full state coffers made the next year's increment look like a good bet. The governor proposed a concentrated, though belated, effort to address a long-standing problem: state university faculty salaries were low relative to those at comparable institutions. Despite the 1988 results, some professors continued to leave Kansas, lured by larger salaries and greater opportunities elsewhere. The Margin of Excellence only began to address the needs of higher education, and there were no guarantees that even this "catch-up" program would be funded in 1989 and 1990.[2]

University salaries, however, reflected only a single side of the multifaceted higher education agenda. Two other long-term issues required attention as the governor, various administrators, and legislators jockeyed for position over the summer of 1988. First, there were the community colleges, nineteen of them to be exact, which often competed for higher education funding with the six Regents institutions. Even given Kansas' substantial geographic reach, no rational plan would have provided for so many state-funded institutions. The community colleges (and the universities) seemed impervious to reorganization, which all would have regarded as a political attack. Still, the community college–university tension was simply politics as usual. The governor's proposal to add Topeka's Washburn University to the state's higher education system, however, was viewed by all as a major challenge to the status quo.

As the last surviving municipal university in the nation, Washburn had become a true anomaly in higher education. Precariously funded by tuition, local property taxes, and state grants, it had remained outside the

Kansas Regents' University system. Although various proposals had surfaced to bring Washburn into the state system, legislators had exhibited little desire to make a long-term commitment of resources to one more institution in a state already overburdened by its higher education obligations.

The 1988/89 revenue glut offered Mike Hayden, a longtime supporter of incorporating Washburn into the state system, an opportunity to move the issue onto the legislative agenda. The governor's chief ally in this endeavor was Rep. Bill Bunten (R-Topeka), the normally tight-fisted Appropriations Committee chair. According to Bunten, "The truth of the matter is that this is the year that Washburn comes into the system. It either comes in this year, or it doesn't come in for a long time."[3] Most observers agreed that sooner or later Washburn would become a state school, but the circumstances for its entry into the system were not clear at all. Its president, John Duggan, summarized the arguments: "Either we go in when we're strong with pretty good funds, or eventually . . . on the brink of bankruptcy. Then the state will have to pay a lot more for keeping the institution going."[4]

Despite the short-term availability of revenue in 1988/89, legislators from both university districts and community college locales generally objected to Washburn's inclusion. Hayden responded by linking Washburn's fate to those of the other higher educational institutions as he cobbled together a comprehensive package for legislative consideration.

Building on the 1988 passage of the Margin of Excellence, Hayden appropriated the MOE label to represent his entire set of higher education proposals — more funding for community colleges, higher salaries and additional resources for Regents' universities, and the inclusion of Washburn in the university system. The dance among interested parties — Washburn, the state's Board of Regents [for six universities], the community colleges, the governor, various lobbyists, and dozens of legislators — was something to behold as consideration of the so-called Margin of Excellence Partnership Act unfolded. On its own, the Washburn proposal was a nonstarter. Hayden's only chance of success was to maintain the linkage among the package's components. Somewhat surprisingly, the Regents offered their formal support in mid-February for the governor's entire proposal, largely to keep alive the $16 million in MOE funds ticketed for the university system.

A few days later the governor reciprocated by backing virtually full (95 percent) funding for the Margin of Excellence in a speech at Lawrence, home of the University of Kansas. Nevertheless, most legislators retained their skepticism toward linking funding for community colleges, the universities, and Washburn's entrance into the system. In early March the governor's top education staffer, Denise Apt, refused to wield a veto threat in response to Senate questions on Washburn linkage. More importantly, Hayden had made few comments on the issue since his State of the State message on January 9, when he had endorsed a comprehensive approach.

The Washburn-MOE package remained intact as the legislation began to move through the Kansas Senate, but the threads holding it together were beginning to fray. In mid-March the Senate Ways and Means Committee barely (7–6) endorsed the proposal, with one key Republican senator suggesting that he might reverse his position on the floor. Simultaneously, the House Appropriations Committee, chaired by Washburn advocate Bill Bunten, cut its recommended faculty salary increases by one percent. The implied threat was clear; Rep. John Solbach (D-Lawrence) observed that "this is the first shot in the battle of the regents budget and whether Washburn comes into the system."[5]

But the governor would not cement the ties between Washburn and the Margin, saying merely that he would "reevaluate" his position if Washburn remained outside the Regents' system. Indeed, a looming Senate showdown would come down to whether legislators could exclude Washburn, pass the rest of the MOE, and remain confident that Hayden would sign the resulting legislation. As Lawrence Sen. Wint Winter, Jr., often referred to as "the Senator from KU," optimistically put it, "I don't believe there's any way . . . the governor is going to veto the Margin of Excellence. I think that would be politically unacceptable [and that] he's trying to get as much mileage out of that as he can without saying he'll veto it."[6]

Editorial writers tossed around terms like "snake-oil sellers"[7] and "the Washburn bribe"[8] to describe the governor's package, which appeared to reflect the general unpopularity of the Washburn proposal throughout the state. On March 22 the Senate, in an unrecorded vote (24–16), rejected bringing Washburn into the state system, while approving legislation that would support the remainder of the governor's higher education initiative. Even though Washburn lost the legislative war, it subsequently won a consolation prize, as state aid to the institution was increased by $1.5 million per year.

In the end, virtually all of Kansas higher education—the six Regents' schools, the nineteen community colleges, private institutions, and Washburn—came out of the 1989 legislative session as major winners. The state's rosy financial condition allowed legislators the luxury of increasing support to all institutions, thus shoring up a system that arguably provided more higher education than Kansas could profitably use. Finally, with his Washburn initiative, the governor may have snatched political defeat from the jaws of victory as he supported substantial educational spending increases but received relatively little credit. By making Washburn the centerpiece of his MOE partnership he absorbed a public defeat that diminished the impact of his backing for higher education funding increases. Moreover, the long-term problem of too many institutions chasing limited higher education resources went completely unaddressed.

Legislative Pensions

Kansas legislators in 1988 didn't have the guts to go to their bosses and ask for . . . an outrageous pension. But they got it. They quietly slipped the pension into the state's lawbooks, and the governor signed the stinky thing.
— Editorial, *Hutchinson News,* May 30, 1988

The Kansas legislature voted itself a generous pension increase in the waning days of the 1988 session. After eight years of part-time service, legislators could collect more than $8,000 annually at retirement—a 43 percent hike in benefits. Beyond this, the legislators explicitly played games in the timing of various pension decisions; for example, they were not required to declare their intent to sign up for the new, optional plan until November 18, 1988, a few days after the general election. This was no accident. Rep. Vern Williams (R-Wichita), chair of the House Pensions Committee and a central member of the generally frugal rebel caucus, explained, "We said, let's not make this effective until after the election."[9]

Editorialists and legislative challengers made the legislative pension increase a central issue in the 1988 campaigns (see Chapter 3). The pension issue played out differently from campaign to campaign. Some newcomers won on the strength of their opposition to the plan's benefits for legislators, even though these provisions were relatively modest parts of a much larger public employee retirement package that enjoyed broad support.

After the election, various first-term legislators inquired about rolling back the increases, only to be met with questions about the constitutionality of such an action. Even for those who opposed the pension increases, the incentives to accept the enhanced benefits were great. For example, Senate President Bud Burke, who had voted against the hike and labeled it "political dynamite," decided to accept the new plan. "Absolutely, I signed up," he reported. "I thought it was an inappropriate move at the time, but it's there and it's an appropriate level [of compensation], so of course I signed up for it."[10]

Several other legislators made this pair of choices—secure in their knowledge that the voters could not extract retribution until 1990 (for representatives) or 1992 (for senators) in newly reapportioned districts. The actions of these legislators, along with those who supported the increases, made it an uphill fight to repeal the pension provisions that had been so hotly contested.

One serious problem confronting those who would roll back the increases was that those most concerned were first-term members, unfamiliar with the legislative process. As the 1989 session progressed, the four Senate bills and six House measures that would have repealed or modified the pension provisions made little progress through the legislative process. Representative Williams, who strongly defended the 1988 act, continued to chair the committee that would hold hearings on any modifications. By mid-March none had been scheduled, although several legislators had made formal requests. Representative Williams cavalierly observed: "A number of legislators promised to introduce bills. They have introduced bills. They have kept their promise."[11]

Delay was the dominant strategy of Williams and other veteran legislators. Moving any discussion of the pension issue toward the last few days of the session would likely kill it, given the number of ways in which key committee leaders could keep either house from full consideration of a reform measure.

As the legislative clock ticked, hearings were finally held on March 27, at the behest of the Speaker and the majority leader, which prompted Representative Williams to respond, somewhat disingenuously, that their actions reflected "political motivation, pure and simple." He blamed editorial writers for keeping the issue alive.[12]

In the last few days of the regular session, the House Pensions Committee did vote to require increased legislator contributions to their pensions, but in a series of unrecorded floor votes the House refused to alter the pension formula. Asked why no one requested a recorded vote, one legislator replied, "Nobody wanted to get lynched." The pension bill remained on the House calendar, which could have allowed for further consideration, but the overwhelming votes against the bill and its amendments meant that such action, in all likelihood, would not occur. Nor did it.

The 1989 House — noted for its openness, combativeness, and large number of recorded votes — buried the pension issue. The pension controversy had helped several challengers win their seats, but the basic temperament of the Kansas legislature had not changed much from 1988 to 1989 on this issue. The linkage between electoral politics and legislative policymaking is often tenuous; legislative pensions, a key 1988 campaign issue, simply did not have the power, even with a bit of belated leadership support, to obtain much more than a symbolic hearing in the 1989 legislature, largely because subsequent elections remained distant and the benefits involved were substantial for virtually all veteran lawmakers.[13]

DOGS THAT DON'T BARK:
ISSUES RESOLVED AND ISSUES DELAYED

With a large number of major issues on the Kansas agenda in 1988/89, the potential for deadlock was great. In particular, social spending, school finance, tort reform, and reapportionment represented formidable stumbling blocks to a successful legislative session. Although all of these issues were hotly contested, one of the most remarkable accomplishments of the 1989 legislature was to resolve or defer these controversies, thus allowing for consideration of major discretionary issues such as a huge highway package, prison construction, funding the state's water plan, and the enactment of campaign reforms. In particular, impasses over either school finance and property taxes or reapportionment could have ground the legislative process to a complete halt, but lawmakers self-consciously acted to resolve these issues so that other important matters could receive adequate attention.

Children's Issues: Planning Amid Plenty

About 100,000 Kansas children live in poverty. Unless the state offers them hope for a better life, many of those youngsters will wind up in prison or become permanently dependent on welfare. Money spent today could save the state even more dollars in the future.
                                    —Editorial, *Wichita Eagle-Beacon,* May 25, 1988

With state revenues plentiful, Gov. Mike Hayden chose to emphasize childrens' issues in anticipation of the 1989 legislative session. Three weeks after the 1988 legislature had adjourned, the Governor's Commission on Children and Families was established, with recommendations to be presented by December 1. The commission's composition was a work of art, virtually guaranteeing that some action would be forthcoming. In addition, it demonstrated the small town, friends-and-neighbors nature of much politics in a state of only 2.5 million residents. Hayden appointed as commission co-chairs his wife Patti and children's advocate and former senator Wint Winter, Sr., whose namesake would be central to many legislative battles before the session ended.

As commission members, the governor named wives of three legislators, including Lisa Donnini Miller, married to House Majority Leader-to-be Robert H. Miller. In addition, he appointed Judy Frick, a prominent lobbyist on children's issues, and Rosemary Menninger, daughter of legendary Topeka psychologist Karl Menninger. A final Hayden appointment was potentially controversial; he named Carl Gump, the prospective Republican opponent to House Minority Leader Marvin Barkis. Barkis, however, did not rise to the bait. Rather, his top aide labeled the appointment of Gump, an educator and banker, as "political," but allowed that "sometimes political appointments are good; sometimes they are not. Mr. Gump is a good appointment."[14]

With such a send-off, the commission was unlikely to fail. The question was, how many of its ultimate recommendations would eventually be funded?

The commission proceeded in typical fashion for an ad hoc organization: it held six hearings across the state, heard testimony from various experts, and even solicited advice from Kansas citizens through a series of letters to the editor across the state. Given these solicitations, the commission collected numerous "horror stories of abuse, neglect, and children at risk," in Winter's words.[15]

By August 25 the group had selected its central issues—child care, health care, and abuse—and had begun to fashion proposals that Winter argued would be "politically feasible for the governor to endorse and the Legislature to adopt."[16] Three months later the commission ostensibly set the children's policy agenda when it forwarded to the governor a list of nine major recommendations, which included expansion of a maternal/infant program, private employer tax incentives for day care, and increasing low-income family subsidies for child care. At the same time, the commission lobbied for an extension of its own existence, arguing that reform of children's programs, which were scattered over numerous agencies, would require more than a few months' attention.

The commission did not provide cost estimates for its recommendations, contending that it did not have the time to develop the requisite expertise. Perhaps that was the case, but such an omission allowed the governor to reap the praise of Kansas editorialists in November and December, in advance of his budget message, which was sure to bring back to earth many of the children's advocates' lofty expectations.

In fact, the governor's budget was essentially set *before* the Children's Commission made its final recommendations. Lobbyist Lynn Barclay of the Children's Coalition thus noted that "publicly it may have appeared that the governor responded to the commission, but it was the reverse. . . . The governor hit the right areas with his budget, but the amounts didn't address the levels of concern."[17] The mid-January budget detailed a total of $6.1 million in new children's spending—far short of the $42 million identified by the Children's Coalition (a collection of social welfare groups) and considerably shy of the $15 million that Wint Winter, Sr., assumed the governor would propose.

The children's advocates immediately moved beyond the commission's report and the governor's budget. With substantial revenues sitting in the state treasury, Barclay observed that "for the Children's Coalition, the governor's report was irrelevant. We were going to have to shape the agenda ourselves, in part using some of the [commission] report data. The report wasn't going to set the agenda for us." The Children's Coalition did exactly that, viewing the 1989 budget year as crucial to raising the base levels of support for any number of programs. Although the umbrella organization, which represented thirty other groups, presented various well-publicized studies (e.g., a foster care survey) in the session's early days, most of its resources and energy went toward the inside game of lobbying the legislature.

In considering Kansas legislative appropriations politics, inside the system means really inside. Many key decisions are made in three-person (two majority members, one minority) subcommittees. In 1989, legislation affecting Social and Rehabilitation Services (SRS), where most children's programs were located, began in the House. Although House leaders would ultimately play a major role, the key individual in shaping the specific alternatives was a rookie subcommittee chair—rural Republican Rep. Duane Goossen, a Mennonite who was sympathetic to the children's agenda items.

As Barclay put it, "Two lucky things happened during the session. First, Duane Goossen got to head the SRS subcommittee. . . . Second was [Sen.] Gus Bogina's heart attack [see below, and Chapter 9]. . . . Goossen pushed the subcommittee to do a good job. They got to the point that they could understand the nuances, which are not easy to master."[18] In the end, Goossen decided to request considerably more money than the governor's modest $6.1 million in additional funds for childrens' programs.

Much of the debate over funding children's programs took place among Republican legislators. Although Speaker Jim Braden and Appropriations chair Bill Bunten supported the governor's budget, Majority Leader Miller, whose wife served on the commission, and State and Federal Affairs chair Rep. Ginger Barr urged higher levels of spending. Indeed, both Miller and Barr held hearings, in 1988 and in February 1989, respectively, that demonstrated substantial needs in children's programs. By March 1989, children's issues had become well-publicized, to the point that the scope of the conflict had been expanded far beyond the ordinary technical deliberations of the appropriations process.[19] In this context, Speaker Braden negotiated with Minority Leader Barkis and Goossen; faced with a united Democratic minority and substantial moderate Republican support for more spending, the Speaker agreed to a $13 million-plus increase in children's programs. The full committee and the House ratified the subcommittee position, sending the issue on to the Senate, where it faced an uncertain future.

Under the leadership of Senator Bogina, the Ways and Means Committee quickly acted to reduce the children's appropriations passed by the House, as it trimmed $8.3 million in proposed Medicaid spending for pregnant women and children. Bogina argued that the Medicaid program had been in existence for just one year, and thus it was too early to raise its funding substantially. The Senate endorsed the committee position, although many senators envisioned much of the money being restored in conference. Still, that was merely a hope. The long-term expansion of interest in children's issues, the focusing efforts of the governor's commission, and the opportunity offered by a robust general fund balance might well have produced only the most modest of funding increases if Senator Bogina drove a hard bargain inside the conference committee.

If you can't be good, be lucky, the saying goes. The children's advocates had been good, but they were also lucky. Their good fortune came at Senator Bogina's expense. As the legislature prepared for its initial early April adjournment, the senator suffered a heart attack, which required immediate bypass surgery and kept him out of the last month of legislative maneuvering. As arguably the most powerful member of the Senate by dint of his position and encyclopedic knowledge of the state budget, the fiscally conservative Bogina was universally regarded as central in shaping major spending priorities. His absence was, of course, extremely important; comparing Bogina to the star of Kansas' NCAA 1988 basketball champions, Senate President Burke observed, "We are going to see how the Senate plays without Danny Manning."[20] At least as significant, however, was that Bogina's replacement would be the Ways and Means vice-chairman, Sen. Wint Winter, Jr., a longtime supporter of children's programs and son of the cochair of the governor's commission.

Winter's sympathies clearly lay with the spending levels in the House bill. Still, he needed to convince his two fellow Senate conferees to come to that position without seeming to abandon their chamber's position. Winter's task was not that difficult; none of the conferees were Hayden loyalists and all saw an historic opportunity to advance the funding of children's programs. The conference went smoothly, and a package that added $16 million to the SRS budget easily passed both chambers and landed on the governor's desk at first adjournment in early April. Mike Hayden was left with the decision to ratify a substantial increase in spending or risk alienating legislative leaders who had solidly supported additional funding (and whose support would be essential to his other major initiatives).

In many ways, Hayden's choices in deciding which items to veto in the huge ($900 million) SRS budget represented simultaneously the final action on children's policies for 1989 and the initial moves in the endgame politics of late April and early May, when most major agenda items would be resolved. The bulk of the SRS budget was routinely accepted by the governor, but the $16 million in extra children's spending served as a direct challenge to his control of social policy outcomes. Although he could use his line-item veto capacity to block these appropriations, the governor faced the real possibility that his vetoes might lead to deadlock on nonrelated issues — including prison construction and, especially, the highway package.

Hayden could make a reasonable case that he had backed substantial increases and that the legislature's proposals were fiscally irresponsible. In the end, however, such an argument would have proved fatuous, given the tremendous flood of other spending commitments made in the last few days of the legislative session. More important, the governor would have placed the highway initiative at great risk, both by producing a fierce legislative reaction and by potentially alienating various lawmakers, including Senator Winter, who had made a credible threat to vote against the highway plan if the SRS increases were not approved.

Seeking to move the children's issues and the SRS budget off the agenda, Governor Hayden signed the legislation April 25, one day before the wrap-up session was to begin. He used his line-item veto on three relatively minor provisions, none of them central to the children's agenda. Hayden thus mollified the acting chair of the Senate Ways and Means Committee and did not dismantle the deal constructed among key House leaders, including many Republicans. Heading into the wrap-up session, the governor cleared the table for the major legislative battle of the session—passage of a major highway maintenance and enhancement package.

In retrospect, Hayden could take some credit for addressing some important social issues, which might undercut opposition to him from the increasingly well-organized social welfare community. As one public sector lobbyist put it a few weeks after the 1989 session ended: "All of us have fared better than we expected. I think there was [an administration] plan to take some lumps over the first couple of years and then run on the spending of the second half of his term."[21] Plan or not, Hayden did not alienate the social service interests as he took advantage of the state's 1989 financial condition to put off the tough choices that Kansas and all states would soon face in funding social programs.

Tort Reform and Medical Malpractice: A Disappearing Agenda Item

> *How many horror stories will it take before Kansas gets serious about addressing the screaming problem of medical malpractice insurance? . . . Like the companies that provide malpractice insurance, doctors are leaving Kansas in droves. . . . It's time for the state to make a serious effort to address the problem. The Legislature's half-hearted effort . . . —a limit on malpractice awards—failed to pass muster of the Kansas Supreme Court.*
> *The malpractice issue must become a priority in the next legislative session. The health of the state is at stake.*
>
> —Editorial, *Salina Journal,* July 17, 1988

Defining an issue as a crisis is a potent weapon in setting the policy agenda.[22] In rural Kansas, on health care matters, the label was apt. The high and rapidly rising price of medical malpractice insurance, the apparent exodus of doctors, and the abandonment by remaining physicians of certain types of practice (namely obstetrics) all contributed to a growing sense of desperation. That same urgency did not extend to the urban and suburban centers of population, where doctors remained plentiful and malpractice insurance rates, while troublesome, had not produced any crisis in the availability of care. Much of the malpractice battle was perceived as a battle between two sets of elites—physicians and trial lawyers. "The public," wrote Kansas Supreme Court Justice Kay McFarland, "is not aroused."[23]

For the state as a whole, the population may not have been aroused, but rural and Western Kansas citizens could certainly see the apparent effects of high malpractice rates, and virtually all major policy actors viewed tort reform and medical malpractice as key agenda items for the 1989 legislature (see Chapter 4). At the same time, none of the participants eagerly anticipated the battles over defining the key malpractice issues and enacting legislation, save for a few contract lobbyists who stood to benefit from an extended struggle.

As in many other states, Kansas policymakers had long wrestled with malpractice issues, especially escalating insurance rates. Although much of the evidence was anecdotal, some doctors were leaving the state, others were declining to provide obstetrical services, and still others simply declined to move into the state in the first place, especially into rural areas.

The Kansas legislature in 1986 placed caps on both punitive and noneconomic damages in malpractice suits, and required payouts in the form of annuities rather than lump sums. Hard on the heels of the 1988 legislative session (June 3), the Kansas Supreme Court ruled these lids unconstitutional. Anticipating this ruling, the 1988 legislature passed a less restrictive set of caps—$5 million on punitive damages, $250,000 for noneconomic losses, and no limit for economic damages. After the court's ruling, however, virtually no one thought that this second set of lids would pass judicial scrutiny. The initial reaction of the anti-cap forces was aggressive; Tom Sullivan, representing the Kansas Malpractice Victims Coalition (a group funded by Kansas trial lawyers), stated that "we're going to challenge those [new laws] right now." Jerry Slaughter, lobbyist for the Kansas Medical Society, concurred: "One would almost have to conclude that with this court, with the seven people sitting there now, they aren't going to find any tort reforms acceptable."[24]

With the state Supreme Court's position seemingly a given, policymakers turned to other alternatives when the issue came to a head during the summer of 1988. Insurance premiums rose 25 percent in the immediate wake of the court decision, and of the two private malpractice insurers, one firm chose to leave the state, while the other decided to write no new policies and considered abandoning the state altogether. In short, by midsummer a physician could only buy new insurance from the state's plan, whose costs were higher across the board than those of the private carriers.

A Crisis?

Governor Hayden reacted to these developments by calling an emergency meeting—a "medical malpractice insurance summit" for August 3.[25] Using the court decision and the perceived malpractice crisis as focusing events, Hayden could bring all interests together in the initial well-publicized summit and a series of subsequent working meetings. Although the governor did not establish a firm position on a malpractice solution, he used the gatherings to sound out support for a constitutional amendment that would set liability limits. A Western Kansas meeting between Hayden and numerous interests defined the malpractice issue as a rural health crisis, and various editorials endorsed the constitutional amendment alternative. Still, not even the Western Kansas press was united in racing to a crisis characterization of malpractice insurance in Kansas. The *Garden City Telegram*, for example, commented that a "special interest constitutional amendment" would benefit the medical profession at the expense of attorneys and that many solutions existed short of the amending strategy.[26]

A number of alternatives were floated during the fall of 1988, including one written by a four-person team of law professors and doctors. More importantly, perhaps, public opinion came down on the side of limiting liability awards, with 70 percent of respondents to a statewide survey expressing support for such restrictions. Although Governor Hayden, well known for examining poll results before backing policy initiatives, had not explicitly supported a constitutional amendment on malpractice in his January State of the State address, he increasingly became identified with this alternative as the legislative session progressed.

A Two-Year Issue

Despite the frequent characterization of the tort reform problem as a crisis, there was little sense of urgency as the legislature convened in January 1989. The governor had not pushed reform in his initial set of requests, although he had previously identified malpractice insurance as a key agenda item. House Minority Leader Barkis, an attorney, announced his opposition to a constitutional amendment in mid-January. Since a two-thirds majority was required in both chambers to place an amendment on the ballot, Barkis's announcement discouraged thoughts of immediate passage. The electoral calendar also dictated a measured approach, since no amendment would be submitted until the November 1990 general election.

The Kansas Medical Society's Jerry Slaughter saw little possibility of moving quickly, observing that "get[ting] it through one house of the Legislature this year" would still allow for getting it "through the other chamber next year," especially in the context of a crowded agenda. He continued: "With highways, education and prisons [already being considered], it's unrealistic to expect [the amendment to pass this year]."[27] Although many doctors (and editorialists) found delay unacceptable, lobbyists saw malpractice and tort reform as an issue that would help support them through two legislative sessions. Indeed, any issue that brought doctors and other medical professionals, lawyers, insurance companies, and hospitals into the fray was welcomed by the capitol lobbying corps; as of 1989, more than sixty lobbyists represented organizations with specific interests in the malpractice issue. The stakes were high, and the state's most prominent lobbying firms were heavily involved, all expecting at least two years of work.[28]

Legislators and Luck

If lobbyists eagerly anticipated an extended policy debate, legislators faced the malpractice issue gingerly at best. Although rural lawmakers could easily endorse limits on awards, most others found themselves at the center of arguments among contending parties armed with reasonable arguments and substantial resources. Legislators ordinarily seek to avoid conflict, often at all costs. Tort reform was an issue on which compromise was difficult and the potential consequences painful. Although the legislature had passed malpractice caps consistently (1986, 1987, amended in 1988), finding the votes for a constitutional amendment would be much more difficult.

The legislature slogged through its consideration of an amendment along with other possible policies. Rural health concerns continued to drive the issue through the first two months of the session, as the number of counties designated as "underserved" by the University of Kansas Medical Center rose by eight compared to 1988. This annual report provided regular ammunition for those who would limit malpractice awards, and the Senate Judiciary Committee, chaired by the seemingly omnipresent Sen. Wint Winter, Jr., began hearings on a constitutional amendment in late March. Speaking in Western Kansas, Governor Hayden formally expressed his support for a malpractice cap amendment, noting that surveys showed between 65 and 75 percent support for such a constitutional provision.[29]

Nevertheless, the chief opponents of an amendment, the trial lawyers, were unwilling to buy into the "crisis" description offered. Richard Mason, executive director of the Kansas Trial Lawyers Association, asked: "Who are we kidding? If it's a crisis, then five years [of dealing with it] is too much time. We've been led to believe that doctors are leaving by the busload."[30] In short, the issue was not close to resolution, and extended debate and politicking seemed assured as the regular legislative session wound down at the end of March.

Then, in the twinkling of an eye, the malpractice issue—at least in terms of caps on awards—disappeared from the legislature's radar screen. In a decision that caught everyone completely off guard, the Kansas Supreme Court ruled 5–2 that a 1987 law (amended in 1988) placing a $250,000 cap on pain and suffering awards was constitutional. The announcement of the preliminary opinion swept through the legislature, disrupting a crucial Senate highway debate like a spring tornado.

The legislators' relief was palpable. "It's amazing," said Rep. Mike O'Neal, House Judiciary Committee chair, "I can't believe this."[31] Both Winter and Hayden expressed satisfaction with the resolution, as did the Medical Society's Slaughter. Although Richard Mason, the Trial Lawyers' director, was disappointed, he saw it as the end of the issue for the time being. He opined that "it will have no effect on malpractice rates, but we will now find out."[32]

The legislature did address malpractice insurance in another, less significant bill, which would phase out a state insurance fund, but it was the court decision that moved the malpractice issue off the legislative agenda. Ironically, though the decision was a policy victory for the governor, it may have been costly politically. One Republican senator speculated that if both houses had passed an amendment, Hayden would have benefited "because the amendment would have been on the ballot at the same time he was running [1990]. You've got 70–80% [sic] in favor of caps. The governor could have nestled right up to it during the election campaign."

Whatever the political repercussions over the electoral cycle, the short-term impact of the court decision was to allow the legislature to address other health care issues—rural coverage, cost containment. The decision took one complicated, long-lived, and divisive issue off the agenda—a positive result for all save the lobbyists.

Reapportionment: A Draw, Not an Endgame

> *In January, some legislators and other observers predicted that reapportionment would pollute the entire 1989 session. The leadership, however, contained the intense politicking over reapportionment, and the issue didn't contaminate other matters.*
>
> *Enactment of the committee proposal shows that bipartisanship often makes the best politics.*
>
> —Editorial, *Wichita Eagle-Beacon*, April 28, 1989

> *Let there be no mistake, [reapportionment] was totally partisan.*
> —Rep. Donna Whiteman, Democratic caucus chair

If political time consists of trends, cycles, and deadlines, no issue better illustrates this combination than reapportionment. Demographic shifts, constitutional requirements, and the intense politics of the process ordinarily demonstrate the difficulty of converting long-term population trends into districts with immediate political consequences.

That Kansas was redistricting at all in 1989 was unusual. After all, states generally redraw their boundaries in the wake of the decennial U.S. census. Historically, however, Kansas has used its own agricultural census as the basis for the state legislative maps. Mandated by a 1988 constitutional amendment, the 1989 reapportionment would create, in the end, state House districts for a single election (1990) at a cost of more than $3 million for the census. Still, given the growing number of Democrats in the House and the increasing suburban population of the state, the political stakes were high.

Finally, the Kansas census historically had not operated under the same rules as the federal counterpart. Kansas did not count temporary residents (notably students and military personnel) as part of a district's population. Thus Riley County, temporary home to many Kansas State University students and Fort Riley military personnel, suffered substantially from the state's formula. As reapportionment progressed on one track in the legislature, various counties, including Riley, proceeded to sue the state over biases and undercounting in the census.[33] High levels of uncertainty prevailed during the entire process, yet in the end a relatively fair reapportionment map was accepted by the House in a reasonably timely manner. Of all the dogs that didn't bark in 1989, this one was probably the most surprising.

Various elements of political time dictated the pace and results of reapportionment. From a long-term perspective, Republicans were eager to produce a map that would reflect the population shifts of the 1980s. Indeed, Democratic aide Tom Laing observed that these were givens: demographic facts dictated where seats are going to be—Johnson County and suburban Sedgwick County [Wichita]. He noted, in addition: "It was pretty hard to argue that downtown Kansas City [Kansas] and the east side of Topeka hadn't lost population. It was painful, but not unbearable." At the same time, the House Democrats held some distinct short-term advantages. First, along with the dissident Republicans, they were fully prepared to tie up the entire legislative process—dooming any highway package or GOP-Hayden initiatives. Second, the rebels and the Democrats might well have cooked up their own reapportionment brew, which could have wreaked havoc with the regular Republicans' districts. Without question, on this procedural issue the Democrat-rebel combination came to the negotiating table as a formidable force.

The top party leaders, Speaker Braden and Minority Leader Barkis, had experienced a relatively amicable, nonpartisan reapportionment a decade earlier. The House Reapportionment Committee chair, Vince Snowbarger (R-Johnson County), was also well placed to oversee a low-key, low-profile process. Laing observed that "Snowbarger tried to remain professionally cool throughout the whole thing. His Johnson County locale might have helped. He knew he was in good shape."

At the same time, the process remained, by definition, highly partisan. Barkis regarded getting a good map as his top priority for the 1989 session: "Reapportionment was the biggest issue for Democrats. It had to be, if we were to become a majority."[34] Nevertheless, partisan goals would be sought by reducing partisan tensions; Barkis pointed out that "there will be six open seats, four in Johnson County. Why should we be pissing them off?"

Progress came with glacial speed. Although there were hundreds, even thousands, of maps drawn and redrawn and pored over by House members, the key negotiations evolved in Speaker Braden's office, as five legislators met regularly to hammer out an agreement. Included were two Republican leaders (Snowbarger and Rep. Keith Roe), two Democrats (Reps. Whiteman and Joan Adam), and one rebel Republican (Rep. David Miller). Joining them were Laing and the Speaker's top assistant, Mark Skinner. Given the importance of the task, midsession reports of delay were neither unexpected nor of great concern. In mid-March Barkis could optimistically state: "I sense from my conversations with the speaker that he is going to treat us fairly well. And that's all we want."[35]

By late March the party leaders had agreed on general guidelines for redistricting; only then did the House committee hold public hearings. As various maps surfaced, partisan sniping became commonplace, particularly because earlier committee deadlines had passed. In fact, the gang of five legislators and two staffers did not reach agreement on a final map until the legislature's initial adjournment on April 8. Their agreement did not become public until April 24, just before the wrap-up session began.[36] Once the map was completed, the legislative gang sought to hold together their package against all amendments. With only a modest amount of carping in a one-day hearing, the Reapportionment Committee forwarded the bill to the full House April 25; by the next day it was on the governor's desk, passing comfortably through both chambers. The dissenting legislators mainly objected to the existence of the 1988 census or its implementation, not the nature of the map itself. In short order Hayden signed the law and the Supreme Court found it adequate to meet constitutional scrutiny, despite a last-minute challenge by a disgruntled legislator.

Although Democrats complained publicly about the nature of the new districts, Minority Leader Barkis declared that "the map is unbelievable" to the extent it offered Democrats the ability to be competitive in 1990, especially in light of population changes and the Republican control of state government. Moreover, Barkis, his fellow Democrats, and all the Republicans also understood that the map's impact would be fleeting. Redistricting would be on the agenda again in 1991/92, as both houses wrestled with the 1990 census figures in the wake of the 1988 constitutional changes.

The Hound of Property Taxes: Barking, But Unheeded

It's too early *to tell whether Kansans complaining about property classification are Chicken Littles or Cassandras. But until more facts are available about the impact of reappraisal, the Legislature should resist seeking changes . . . approved by the voters in 1986.*
—Editorial, *Wichita Eagle-Beacon*, March 12, 1989

Getting this far [on classification and reappraisal] has been extremely difficult. It is too late *to pause or turn back now.*
—Editorial, *Kansas City Times*, March 13, 1989

Too early to change a new, controversial property scheme? Or too late? Both of Kansas's largest newspapers were correct in their assessments. As property tax reform was being implemented in 1988/89, the governor and the legislature faced a situation in which they could act, perhaps prematurely, to ward off the effects of classification, or they could wait to test the political strength of reactions to property tax reform. As much as for any issue, the streams of problems, policies, and politics flowed together on property taxes in 1988/89, but no policy entrepreneur came to the fore to move a major proposal through the system. Together, the *Eagle-Beacon* and the *Times* got it right: it was too late to make major changes in a partially implemented system, precisely because it was too early to judge the ultimate impact of these changes.

Property Tax Reform: A Long-Term Problem

In 1986 the Kansas electorate endorsed a constitutional amendment that required the classification of real property; this amendment followed the legislature's 1985 decision to order reappraisal. These two linked actions, pressed by Gov. John Carlin, followed from the fact that the state had not reappraised its property in a regular way since 1965. Although all property was to be appraised at 30 percent of market value, residential assessments had fallen to 3 to 8 percent of market value, and commercial property to 11 percent.[37] The simultaneous processes of classification and reappraisal added confusion to an already highly uncertain situation. Many owners of older homes would be faced with much higher taxes, as would many small businesses, but the exact amounts would not be known until new evaluations came in (March 1989), the state school aid formula was rewritten (April 1989), and tax bills went out (November 1989).

Nevertheless, one long-term school finance trend was clear: the state's smaller, predominantly rural school districts were receiving consistently higher percentages of the total state public education monies—from 53 percent in

1976/77 to 72 percent twelve years later. During the same period, the five largest districts went from 34 percent of all funding to 15 percent.[38] In addition, urban and suburban districts anticipated more reductions in the wake of reappraisal and classification, due to the decline of the total valuation in many rural areas and subsequent increases in compensatory state funding.

The classification/reappraisal/school finance set of issues affected virtually every state resident and generated tremendous attention from many key interest groups (the state education association, realtors, school boards, counties and additional governing units, and many others). Despite the clear significance of these issues, it remained difficult to define them as a single, integrated problem. The property tax issue comprised a multitude of related but distinct problems, none of which would dominate the policymaking process in 1988/89. The governor, legislators, and others could legitimately call for a "wait-and-see attitude" as classification and reappraisal were implemented.

Simultaneously, the legislature was sitting on a large pot of money, which might well be used to take much of the immediate sting out of the property tax bite. As an interim legislative committee considered, in October 1988, recommending substantial increases in state funding, Sen. Fred Kerr (who would become majority leader in 1989) urged that reappraisal be completed and that the legislature "handle problems . . . within the scope of what's possible. A big key is school finance."[39]

In the wake of the 1988 election, however, the interim legislative committee voted against increasing funding for the school finance formula by $100 million; instead it endorsed a resolution in November 1988 that would set a goal of 50 percent state funding for Kansas public education. Many legislators saw such goal-setting as an empty gesture. Democratic state senator Phil Martin, a harsh critic of classification and reappraisal, stated that timing was crucial; he concluded, "If we're ever going to get to 50 percent funding of schools, which is really helping reduce the amount of property taxes, this is the year."[40] Likewise, Kansas National Education Association (KNEA) executive director Bruce Goeden saw a window of opportunity in 1989 budget surpluses. He noted: "Everybody knows there's money this year. This is the year to do what's right for the school formula."[41]

Such a framing of the school finance and property tax issues ignored the long-term impact of major increases in state aid, which would compound annually from the additional higher base. Without new revenue sources, a single-year window of opportunity meant very little, although advocates of more state aid might well be willing to incur long-term obligations that would require future tax increases.

As the 1989 legislature opened, however, there was no dominant proposal on the table, either to revise the property tax structure or to pump more state funds into public education. Although he had proposed some interim relief for those districts most adversely affected by classification and reappraisal, the governor offered no comprehensive plan, in part because he had been a key figure in pushing for the 1986 changes. Moreover, Hayden had promised to reduce state income taxes, an action that would remove funds that might be used for school aid. In sum, most key actors wanted to delay any action on the property tax and school finance issues, largely because they did not see the problem as ripe for resolution. But for the governor a delay would prove tremendously costly, as property tax issues came to dominate his 1990 bid for reelection.

Ill-Defined Issues, Dollars, and Delays

Passed in November 1986, the classification and reappraisal of Kansas property was to have been completed in just over two years, with tax bills to go out three years after adoption of the constitutional amendment. There would be no phasing-in of classification and reappraisal. Such a schedule allowed for little adjustment; actions all bumped up against deadlines as county officials, often ill-prepared, raced to reappraise and classify every piece of property within their jurisdictions. The initial deadline for sending out reevaluation notices was March 1, 1989, virtually the midpoint of the legislative session.

As they waited for the March 1 information, legislators and interests jockeyed for position, uncertain of what the notices would bring or how property owners would react. Realtors forecast doom ("Main Street cannot afford to have taxes double and triple."[42]), while editorialists batted about the prospective problems of shifting tax burdens and state school monies. The real estate interests sought to suspend classification until reappraisal had been completed, but reappraisal might never have been approved had it not been tightly linked to classification. Separating these procedures was unlikely, because of both their constitutional mandates and their political bonds.

Democratic legislators approached the property tax problem with a set of proposals to ease the pain by targeting funds for those homeowners most adversely affected by the changes and those least able to pay. The Democratic plan, introduced *before* the windfall return was considered in the House, was a version of the "shock absorber" proposal initially offered by Governor Hayden. "If the increase in property tax after reappraisal is more than 50 percent [for low-income families]," said the Taxation Committee's ranking member, Rep. Joan Wagnon (D-Topeka), one day after the House emasculated the governor's initial windfall package, "the state would pay half that increase the first year and one-fourth the second year."[43]

With a constitutional remedy unlikely and the problem still muddled, legislators were unwilling to act precipitously. State Senate President Bud Burke summarized the feelings of many lawmakers, noting that "everybody's getting nervous. But throwing money at the problem isn't going to resolve it. . . . Right now it's henny penny the sky is falling over here. If someone could define the problem for me, I'm ready to act."[44]

All sides in the property tax battle desired some kind of delay. A coalition of realtors, restaurant and motel owners, and some local chambers sought to restrain the imposition of new classes of property, while a range of other interests and governmental figures argued for a "wait-and-see attitude" in coming to terms with the new policies. Among these policies was a new exemption for manufacturers' and merchants' inventories, effective January 1, which provided great tax benefits to major interests like Boeing and Wal-Mart.

The real estate sector's group—Kansans Reappraising Classification— adopted a grass-roots approach to lobbying the legislature, with 7,700 local realtors providing the core of the coalition. The advocates of waiting were not as well organized but held much more important strategic positions— including the governorship and most of the key legislative leadership slots. The realtors were thus faced with the difficult task of convincing the dominant forces in state policymaking that the constitutional mandate for reclassification should not be implemented.

As the reappraisal process ground on, uncertainties multiplied. Six counties missed the March 1 deadline, substantial computational errors occurred, often due to untested computer programs, and valuations across counties became increasingly open to question. Although some horror stories began to make the rounds, few policymakers wanted to attack a problem that remained ill-defined. The *Wichita Eagle-Beacon* concluded that "eventually, the classification amendment may need fixing, but not until Kansans know how badly—or if—it is broken."[45] The *Kansas City Times* argued that "it would be fool-hardy to reopen the debate, [since] it won't be known how [taxpayers will be affected] until later this year. Getting this far has been extremely difficult. It is too late to pause or turn back now."[46]

With sentiments like these finding their way onto the legislators' desks, the realtors' grass-roots campaign faced an uphill struggle. For a March 21 demonstration on the capitol steps (a seven-television-camera day, tops for the session), the realtors brought in both their local members and their homeowner constituents. "The crowd, dressed informally, was a sharp contrast to the usual well-groomed lobbyists who dominated legislative hearings. They booed and applauded . . . with as much vigor as an audience at an evangelical revival meeting."[47] In the end, their message was "delay this thing until we know where we stand."[48]

As if there were not enough uncertainty, on the day of the rally the state Department of Education produced figures that projected large *tax rate* decreases in the wake of reappraisal (for example, about $35 per $1,000 of assessed value in much of Johnson County). At the same time, because *appraised values* had risen substantially, no one could predict with confidence what the ultimate effects would be on November's tax bill. One day later (March 22) the Department of Education provided the initial computer runs that projected changes in state aid for all Kansas school districts. Ordinarily these benchmark projections would have been available in January, but reappraisal delayed their release until two weeks before the legislature had scheduled its first adjournment (April 8). The computer runs also encouraged apparent "winners" in classification to voice their opposition to delaying its implementation. Many local school boards, along with many rural groups, argued that the property tax protests had been overblown. In large part, such sentiments derived from the fact that agricultural interests had won substantial concessions for farm land, which was classified on the basis of its use value, not its market worth. Kansas Farm Bureau lobbyist Paul Fleenor could easily conclude that complaints have represented "a few voices in the wilderness."[49]

Few elected officials were willing to make such claims, but most legislators chose the "wait-and-see" strategy, for good reason. As columnist John Marshall pointed out, the governor and the many legislators were "telling everyone not to panic but [to] wait for the true tax bills next fall. But a special law tacked onto reappraisal forbids local governments to raise even a penny in new taxes for another year. . . . For now . . . the legislators and the governor can claim in 1990, an election year, that they reformed taxes without raising them."[50]

For such a strategy to work, however, adequate short-term funding would have to be provided for school districts in 1989/90. With the legislature approaching its final days, great uncertainty remained concerning the policy and political implications of reappraisal and classification. In 1989, even after the windfall's return and major increases in social spending, many decision makers chose to believe they were still sitting on a large pile of cash. Their beliefs were reinforced on April 5, when the consensus revenue estimating group increased its evaluation of the state's receipts for FY 1989 by more than $9 million.

Short-Term Problem Solving: When in Doubt, Throw Money

As the late-March property tax protests became increasingly vocal and centered in Topeka, pressures mounted on the legislature to do something to address the forthcoming jolt to homeowners and small businesses. Although Republican legislative leaders in both houses had little desire to challenge classification, the House remained essentially out of control. While key resolutions remained mired in committee, many legislators called for a vote on a constitutional amendment that would revise classification and delay its implementation.

The rebel Republican-Democratic axis in the House again demonstrated its strength as the alliance mustered consecutive majorities of 62–61 (on Republican rebel Rep. Kerry Patrick's motion) and 65–58 (on one by Minority Leader Barkis) to pull two different property tax relief measures out of the House Taxation Committee. Seventy votes were required to succeed, and both measures died. The rebel plan, placing a constitutional amendment on the state's ballot, would ultimately have required a two-thirds majority. At the same time, the rebel-Democrat combine continued to demonstrate its capacity to wreak havoc on the House floor. Indeed, the Barkis motion obtained the support of all 57 Democrats and eight Republicans.[51]

In addition, a Patrick floor amendment on the same day (March 28) succeeded in reducing the corporate income tax. Although the impact of a modest reduction was unclear, the politics was straightforward; with only two weeks left in the regular session the rebels demonstrated that they could continue to embarrass the Republican leadership, while Democrats could reduce the amount of general revenue available to the governor. As loyalist Republican Rep. Fred Gatlin noted, "Remember, the fiscal note on a tax bill goes on and on and on." To which fellow Republican Gene Amos responded, "I voted for [the corporate tax reduction] because property taxes, after reclassification, will go on and on and on."[52]

After its votes on classification and corporate taxation, the legislature acted on an expensive ($500-million-plus) school finance package; it had been stitched together with two key compromises that allowed supporters to ward off several attempts to amend the bill. First, the legislation finessed the issue of whether to use pre- or postreappraisal property valuation figures by agreeing to a two-year average. Second, the legislators agreed to a "hold-harmless" provision that meant that no school district would experience a decrease in state aid for the 1989/90 school year. Senate Education Committee chair Joe Harder noted the long-term costs of such actions: "It isn't defensible to use two-year averaging. But politically, it's very popular. And I think every time you have a hold-harmless it destroys the purpose of [statewide school finance] equalization."[53]

The school finance bill, often the most intractable issue faced by the legislature, was on the governor's desk by the first adjournment (April 8). Although there were losers in the process (districts such as Derby, where most of Boeing's assets had been removed from the tax rolls), the legislators had built solid majorities by spending $6.2 million more on education than Governor Hayden had requested.[54] The central issues of tax increases and equalization of educational spending had not been addressed, but these potentially divisive items had been removed from the legislative agenda for 1989.

The governor benefited from this outcome, as he could focus on highways and prisons in the wrap-up session. The Democratic minorities had won substantial increases in state funding and further reduced the state's ending balances. This worried Speaker Jim Braden, who had offered continuing warnings to his Republican colleagues for months; he concluded that, as of March 29, "we've overspent the governor by $40 million or $50 million. We're going to have serious problems next year, folks."[55] Next year, of course, would bring reelection contests for the governor and every House member.

The Circuit-Breaker: Symbol as Substance

All sides agreed that some amelioration was due those Kansans most adversely affected by reappraisal and classification. The governor had consistently advocated a "shock absorber" fund to ease the transition to the new property tax system. But as the session wound down, the dominant metaphor changed — to a "circuit breaker" that would limit increased tax bills — as did the context for spending down the state's rapidly shrinking balances. The circuit breaker had been incorporated into the windfall bill passed in February, but how much state money should be committed to the program to reimburse low-income homeowners whose property taxes rose by 50 percent or more? The question remained.

Acting Ways and Means chair Sen. Wint Winter, Jr., argued that a modest $10 million would be adequate, in that most payouts would not occur until property taxes were actually paid, in December 1989 and June 1990. Other senators saw much larger unfunded liabilities that reflected the $24 million cost that was anticipated in February, when the authorizing legislation was passed. Senate Minority Leader Mike Johnston observed: "There is no doubt that this is an entitlement. . . . [Thus,] we will make an estimate on what this will cost and appropriate that amount of money."[56] Winter countered that the $10 million figure was "what I thought I was voting for when it came to the Senate" in February. Since that time, other more expensive estimates had been made, but no one knew what the costs of the circuit breaker would be. With the state's ending balances shrinking and other spending priorities remaining, the Senate decided to set aside only $10 million for the program, regardless of the potential unfunded liability. In the end, the politics of property tax reform dictated that the circuit breaker be adopted and funded, but the policy desires of legislators and the governor made it difficult to take any more funds off the table. So $10 million was appropriated, even though most actors involved anticipated more substantial liabilities.

LET THE (END)GAMES BEGIN

By the time the Kansas legislature adjourned on April 8, in anticipation of picking up again April 26 for its wrap-up session, it had dealt with a truly remarkable spectrum of major issues, including school finance and property taxes, reapportionment, social welfare and children's policies, and higher education funding. In an ordinary year, state policymakers might well have patted themselves on the back and considered their job well done. But 1989 was no ordinary year.

Federal Judge Richard Rogers was demanding that the state reforge its corrections policies; Governor Hayden and a raft of legislators, localities, and lobbyists were apoplectic over the real chance that a major highway bill would not pass, and advocates for funding the water plan and enacting campaign reform continued to see 1989 as their best chance in years. For all the major accomplishments, the legislature's agenda remained full as it adjourned on April 8. The endgame politics of 1989 were about to begin.

8

Endgame I: Highways

For all the major issues that Kansas policymakers addressed in 1988/89, the state's agenda centerpiece — from May 1988 through May 1989 — comprised a set of highway construction, renovation, and maintenance proposals that would ultimately become parts of the largest taxing and spending package in state history. Much as the state's 1973 legislative session was identified for years to come with the development of a statewide school aid formula, the 1989 session would be remembered for its decision to embark upon a large-scale highway construction program.

The highway issue, like reapportionment, exemplifies the overlapping elements of political time — long-term trends, cycles, and deadlines. Moreover, no agenda item more clearly represents Kingdon's notion of coupling the problem, policy, and political streams within the policymaking process. Yet even after a year of intense politicking, it remained unclear that a major highway program was indeed an "idea whose time had come."[1]

For various towns in Southeast Kansas, for a number of other cities, for heavy construction firms, for a gaggle of legislators, and especially for Governor Hayden, the 1989 session represented the best chance in the foreseeable future for the state to approve a costly comprehensive highway package. After the 1989 tax cuts and spending spree, fewer funds would be available, and rural interests would lose seats in the 1990 redistricting. Politics also dictated action in 1989, because obtaining a highway package would go a long way toward defining Mike Hayden's first term in office as a success. Highway improvements as part of an economic development emphasis had stood at the top of the governor's personal agenda since he won the 1986 election. His first attempt at passing a major highway program had run into a brick wall in an August 1987 legislative special session. In 1989 there was no certainty that the legislature — especially the raucous, uncontrollable

House—would give Hayden the victory he longed for as both a committed policy entrepreneur and a strategic politician with his eye on the 1990 election.

TRENDS AND CYCLES, 1983–1988: DEFINING THE PROBLEM

In 1983 the Kansas legislature passed a modest highway bill that emphasized maintenance, but little new construction went forward with state funds. No major highway legislation had passed the legislature since mid-1976. As Governor Hayden laid out the issue, action during the 1989 legislative session was crucial, because

> you have the opportunity to pass a comprehensive plan only once in every few years. The last . . . program was in 1983. The legislature takes a leapfrogging approach to highways. It waits until its back is against the wall and then raises registration and license fees to cover the costs. We needed to break that cycle for a comprehensive plan and for once get out ahead of inflation.[2]

The 1983 program was widely viewed as inadequate in two distinct ways. First, it did not escape the "leapfrogging" problem of matching revenues to needs. Second, and crucial in 1988/89, it did not address key long-term economic development issues. In particular, Southeast Kansans saw their region at a great competitive disadvantage because of its poor road system, and Hutchinson residents desperately wanted to be connected to Wichita by a four-lane highway. These issues had festered since the interstate highway system was built in the 1960s. The emphasis on economic development in the 1980s provided advocates with another argument for new construction.

But as a large agricultural state with a modest, stable population, Kansas already possessed a substantial highway network—about 10,000 miles total, 1,234 miles of which had been designated in 1969 as part of a major "Freeway and Express Highway" system. Economic slowdowns in the 1970s, however, had brought new building and significant upgrading to a standstill.[3]

As the federal government's interstate highway program neared completion, attention turned to maintenance and its attendant state financial responsibilities. In 1984 Congressman Bob Whittaker, a Republican who represented Southeast Kansas, called a meeting at Fredonia, Kansas, to begin an organized push for better roads. Whittaker's initiative recognized the need for federal-state cooperation and substantial new state funding, but it suffered from a perception that regional, not statewide, issues were at stake.

As a gubernatorial candidate in 1986, Mike Hayden had embraced a substantial highway program as one of his central campaign themes, and he articulated it consistently in his successful election effort.[4] With his rural roots, Hayden represented interests that wanted better roads, which often placed him at odds with Johnson County Republicans, whose highway improvements had been made largely within the context of the federal interstate system.

From start to finish, the highway program, along with the death penalty, was the agenda item with which Hayden was most firmly identified. Hayden's 1986 election assured highways of a major place on the state's policy agenda, but in no way guaranteed the passage of a major program. In fact, the highway program's fate remained in doubt up to the final two days of the longest legislative session in the state's history.

Although the state's uncertain fiscal condition had prevented Hayden from articulating an extensive highway program in the regular (January through April 1987) legislative session, he wasted little time in pushing energetically for a large-scale package. In January 1987 he attended a new governors' conference where Virginia's Governor Baliles "talked about how he'd appointed a task force and then called a special session to enact a significant highway plan." Former Hayden aide Ed Flentje noted, "I think Mike came back, convinced that was the way to go."[5]

Attempting to follow the Virginia model proved a short-term political disaster for the governor. In 1987 there was no consensus that a substantial highway program was needed; such a proposal was part of Hayden's "discretionary agenda."[6] Although many state legislatures regularly meet in special session, Kansas has historically resisted this trend. However, Hayden called such a week-long session for August 1987. This time, all attention was directed at the governor's $1.8 billion road package, which "was so precise . . . that there was no room for maneuvering."[7] New projects were specifically designated; opponents could argue both that his proposals were too large and that they did not promise benefits to many specific areas. All in all, neither members of the public nor governmental elites were adequately prepared to consider a set of large-scale changes in spending and taxing (user fees, bonding). Hayden's own legislative party offered no solid base of support. To carry his legislation Hayden enlisted Senate Minority Leader Mike Johnston, from Southeast Kansas, even though Republicans controlled both houses of the legislature.

After six days of flailing about, the special session mercifully adjourned, without adopting even a face-saving minimal program. The governor's defeat was complete. Hayden had failed to generate adequate support — either popular or legislative — for his proposal; there was no sense of urgency. Delay seemed a reasonable response to his initiative, and delay continued to be the watchword during the 1988 legislative session, when the highway issue simply did not attract any serious attention.

Still, Kansas' long-term transportation and economic development needs were perceived as substantial, and Hayden continued to advocate constructing or improving hundreds of miles of roads. In retrospect, the 1987 special session may well have contributed to the "softening up" process of policy development.[8] Flentje concluded that it might not have been possible to "have highlighted that issue or set expectations that high [$1.8 billion] without the special session."[9] Indeed, although the special session did collapse, the highway issue had been well publicized and better defined: addressing Kansas' needs would be a costly proposition.

One top House Republican aide saw the special session as a "public relations disaster" for the governor, yet there were some positive implications: "By calling the 1987 special session, Hayden increased everyone's awareness of the need for improved highways. During the 1988 [legislative] election, there was more of an awareness. In 1987 the debate was over 'Do we need a highway plan or not?' In 1989 it went, 'Yes, we need one — but what size?' "[10] At the same time, the emergence of the highway issue focused attention on the governor as leader. If the public had grown to accept the need for a major program, it would expect the program's most visible proponent to provide the requisite energy to gain legislative approval. As the policy opportunity became more tangible, the political stakes grew for Mike Hayden.

If converting agenda items into policy outcomes is indeed the coupling of problem, policy, and political forces at an opportune time,[11] the 1987 special session had been premature. The problem had not been adequately defined, and thus the governor's very specific set of policy solutions was seen as inappropriate. In addition, there was no overriding political reason for most legislators to adopt a comprehensive highway policy. But the special session did contribute to increasing interest in the problem. Likewise, it demonstrated that project-specific proposals might well produce more opposition than support. As Hayden and his allies regrouped in 1987/88, they moved to (1) define the highway problem in more compelling ways; (2) render potential solutions more difficult to attack; and (3) build grass-roots political support for a large-scale plan. In the end, these were necessary actions, but they were not sufficient. What Hayden and the highway advocates lacked was an adequate plan to build a legislative majority for a major highway package.

SPECIFYING ALTERNATIVES AND BUILDING SUPPORT: MAY–DECEMBER 1988

After Hayden's special session defeat in 1987, major highway issues simply disappeared from legislative consideration during the spring of 1988. The governor remained committed to an initiative, but a substantial highway program was not on anyone's immediate agenda; it was an idea whose time had not yet come. Yet the ink was scarcely dry on the 1988 legislature's work before prohighway forces began a prodigious public lobbying campaign to move the issue front and center for 1989. During the next year three overlapping sets of policymakers would move the highway issue to the top of the state's agenda, frame specific alternatives, and eventually win approval for a $2.65 billion program. These policy activists included (1) state-level public officials (Governor Hayden, his secretary of transportation, and various legislative leaders); (2) grass-roots lobbying forces (regional groups, local chambers of commerce, and especially Economic Lifelines, a well-funded statewide highways group); and (3) a few key inside lobbyists who came on board relatively late in the process.

Although Hayden and an interim legislative committee would begin to frame the specifics of a highway program in late 1988, the key agenda-setters through much of the year were the grass-roots lobbying groups. The term "grass-roots lobby" connotes a sense of spontaneous popular support for a given issue.[12] This may occasionally be the case, but much more frequently such lobbying merely represents one tool of political elites and established interests to press their positions. Although various localities did create grass-roots organizations, these essentially reflected the interests of local economic elites. Economic Lifelines (EL), the umbrella grass-roots group, depended almost exclusively on the contributions of local and regional groups as well as major corporate support (such as heavy contractors and the Kansas Power and Light Company). Indeed, at the governor's request, KPL "loaned" the EL group an executive (Rick Kready) to head its efforts.

There was never any broad, spontaneous public demand for sharply increased highway funding. As one top Department of Transportation official put it, "Citizens react to driving surface conditions, which have not been bad since the 'pothole' era of the Carlin Administration [1979–87]."[13] At the same time, editorialists spilled more ink on highways than any other single issue between May and December. Combined with the grass-roots efforts of Economic Lifelines, the editorial emphasis helped make highways the leading concern of the public in a February 1989 statewide survey. Even though citizens did not demonstrate or write piles of letters on highways, the grass-roots lobbying efforts and the barrage of editorials, along with the publicity generated by the special session, succeeded in making highways an important issue across the state.

The initial phases of the grass-roots efforts emphasized two complementary strategies for obtaining extensive news coverage of the highway issue. First, various local and regional groups, such as those in Parsons and Pittsburg (Southeast Kansas), Wichita, and Hutchinson, enlisted major local elite figures to head their organizations. In Pittsburg, for example, the economic development group Pittsburg NOW! was headed by the Pittsburg State University president, one of the city's most visible and influential citizens. The group thus gained legitimacy and the capacity to make news.

Left on their own, regional groups were unlikely to embrace either a coherent set of proposals or a well-organized plan to press for action. A statewide effort required more unity and less particularism; the Economic Lifelines umbrella organization admirably filled that bill. Economic Lifelines brought together two types of groups into a major coalition. It allowed regional groups a vehicle for organizing their disparate interests in a reasonably coherent manner, and equally important, it provided a base for major statewide interests to join in promoting a unified stance on highways.

This is not to say that Economic Lifelines — with a $240,000 budget in 1988 — was a complete success. Not at all. It harbored many diverse points of view and many distinct, even competing, interests (the National Education Association and the state Chamber of Commerce and Industry). It was also much better at setting the agenda than at specifying alternatives or convincing legislators to vote for a given plan.

Economic Lifelines and the Problem Stream

Commenting on an October 1988 preview of a video to be shown to local civic groups across the state, Economic Lifelines grass-roots coordinator and spokesman Rick Kready noted that the EL program "is not a highway plan. What it is is a study of highway needs."[14] Although the issue had already been aired in a special session and the next session of the legislature was only three months away, Economic Lifelines saw its role not as offering a specific set of proposals, but as demonstrating to decision makers that a serious highway problem existed.

The EL approach evolved in stages during the fall of 1988. First the group hired David Lane, a Wichita marketing consultant, to conduct seven ten-person focus groups across the state. Lane concluded that there was substantial support for a highway program, even though none of the groups were drawn from the northeast corner of the state, where the issue had received relatively little attention. Lane observed that "they [the public] want political leadership to get organized, get it done without squabbling."[15]

Using these limited data, EL spokesman Kready then traveled the state, seeking to convince local elites that there was, indeed, strong support for a large-scale highway plan. The evidence was extremely sketchy, but the study and Kready's presentations hit a responsive chord in much of the state. In Hutchinson, which would benefit greatly from new construction, the newspaper likened Kready to Sir Galahad, as he searched for the holy grail of statewide unity on highway policy.[16]

The positive publicity aided greatly in moving highways to the top of the state's policy agenda; more editorials (usually highly supportive) were written on highways than any other subject between May 1988 and January 1989. Still, the support of some focus groups and the enthusiasm of local elites in favorable communities were weak reeds upon which to construct adequate backing for an extensive, expensive program.

The final element in defining the highway problem in terms of public sentiments came in a statewide survey conducted for EL. The results generally supported maintenance and some enhancements of existing roadways (converting two-lane roads to four lanes, for example); increased fuel taxes were seen as the most appropriate way to pay for the program. Only 4 percent favored raising sales taxes.[17] The survey results were released in late December, immediately before the legislative session, but received almost no press attention. The unrepresentative, almost boosterish results of the earlier focus groups obtained much greater coverage than the more scientifically sound survey findings. By design or good fortune the timing of the focus group results encouraged much more detailed coverage than did the end-of-the year polling data. EL could use the survey to bolster its case, but by December the legislature's interim committee had already placed a substantial new program on the table. Although EL would continue to define the problem of highways, emphasizing both economic development and safety, the policymakers had already turned their attention to the emerging set of policy alternatives.

The Legislature and the Policy Stream

If the task of Economic Lifelines was to offend no one while building general support, the job of the legislature's interim committee was to piece together a set of proposals that would stand a chance of becoming law. The interim Transportation Committee, composed of fifteen representatives and senators, met throughout the summer and fall, but no specifics were presented until after the November general election. Instead, the committee — generally committed to a large-scale program — contributed to defining the highway problem as fiscal; the state would not have adequate funds to match federal grants and continue its ongoing maintenance program. One top DOT official made the basic case that "the 1989 Kansas Legislature will need to make a decision — either some kind of additional revenue is going to be needed, or we're going to have to reduce the [maintenance] program."[18] In fact, the immediate choice for 1988/89 was not nearly so stark, but prohighway legislators strenuously pushed for such an "either-or" interpretation, with its implication that some kind of program must be in place by the start of FY 1990 (July 1, 1989).

The legislature's interim committee received relatively little attention over the summer and fall of 1988. Three members — Senators Bill Morris and Jim Francisco and Rep. Rex Crowell — dominated the process of constructing a specific plan.[19] Rural Republican Crowell and Wichita's Morris were crucial, given their roles as chairs of the standing House and Senate Transportation Committees, respectively. A Wichita Democrat and ranking Transportation Committee member, Francisco provided partisan balance for the trio's proposals. Although these individuals would not ordinarily be ranked among the most powerful legislators in their chambers, they did work well together to produce an initial proposal from which alternatives could evolve during the regular session.

A general picture of the possible highway proposal began to develop in the days before the November election, but the committee released its recommendations, drafted by the three leaders, two days *after* the election. No legislator was going to be placed in jeopardy by the interim committee's plan. The $2 million-plus proposal emphasized maintenance and enhancements, not new construction.[20] Motor fuel taxes would rise by seven cents, the sales tax would increase by one-fourth cent, and vehicle registration fees would go up. Bonding was also incorporated into the plan, as opposed to a "pay-as-you-go" approach. Through his press secretary, the governor labeled the proposal a "good work product for the Legislature to debate and consider." Overall, however, Hayden continued his hands-off approach to the development of alternatives, consistent with his view that his imprimatur would hurt more than help any set of proposals.

The committee's wisdom in delaying the unveiling of its plan until after the election quickly became apparent. Various interests, especially in the Wichita area, attacked the package as too small and without adequate new construction funding (only $200 million). Hayden, conversely, saw it as somewhat too large but a reasonable starting point for negotiations. Indeed, Hayden's reaction provides solid evidence that he desired a program in the $2-billion range, spread over a decade, which would allow him to claim a major rejuvenation of the state's roads without making too much of a long-term fiscal commitment.

Almost immediately, however, the package began to grow rather than shrink toward the governor's desired figure. Ten days after its initial announcement, the interim committee, chaired by Rep. Crowell, endorsed a $2.7 billion, ten-year plan that included a half-cent increase in the state sales tax. The additional funding would largely go toward new projects, although none were specified. As opposed to Hayden's special session proposal, which had laid out the actual routes for new construction, there were no early winners and losers in this process. Legislators could simply report that the Department of Transportation would make the final decisions on the basis of criteria that were supposedly nonpolitical.

The escalation of costs came after many legislators, interests, and editorialists reacted to the lack of new construction in the original committee recommendations. Thus the size of the revised package reassured these actors that their needs would be met, despite the absence of a detailed laundry list of new construction projects. Throughout the policymaking process on highways, legislators and other advocates pursued the dual strategy of not formally specifying projects while encouraging expectations that certain roads would be built.

Further modifying the Crowell-Morris-Francisco plan in his January State of the State message, Governor Hayden eliminated any new sales tax funding; rather, he relied on the same mix of fuel taxes and increased registration fees as the interim proposal and advocated earmarking all sales taxes on new and used vehicles for highways. Although there was some resistance to increased fuel taxes and user fees, the governor's program overcame these objections with its endorsement by the Kansas Motor Carriers, whose highly respected executive director, Mary Turkington, proved a tireless and effective advocate for a large-scale highway package.

Still, gas taxes and user fees would not raise enough revenue; Hayden called for the injection of considerable general fund monies. Earmarking was designed to make the idea more palatable, but the fact remained that the introduction of general fund revenues led many other interests to question whether they were competing with powerful highway forces for the same state dollars.

By the start of the legislative session, Hayden could endorse a comprehensive interim committee proposal, with the rejection of a sales tax hike as his own personal mark. Then, after two years of intense identification with the highway issue, Hayden retreated into the background as the legislative process began. Though he perceived highways as the most important issue of the year and perhaps of his four-year term, the governor understood that his active involvement would almost certainly hurt his cause. EL and the bipartisan interim leadership wanted to reduce animosities — regional, urban-rural, and partisan. Hayden, with his rural western Kansas and highly partisan Republican background, would only open old wounds. Therefore the governor would have to keep a low profile, which meant he would stay on the sidelines, even in the final days of the legislative session.

Channeling the Political Stream: The Insiders Take Over

By the early days of the 1989 legislature, the highway problems for Kansas (federal matching fund qualification, economic development) and a potential solution (a $2.7 billion, ten-year program) had been well articulated.

Highways sat atop the agendas of the governor, legislators, lobbyists, the media, and the public. Yet little had changed from August 1987, when the governor's special session proposals went down in flames. Few decision makers required convincing that the highway issue must be addressed, but there was no agreement on what an appropriate level of spending might be. The 1989 politics of highways revolved around constructing a bill that would spend enough money to attract majorities in both houses, but not raise taxes so much that legislative support was threatened. There was no precise formula to obtain such a balance. Rather, the coalitions were laboriously constructed throughout the entire legislative session, especially within its last three weeks. And the key players were not legislators, but lobbyists.

In the first month of the 1989 legislature, amidst the wrangling over rules and the return of the windfall, highway advocates offered a host of options that raised the ante on highways. In mid-February, one day before the windfall issue was resolved with a large tax cut, Pat Hurley, a principal in the state's largest contract lobbying firm, presented the Economic Lifelines highway proposal to the House Transportation Committee. Included in the $3.3–$3.5 billion package was a half-cent sales tax increase; half of this would go to local school districts in a straightforward attempt to broaden the base of support, both among House Democrats and from the Kansas National Education Association.

Although the $1.8 billion in new construction Hayden had proposed to spend during the special session was not strictly comparable to the 1988/89 Economic Lifelines package, the huge commitments of this latter proposal made it extremely vulnerable to the same sort of criticism. Sometime rebel Republican Rep. Dennis Spaniol made a thirty-second speech that angered highway advocates by simply observing that "during the past two years, the plan has escalated in size from $1.7 billion to $3.5 billion. To date, no explanation has been given for the enormous growth."[21] Noting that he might request a Legislative Post-Audit report on DOT figures, Spaniol incurred the wrath of both Secretary of Transportation Horace Edwards and Speaker Jim Braden, who said to the legislator, "Let's not do this today. If you want to kill a highway program, this is the way, so let's talk this over."[22] Braden thought he had deterred Spaniol, but once again he misjudged the rebels' willingness to take on the leadership.

Such a reaction to a modest request in a short speech typified both the Speaker's lack of control over the House and a more general failing in the consideration of highway legislation throughout the 1989 session. There was precious little serious deliberation over the broad issue of transportation policy for the coming decade. Rather, highways became defined simultaneously as an acid test on economic development and the future of the state of Kansas, and a set of specific benefits that would be spread around the state in a manner that would produce majorities in both chambers. Both the very general notion of economic development and the very specific allocation of concrete (literally) benefits received little scrutiny throughout the process, largely because the opposition to the highway bill, while substantial, remained unfocused and unorganized during the entire legislative session. House Democrats in particular never coalesced around any specific program. Thus, despite substantial opposition to large-scale plans, no coherent alternative was presented.

Although the problems had been defined and policies placed on the table when the legislative session began, there was no indication of an overall political strategy for passing a substantial highway package. The governor stood in the wings; Economic Lifelines had produced awareness of the highway issue but offered little legislative leadership; legislators Crowell, Francisco, and Morris did not have sufficient clout to move the bill through the process, especially in the House; numerous key interest groups, including the Kansas National Education Association (KNEA) and the Kansas Motor Carriers Association (KMCA), had come on board in the fall. Still, no single individual or group seemed capable of imposing coherence on a legislative process that by March was unpredictable in the extreme.

Enter the contract lobbying firm of McGill and Associates. Over the years the firm had sought active involvement on the highway issue but had begun to participate only in the summer of 1988, when the Kansas City heavy contractors pulled them into the process. McGill principal Pat Hurley recounted that "the 'heavies' were our way in. They got us to the table."[23] Although Economic Lifelines had the umbrella lobbying organization, Hurley judged that the key players by the fall were "the heavy contractors, the state association of contractors, and the Wichita-area chamber (WI/SE)."

The size of the highway package became McGill and Hurley's first target in building a strategic political plan; although various alternatives were bandied about, the lobbyists employed policies as means for coalition building. Hurley noted that "if the plan was too small, there would be geographic division, if it was too large, there would be too much money out of other folks' pockets. *Our charge was to produce the biggest possible package for the heavy contractors* [emphasis added]."

The significance of the road construction side of the equation was equaled by the tax mix. Here the lobbyists made use of the Department of Transportation's figures to build their package. On January 31, the DOT released a grid of highway finance alternatives that included six revenue sources:

- motor fuel increases
- registration fee increases
- sales tax transfers (from the general fund)

- sales tax increases
- increases of portions of sales or motor fuel tax increases to a special city/county fund
- bond sales

This specific listing of potential revenue sources served as building blocks for Hurley and other lobbyists as they constructed their own proposals for a large-scale plan. Hurley pointed out that "everything we proposed . . . we drew from [the DOT matrix]. We'd go into a hearing and say 'here's what we want to do'— even the 10 percent transfer from sales tax revenues. And [Budget Director] O'Keefe would come in and argue against it. But we'd show them the DOT matrix, and that was all [the legislators] needed." In the end, the highway lobby was able to "wrap the [revenue] numbers in [the Administration's] credibility."

The decision to seek a half-cent increase in the sales tax, a quarter cent of which would go to K-12 education, helped bring the KNEA on board for the duration of the roads fight. Still, the House of Representatives harbored only forty-five or so strong supporters of a major highway bill, and the House was where the package began its tortuous legislative journey in February and March.

THE HOUSE: THE LONG AND WINDING ROADS

As the House began consideration of a highway program, first in Representative Crowell's Transportation Committee and later on the floor, the context of the chamber became extremely important. The House was essentially beyond the control of any single force. The GOP leadership had lost on rules and, following the governor's lead, had been unable to dictate the outcome on the windfall's return. After the Transportation Committee's hearings, Representative Crowell could only say that "right now [February 27], we're all over the road [sic] on this. . . . I never thought it would be easy, but I think we can get something [with a sales tax increase] out of committee."[24]

The committee did provide the House a golden opportunity to consider a comprehensive highway bill; it sent to the floor, on a March 2 voice vote, a $3.97-billion (labeled $4 billion by headline writers), 13-year highway program. Not all Kansas road needs were addressed, but no highway advocate could argue that the committee had pulled its punches. Rather, it had endorsed additional sales taxes, gas tax increases, and bonding—all of which faced serious opposition in the House. Despite the size of the proposal, the key actors agreed that simply passing *any* highway legislation in the House was the most important single step in the entire process. "That's why the bill was started in the House," observed Governor Hayden, who remained at more than arm's length from the highway issue, at least in public.[25] "I came out with a plan in 1987," he noted, "and it drew a lot of partisan criticism. I don't want that to happen again."[26]

Still, the highway bill was universally regarded as the issue that would most reflect the success or failure of both the Hayden administration and the legislature's leadership. Although their success would ultimately be judged on the size of the roads package, their short-term goal was to pass virtually anything resembling a major highway bill through the Kansas House. No matter how loudly editorialists, Economic Lifelines, and various regional groups might beat the publicity drum, the fate of a large-scale proposal lay in the hands of an unruly, fractious House chamber.

As the debate began in mid-March, expectations for a House bill were modest — between $1 billion and $1.5 billion. In fact, there was the real chance that nothing, or only the most minimal maintenance program, would emerge, which might well doom a major highway program for years to come.

The disorganization of the House and both its parties dominated the legislative politics of the highway bill. Democrats could never develop an adequate party position on this legislation; no single legislator took the issue as his or her own, save for ranking Transportation Committee member Rep. Herman Dillon, who was unable to generate any substantial support for an alternative approach. Minority Leader Barkis, who favored and introduced a small package, was simply less effective at building a policy coalition than he was at delegating this task to one of his party lieutenants. The minority remained profoundly divided on highways, as many Southeast Kansas Democrats were among the strongest advocates of a large package.

If the Democrats' lack of organization on highways was atypical for the session, the Republicans' disarray was not.[27] On March 16, Representative Crowell led off extensive discussion in the Republican caucus by reviewing the committee's $4 billion proposal. Speaker Braden immediately suggested that there was not enough support to pass such a package, and he pressed for a bill that would pass the House. Conversely, Crowell attempted to defend the large-scale committee proposal. Various rebel Republicans attacked the plan as too costly and overly reliant on debt financing. More conventional criticism came from Appropriations chair Bunten, who saw highway expenditures as cutting sharply into the state's fiscal year ending balances in the general fund since sales tax revenues were to be dedicated for roads.

In addition, the figures for various alternatives, including the committee's plan and a leadership substitute, remained very soft and open to interpretation from all sides. The waters were further muddied by Johnson County Republican challenges to the formula for distributing state highway funds. Majority Leader Robert H. Miller captured the essence of the fragmentation within the House on highways with his observation that all 125 House members have "problems with this bill. If anything is going to pass this session, that something's got to pass today. What we've been working on with Rex [Crowell] is to reach that short-term goal. It's essential to keep things alive. We need 63 votes."

That was the nub of the highway issue as of March 16, 1989: some kind of bill had to pass the House. Period. Speaker Braden wrapped up the caucus by asking first for a show of hands as to those who could not vote for the Crowell bill. At least twenty-five (of sixty-seven) members raised their hands. What, then, about the smaller leadership substitute? Seventeen hands went up. Braden concluded that the substitute had more backing, reported that the leadership would work over its bill in the next few hours, and ended the caucus with a request "for your support for getting the amendment on. We'd appreciate your vote, even if you think you can't vote [favorably] on final action tomorrow." There was nothing close to a consensus among the Republicans, and Braden was pleading to keep the bill alive, all the while knowing that Democratic votes would be essential for such a result. Not only would Democrats provide the crucial support for highways, but enlisting minority members would also give political cover to Republicans in defending a set of tax increases.

On the House floor, five-plus hours of debate focused on the specifics of the Transportation Committee proposal; it failed to address many broad questions regarding what kind of transportation system the state should have. Given internal Democratic divisions and the lack of a coherent alternative plan, the minority could not force any general reconsideration of the questionable economic development assumptions of the committee proposal. What the Democrats did have, however, was a core of votes that, when added to those of dissident Republicans (of both the regular and rebel camps), could severely reduce the scope of the highway plan.

Two key amendments slashed the program to $1.28 billion. First, Representative Crowell, reluctantly acting on behalf of the Republican leadership, reduced the size of the package from almost $4 billion to approximately $1.9 billion and eliminated the sales tax component of funding. Then rebel Republican Kerry Patrick struck once again. He proposed an amendment to strip $650 million in bonding; it passed 69–50, with bipartisan support.[28] The House actually approved some further reductions but then reversed itself and ultimately settled on the $1.28 figure in a preliminary vote of 86–33.

With the House's decimation of the Transportation Committee bill, the governor, the leadership, and the prohighway forces lost the legislative battle but took the first step toward winning the war for a comprehensive roads program. Hayden's absence occasioned substantial criticism from Democrats, rebel Republicans, and the press. On the day of final passage (a 68–55 vote on March 17) the governor held his first press conference in two months, arguing that he had not endorsed any specific plan and that "highways should not be addressed in a partisan manner."

Regardless of the rhetoric, the fact remained that a substantial highway bill had passed the House, the largest stumbling block in the legislative process. Aside from their presence on subsequent floor votes in the House, opponents of a major highway program were essentially cut out of the process after March 17. In the conference committee the House would be represented by strong highway proponents, including Representative Crowell, who predicted with some accuracy that the House would eventually pass a $3 billion bill.[29] These Republican conferees never actively defended the House majority position. Rather, they worked hand in glove with Senate conferees to pass the largest bill possible. Although Democrats and dissident Republicans could express themselves on the floor and in votes on a succession of proposals, they could not affect the negotiation process at all. Thus, no matter that the leadership had taken a beating on highways, *a* bill—a vehicle—had been passed. Secretary of Transportation Horace Edwards could legitimately, if disingenuously, state, "I'm pleased with what came out of the House, and we can certainly make a great start with it."[30]

THE SENATE: ROAD RECONSTRUCTION

The Senate Transportation Committee took up the highway bill the next week and quickly forged a $2.8 billion package, which included a half cent sales tax hike and a billion dollars in bonding.[31] There was virtually no deliberation about overall highway needs, either in the Senate committee or on the floor. The package quickly gained approval on the floor, although core support there was never much stronger than twenty-two (of forty) votes. DOT analyst Deb Miller noted that "we gave [the program] to the [Senate] Transportation Committee, and nobody asked a question [about new construction projects, which were labeled program enhancements]. The Senate's byword was speed. It was a 20-minute presentation. Nobody knew, read anything about enhancements."[32] Indeed, she observed, details simply went undiscussed, because "the highway program was less about highways than it was about the economy of Kansas." Echoing those sentiments, the *Wichita Eagle-Beacon* opined: "Highways are not simply concrete, contracts and bonds, but investments in future prosperity so Kansas will have the dollars [to support programs for] the poor, the young and underprivileged."[33]

The Senate's speed did not move the highway legislation immediately back to the other side of the capitol. Key lobbyists and legislators urged Speaker Braden to postpone a vote on the Senate package until the wrap-up session, which would begin April 26. The job for the capital lobbyists, the grass-roots groups, the legislative supporters, and the governor was well defined. They had to convince sixty-three members of the House to vote for a highway package resembling the Senate's version. As Representative Crowell put it, "I think there is substantial support for a larger program than the House passed. How much we'll have to cut back to get a majority [of House votes], I just don't know."[34]

THE HIGHWAY ENDGAME: SQUEEZING OUT SIXTY-THREE VOTES

When the Kansas legislature adjourned on April 8, to reconvene April 26, virtually all actors agreed that the House votes to support a large-scale highway package simply were not there. Despite a year-long grass-roots lobbying campaign, a chorus of prohighway editorials, the lobbying of key Topeka insiders, the governor's backing, and substantial minority party support in both chambers, the road bill was in deep trouble. As of early April, there was little in the way of strategy left to work out; it was all tactics. Lobbyist Pat Hurley noted: "We had to convince the Speaker not to bring it up [before the first adjournment]. We wanted to keep both [highways and sales tax support for K-12 education] alive during the regular session, so we could go out and work for it around the state before the veto session."

Hurley, McGill, and other lobbyists made an explicit "window of opportunity" argument. Hurley recounted: "What we said [in a series of meetings with local elites] was 'This is it. You'll never have another chance to get this much.'" But timing arguments in themselves would not be enough. Legislators and savvy local leaders were generally inured to such rhetoric. Instead they wanted reassurances that their areas would benefit from the highway plan. This posed real problems, since all key policymakers had agreed not to designate specific new roads or projects in advance.

What the highway advocates could do, however, was to demonstrate where the bulk of the "major modifications" and maintenance monies would go (approximately $2 billion), even if iron clad promises of new building (system enhancements) could not be made. Using the DOT maps locating modifications and maintenance spending, the Hurley-McGill forces focused their efforts on Republican legislators. Hurley argued that, at least for the Republicans, "we could, to a person, tell you why they voted for the program. It wasn't pork in a traditional sense, . . . but you had to get specific. It was a lot like school finance. The computer printouts tell them how to vote." This knowledge was buttressed by calls from local notables, spurred by the grass-roots lobbying. A number of local groups came to Topeka to hear the highway advocates' pitch, and grass-roots lobbying efforts merged seamlessly with insider appeals. Many of the principals knew each other well, and Topeka was not all that distant in either miles or culture from Southeast Kansas, Wichita, or any other Kansas locale.

Beyond the particulars of the DOT map, many actors assumed that, if new construction funds could be kept reasonably high, there would be enough money to address a core of significant new projects, especially in Southeast Kansas and in the Wichita-Hutchinson corridor. One lobbyist observed: "It was widely believed that if the [new construction figures] dipped below $600 million that Hutch would be the first to be dropped."[35] Understandably, Hutchinson lobbyists worked hard to maintain the largest package possible, and the *Hutchinson News* listed four major projects that might well be funded if the Senate's version was adopted.

In the two-plus weeks between the legislature's initial adjournment and the April 26 beginning of the veto (or wrap-up)[36] session, lobbying efforts of the McGill-Hurley coalition reached a fever pitch, both in Topeka and around the state. As the lawmakers returned to Topeka in the days before the wrap-up session, some optimism was voiced that a large package could be passed. The lobbying had helped, and so had the relatively modest property tax complaints that the legislators had experienced. Had they encountered a firestorm of property tax protests in their districts during the April 8–26 recess, the lawmakers would have found it much more difficult to raise taxes and spend large sums on highways. The delay in taking up the roads legislation had thus provided one unplanned benefit: temporarily, at least, the property tax issue had been put to rest.

But in order for highway advocates, the Senate majority, and the governor to emerge victorious, the House would have to pass a large highway bill. The key vote here may have been the initial one — on a $2.8 billion conference committee "compromise," which was $1.5 billion more expensive than the House version and a mere $1 million less than the Senate's. In short, it was not a compromise at all. The House conferees had essentially adopted the Senate's position and completely abandoned the House's $1.28 billion proposal. The majority's position went undefended as the House Republican leadership appointed two large-program supporters, including Transportation Committee chair Crowell, to the first conference committee (and all succeeding conferences).

With Senators Morris and Francisco among the three Senate conferees, each successive conference put forward the largest package that might conceivably pass the House. Metaphorically, this was a "salami" strategy; the conference committee would slice a bit off the Senate's proposal and return the bill, virtually intact, to the House.[37] The first House vote after the legislature returned indicated that this tactic might succeed. The House narrowly defeated the $2.8 billion conference bill, 63–61. Highway supporters appeared to need only two more votes to insure a large program, which virtually guaranteed that no serious attempts to compromise would come before the House. Instead of a bill that "split the difference" between House and Senate versions, the Senate bill would continue to serve as the dominant highway alternative.[38]

House leaders saw themselves as free to pry loose two extra votes without making the major concessions that might alienate enough senators to lose the prohighway majority in that chamber. If Governor Hayden had had any substantial clout, he should have been able to change two votes, but this proved impossible. Rather, after making some minor adjustments in conference, the House leadership began to lose support, rather than the reverse. "People keep flaking off," observed an increasingly frustrated Representative Crowell.[39]

The second, basically unchanged, conference committee report passed the Senate, 22–16, but failed in the House, 55–70. Highway advocates had apparently lost ground. Some of this fall-off reflected internal legislative maneuvering on other issues, but it was becoming clear that the House did not contain a majority for a $2.8 billion highway bill. The House leadership did not have accurate vote counts, either from allegedly supportive Democrats or their own forces. Economic Lifelines kept providing the leadership with optimistic vote projections that proved unreliable. Adding insult to injury, Majority Leader Miller voted against the highway bill, as he would continue to do. Not even the leadership itself was unified on this large-scale proposal.

Tensions ran extremely high, since the highway bill was the centerpiece of the governor's program and the issue that House Speaker Braden had to move through the process if he was to regain any measure of control of his chamber. The Senate's perceived need for a large program (to retain majority support) now had to be balanced by the House's requirement of some actual cuts.

As the possibility of failure became a reality, lobbying efforts escalated, both inside the capitol and through grassroots and editorial efforts. In the Hutchinson area, for example, both a fellow legislator and the local paper harshly criticized Democratic Rep. Donna Whiteman, who voted against the bill and hoped to inject income tax reform into a final package.

After the two unsuccessful attempts to pass one version or another of the Senate bill, the specter of the 1987 special session's collapse was raised. Even though the quarter-cent tax for public education had already been abandoned, the combination of a quarter-cent sales tax boost for highways and substantial bonding sustained the House opponents. Senator Morris, who sat impassively in the balcony, watching most of the House highway debates, stated that the defeat of the major highway plan might well mean that any program

— even for adequate maintenance — would be deferred for several years. The legislature's actions in the session's last three days would be decisive.

With two defeats in the House, the Senate conferees began to see a need to compromise, and House Republican conferees proposed a modest reduction in bonding to hold the overall cost to approximately $2.65 billion. This smaller size offered some general hope that the House would agree to the package; more specifically the key leaders — especially the Speaker and the governor — thought that all the necessary side deals to cement the package had been made. Proponents argued that this was the last chance to vote in favor of highways; opponents disagreed vociferously. Republican rebel Rep. Tim Shallenberger argued: "Give us one more chance at least. . . . If you've ever voted 'no,' vote 'no' on this now," and he implied that a more substantive compromise might be right around the corner.

Crowell responded, "I sincerely believe this is the most we can reduce this before we start losing votes [in both the House and the Senate]." Faced with the prospective passage of the bill, many House Democrats looked deflated as they saw large commitments of future revenues going to highways. Their inability to develop an attractive alternative made their dissatisfaction all the more tangible.

The House, however, had not lost its capacity to surprise. Before a packed audience of lobbyists, DOT officials, and gubernatorial staff, the House voted 63–61 to return the bill to conference.

Pandemonium reigned.

Prohighway Republicans looked over at their rebel colleague, Rep. Kenny King, an anticipated "yea," and began to chant "King, King, King." King ignored them. Representative Crowell approached his desk and argued with him to change his vote. King refused.

Crowell announced, "That's it."

Speaker Braden agreed, "That's it. I'm ready to go home."

A reporter asked, "That's really it?"

Braden replied, "As far as I'm concerned. Let's say that I'm disgusted, absolutely disgusted."

But it wasn't over. Braden motioned for King to come to his office, and they virtually raced there, followed by Kansas Public Radio's Rob McNeeley, who recorded King's angry steps and the muffled shouts behind closed doors. Shortly thereafter Rep. Artie Lucas, another unexpected "no" vote, moved for reconsideration; this time he and King supported the package, which passed 63–59, after much vote-shifting. Sixteen Democrats supported the measure. The drama ended with Democratic Rep. Herman Dillon seeking recognition to explain his vote; ignored throughout the process, Dillon, the ranking minority party Transportation Committee member, was again snubbed by the Speaker, who shouted to Dillon that "I didn't hear you."

Reps. Rochelle Chronister and Crowell joined in a victory embrace, supporters breathed a collective sigh of relief, and opponents simply sighed after a battle that they were probably predestined to lose. Kansas had its highway program. Supporters could relax. The governor could claim victory, and he did, almost immediately. With the highway gridlock broken, other agenda items could be acted upon. And within a day regional newspaper stories began to detail various scenarios for the spending of local highway funds, even though the DOT would not make these decisions for months.

HIGHWAYS AND POLITICAL TIME

The politicking, agenda-setting, and decision making on highways offers a rich, complex example of how political time frames the policymaking process. Population trends, electoral cycles, immediate highway funding requirements, and anticipated political reactions, to say nothing of the intense deadline pressures of the legislature's final days, all affected the process and its results.

The long-term trends in Kansas population and economic development have increasingly favored the urban and northeast parts of the state at the expense of many of the rural areas. With a substantial interstate highway system in place, population-gaining Johnson County simply did not value investment in roads as much as it did in, say, education. For much of Kansas, however, improved roads meant one last chance for the surge of economic development that might allow cities and counties to prosper and halt the exodus of another generation of sons and daughters. In a typical editorial the *Hutchinson News* argued that the highway program "is a key to preserving existing jobs, and in helping ensure that the rest of Kansas gets a piece of the economic action enjoyed by other areas in the past generation."[40] This remained the overwhelming perception of highway program backers, even though there was little evidence in Kansas or in other states that highway construction provided any significant stimulus to economic development.[41]

Long-term trends rarely define issues completely or determine when they are acted upon. Various cycles play much larger roles, and three particular cycles defined highways as a 1989 issue. First, reapportionment meant that the next Kansas House would have additional suburban Johnson County representatives who would probably oppose a major road program. Second, Governor Hayden's hopes for reelection in 1990 depended in part on his ability to build public support with a victory on highways. Such a triumph would help to ensure adequate funding for his reelection bid, as transportation interests would contribute substantial funds to his campaign. Third, the legislature was willing to believe that routine maintenance would not be performed on Kansas highways, absent new legislation that pumped funds into these efforts. As the DOT's Miller noted: "Before 1983 [and its program] we completely wiped out any maintenance. Then, the DOT was literally desperate. This year, I didn't think the state was desperate enough. We could have matched [the federal money] and reduced our 'substantial' maintenance level. The perception was — even among a lot of legislators — that we were flat broke."[42]

In short, the highway maintenance cycle, the gubernatorial election cycle, and the reapportionment cycle all moved highways onto the state's agenda. That accomplished, the decision on roads was framed by the general sense that 1989 might represent the best chance to pass a large program and the specific requirements of enacting major legislation within the time limits of the legislative session. Deadlines forced action, even in the House, whose members were profoundly suspicious of the scale of the road package. But legislative leaders and the governor could make specific time-based deals that were good only for very limited periods. Thus getting on the highway bandwagon offered significant rewards for several wavering Republicans, especially those whose constituents were most hurt by reappraisal and classification.

Still, timing was not everything. Two key questions remained after the highway bill was signed into law. First, why was the program so large? Second, how much credit was legitimately due Governor Hayden, both as policy entrepreneur and strategic politician?

In talking to principals about the highway legislation, my opening (and sometimes only) question was: "Why was the highway bill so large?"[43] Although some respondents protested that the state's needs were very great (and thus the size), few actors thought that such a huge package would be adopted. Even McGill and Hurley, who helped engineer the acceptance of a large plan, admitted that "at the end, we were astonished ourselves that that big a program got through."

Most basic was the need for a plan large enough to attract an adequate amount of support. As former legislator Jim Maag succinctly put it, "You had to make the train long enough to get enough passengers on."[44] The Republican leadership took advantage of this notion to keep the train as long as possible, never having to discover if a smaller vehicle would push off some of the Senate supporters. In fact, the larger size of Senate districts (three times that of House units) might well have allowed most senators to support a smaller program. The smaller House districts stood a much better chance of total exclusion in such a package.[45]

The leaders of both chambers could build on the large Senate bill because they never had to worry about compromising with House conferees, who consistently fought for the Senate position. Thus the House majority that voted for a $1.28 billion program was entirely cut out of the negotiating process, largely because of continuing deep Democratic division on this issue. The supporters of a smaller program could only assert themselves in floor debate and through their votes on passage, as they responded to the series of conference offerings.

The decision not to specify new construction projects was critical, as was the continuing ability to convey the expectation that certain projects would receive priority status in the "nonpolitical" selection process. The lobbyists could sell both the reality of specific maintenance spending and the hope for substantial new construction projects.

Finally, highways consumed an extremely large chunk of funds because the governor could not hold down the size of the program. For more than two years Mike Hayden had pushed vigorously to place highways at the top of the Kansas policy agenda. At the same time, he came to recognize in late 1988 and early 1989 that his personal involvement would be a potentially fatal liability to a major roads bill. Topeka veteran Maag notes that "it takes every governor some time" to make the transition from legislator to executive; "The governor is much better off in letting his lieutenants do the negotiations or compromise on issues."[46] Although Transportation Secretary Edwards was generally well respected by legislators, Hayden's personal staff carried relatively little influence on highways, especially in the House.[47] Indeed, while he kept himself informed on highways, Hayden was not a major coalition builder, although he did make the key strategic decision not to designate specific new construction projects.

Both in developing alternatives and especially in closing the deal during the session's last few days, Hayden played only a modest role. He participated in endorsing a few side payments in legislative bargaining (school finance relief, for example), but he did not influence many votes as the lobbying team and the House leadership went about their gritty efforts to piece together a majority. One lobbyist noted that Hayden "was desperate for success" and would have been willing to settle for a much smaller bill. Politically, a more modest package might have served Hayden better, in that less new tax revenue would have been required as well as less in general fund transfers, which would have given him more flexibility in the election year of 1990. By keeping himself out of the process, the governor made himself totally beholden to the legislature's policy decision, because he would receive credit or blame for the final outcome.

In May 1989 Mike Hayden signed the highway bill in the small Southeast Kansas town of Fredonia, where the roads issue had first been raised four years before. The governor had moved it onto the state's agenda, the legislature had shaped its content, and lobbyists had built support for the package from May 1988 through its final passage on April 30, 1989. Highways had dominated the politics of the legislative cycle. Roads advocates had taken advantage of the window of opportunity to pass a bill larger than almost anyone had dreamed possible. The governor apparently had won a defining victory for his administration. And for all who labored under the capitol dome, the end of the session was, at long last, almost upon them.

9

Endgames II:
Preparation and Exhaustion

Decision-making actions during the last few days of nearly every legislative session in almost every state follow a predictable pattern that belies the apparent chaos beneath capitol domes. As vital pieces of legislation accumulate on the calendar, editorials blast the legislature for its annual unwillingness to settle issues in a more timely, rational, efficient manner. For most legislators, however, business goes on as usual. The end of the session is, well, the end of the session. The last few days provide a series of opportunities to "close the deal" on a wide range of policies. Legislators do get tired, irritated, and impatient, of course, but many also get to see their policy preferences enacted into law. Thus they regard the session's final days and hours as the last in a series of elements integral to the regular legislative process.

Kansas House Speaker Jim Braden and Senate President Bud Burke both alluded to everyday life in describing the end-of-session crush.[1] Burke noted: "Just like families or businesses, we put off decision-making as long as possible. People have to be out of time and have only two options. Choices are more clearly defined when we're at the end of the session and other options have been eliminated. That's why you can focus on why Choice A is okay." Braden sharpened the business analogy in his discussion of the apparent logjam in the final days, stating: "It's like having a piece of property to sell. You don't make your best offer right away. But when there's a deadline, you can't wait. You have to move. No one's going to take bottom dollar early in the negotiation."

These metaphors provide some insight as to why legislative leaders and other key players do not necessarily share in all the confusion that appears to envelope the end of the session. They are the brokers who can control scheduling, make deals, have access to vote counts, and negotiate coalitions across policy arenas. Even when Braden felt betrayed by broken promises on several highway votes, he could and did resurrect the road legislation, bringing the issue to a vote time and again. Despite his inability to muster a partisan majority on numerous occasions during the session, Braden could still guide the legislative process in his role as Speaker, his powers enhanced by the impending adjournment.

There are predictable types of endgames, such as "splitting the difference" in negotiations over money (or anything that can be divided) or explicit "logrolling" (one policy outcome traded for another to build majorities).[2] Still, almost all end-of-session activities are singular, since the mix of legislators and interests and the particular context of policymaking are rarely the same. This was especially true in 1989, as the ordinary sticking points, such as school finance and social welfare spending, had been settled, and discretionary items dominated the agenda.

Resolving the highway issue allowed legislators to view the end of the session with optimism. Former legislative leader Jim Maag pointed out that "you break a psychological logjam in every legislative session. In [1989 the legislators] would have never gotten the water plan through, or campaign finance, if the highway bill hadn't gone."[3] But the highway package had passed, and the legislature was ready to finish its run by addressing prison construction, water plan funding, and campaign finance reform, three issues that had bedeviled Kansas policymakers for years.

PRISONS: HERE COMES THE JUDGE

In the Kansas policymaking environment of 1988/89, few policy entrepreneurs came to the fore. Even on highways, Governor Hayden was only one of many influential individuals. Still, policy entrepreneurs can be central to state-level policy development, much as they are on the national scene.[4] In the 1980s Kansas prison policy was increasingly dominated by Federal District Judge Richard Rogers, a former state Senate president, who used his position and comprehension of the legislative process to force the state to address the difficult issue of prison overcrowding.

From 1981 to 1987 the Kansas prison population rose by well over 100 percent, from a base of 2,449 inmates in 1981 to 5,437 in 1987.[5] All policymakers were acutely aware of the overcrowding problem, which had been raised as early as 1977, when seven inmates sued the Lansing state prison over this issue. The legislature itself was responsible for part of the prison population growth because it had toughened some minimum sentencing standards in 1982, although these were softened a bit in 1984 when the inmate population grew by 643 that one year.[6] By the late 1980s, the trend toward larger prison populations was both dramatic and continuing, as state politicians joined national officials in urging a "get-tough" approach to crime.

The legislature did adopt a modest community corrections program to alleviate overcrowding, among other goals, but this measure did not stem the growing prison populations. In 1988 Judge Rogers reopened the original inmate lawsuit, and on April 1, 1988, he mandated the release of four hundred prisoners from state prisons by September 1, in order to reduce overcrowding. In the next year, these two elements of political time—the long-term trend of rising numbers and the short-term imposition of judicial deadlines—combined to drive corrections policy in Kansas. By the last hours of the 1989 legislative session, Kansas had not only decided to build two new prisons but had also set in motion procedures to revise its sentencing guidelines and overall corrections policies.

Construction and Corrections: Agendas and Alternatives

The 1988 legislature reacted to Judge Rogers's April 1 order by increasing the number of prison beds, building and converting facilities for low-risk prisoners, and expanding community corrections programs, at a total cost of $39 million. Although these were band-aid approaches to the problem, they were scarcely insignificant. The *Emporia Gazette* editorialized:

> After decades of treating the prison issue like a pregnant girlfriend, the lawmakers mended their ways in the 1988 session. They had little choice. They were looking down the wrong end of a double-barreled 12-gauge pointed at them by Federal Judge Richard Rogers.

It concluded: "Surely [the legislation] will be enough to let Judge Rogers lower his shotgun."[7] In a similar vein, Sen. Ed Reilly, who represented the Lansing prison district, argued that "an easing of the prison population crunch to the point of building a new prison would be ludicrous."[8]

At the same time, however, the Kansas Department of Corrections hired an Oklahoma firm to provide 350 "residential custody beds" as part of the "state's rush to comply with the federal court order."[9] The overcrowding issue was not about to go away, despite the substantial efforts of the 1988 legislature.

The 1988 appropriations reflected an incremental approach to the overcrowding issue by adding beds to existing prisons and converting other facilities, such as a mobile home manufacturing plant, to corrections use. The judge's resolve appeared to mean that large-scale changes would be essential.[10] Two related questions came into focus: (1) How many new prison beds must be provided? and (2) Would Kansas simply build more prisons or would it broadly reassess its approach to corrections policy?

In 1988 Governor Hayden appointed a Coordinating Council for Criminal Justice, which was to address all issues surrounding the growth of prison populations. Made up of the Attorney General, the Secretary of Health and Rehabilitative Services, and other well-qualified individuals, the council was headed by Department of Corrections Secretary Roger Endell, who came to Kansas in late 1987 from Alaska with a reputation as a builder of new prisons. His major task in Kansas was to direct the efforts to build the state's first new maximum security prison in 125 years. Still, he and virtually all other observers agreed that construction itself was not the answer. After all, funds that went to new prisons were lost to other purposes, and new facilities would require continuing, expensive maintenance. One council member, Democratic Sen. Frank Gaines, expressed the general reluctance to build: "Everybody in the Legislature says, 'I don't want to spend $55 . . . or $60 million [on new prisons].' I don't want to spend it either."[11]

As the state moved to meet the September 1 deadline for reducing the number of prisoners, the Kansas corrections system remained tremendously overburdened; in mid-August, after a number of early releases, the state's prisons, built to house 3,982 inmates, contained 5,811, approximately 150 percent of the optimal population. Endell observed that "effectively, there's been a cap placed on the [prison] population. . . . I cannot add anyone to the penitentiary without taking someone out."[12]

As long as the judge was going to mandate prison construction, various hard-pressed communities began to see the overcrowding issue in economic development terms. Thus both the carrots of new facilities and new jobs and the stick of Judge Rogers's mandate drove prison policy in 1988. In addition, those who wanted fundamental corrections reform could hold new construction hostage as they sought their own policy ends. In the end, four sets of forces interacted to shape prison policy:[13]

- Judge Rogers's requirement to curb overcrowding
- The lack of general support for prison spending
- Economic development opportunities for some locales
- Sentencing and community corrections reform opportunities

Despite the complexity of corrections policies, the bulk of the public debate revolved around the number of prison beds the state should add in order to meet Judge Rogers's standard for overcrowding, which was never completely clear. Even as the state met the September 1 deadline, Hayden correctly predicted that the judge would "tell us the state needs to go ahead and provide more beds."[14]

Prison Beds: Something to Count On

When policymakers, especially legislators, deal with numbers (tax rates, appropriations, pollution levels) rather than either-or propositions (abortions, gambling), compromises are relatively easy to reach. In 1988/89, much of the prison debate revolved around the number of prison beds the state would provide in the next few years. In practice, this debate became centered on the number of beds it would take to satisfy Judge Rogers. If he was content, the state would be allowed to maintain control over its prison system, rather than submit to the governance of a court-appointed special master.

DOC Secretary Endell began the bidding in the 1988 legislative session by proposing 1,200 beds. Although the legislature quickly rejected this number, the 1,200 figure resurfaced in August, when Governor Hayden appeared to endorse it by observing that "no one's proven the [1,200-bed] needs are not there."[15] In the meantime, the judge had called for further prison population reductions and allowed inmates from two additional prisons to join the original lawsuit. Hayden, mindful of the costs for 1,200 beds, backed away from this position, which left Endell as the chief construction advocate, a role he would continue to play through May 1989.

In mid-September Endell formally proposed building two new prisons with a combined population of almost 1,400; Hayden continued to keep his distance and by the end of September labeled the plan as too costly. As with the highway issue, Hayden remained at arm's length from the policy development process on prisons, but for different reasons. The governor feared his involvement in road policy would reduce the chances for passing a comprehensive package. With the prison issue, Hayden's involvement was simply not needed. Judge Rogers was prodding the state for action, and Hayden had already made his crucial decision by selecting Endell, a prison builder, as his DOC secretary. Given their costs, prisons remained a no-win issue, however, and Hayden was content to allow Endell to make the arguments concerning the size and location of facilities.

Through the fall, the coordinating council and Judge Rogers kept corrections high on the state's agenda. The council began to draft sentencing guidelines while the judge held hearings in October on prison overcrowding. The sessions produced the usual horror stories (two inmates in a 40-square-foot cell) and discouraging statistics, which prompted Judge Rogers to state on October 26 that "we'll try to get something out as quickly as possible."[16]

Three weeks later a legislative interim committee proposed a 750-bed prison that could be expanded to 1,300 beds. The committee rejected Endell's proposal, which by late fall had grown to two 752-bed facilities. Still, Endell, the coordinating council, and the interim committee had all developed specific alternatives, which filled the policy "garbage can" to the brim.[17] The *Wichita*

Eagle-Beacon editorialized that "the 1989 Legislature should have feasible, realistic choices for corrections. Considering the Legislature's history of delay and avoidance of the prison population, that's solid progress."[18]

In late December Rogers kept up the pressure by ordering another reduction in the state's prison population (by four hundred reformatory inmates). Governor Hayden followed this decision by including a new prison (750 beds) in his January budget. With such a concrete alternative before the legislature, twelve communities began positioning themselves to obtain the new prison. As a statewide issue, the prison question was dominated by the judge's mandates. Simultaneously, however, the subtheme of economic development grew more prominent, both in the bids for the new state facility and in the nascent proposals of a few communities to build private prisons that would serve either Kansas or other states. By mid-December the Department of Corrections had established an initial ranking of sites, with El Dorado, near Wichita, as its favored location. Nearly everything seemed to be in place. All that remained was for the legislature to pass the requisite bill, an action that would not be taken until the waning hours of its longest-ever session.

The Politics of Prisons

If the overcrowding problem was clear in January 1989 and the potential solutions well developed (more beds, sentencing reforms, community corrections expansion), the politics of prisons remained convoluted. Judge Rogers had led the legislative horse to water but could not easily make it drink. The basic sticking point was elementary: legislators simply did not want to spend up to $100 million to construct a new prison; nor were they willing to commit subsequent millions for annual administration. Nevertheless, virtually everyone understood that the overcrowding problem must be addressed if the state wanted to guarantee that the judge would not appoint a special master to administer the prison system.

As Senate Judiciary chair Wint Winter, Jr., observed: "Rogers is running prison policy. . . . It's so political. . . . Governors have a lot of control, but are afraid to make any major policy proposals due to the unpopularity of the issue." In mid-February Rogers continued to employ his leverage by ordering further substantial reductions in prison populations, effective July 1, 1991. The judge explicitly noted that "a lack of funds shall not be an excuse for failing to comply with his order."[19] This order forced the state's hand and raised serious questions about the adequacy of a 750-bed prison to deal with the overcrowding problem. Even Sen. Gus Bogina, the tight-fisted chair of the Ways and Means Committee, saw the need for a larger prison, stating, "I have problems accepting it, but I don't have much choice."[20] The legislature quickly passed a bill that provided almost $3 million in planning money for a new prison; in many ways this initial commitment of such a large sum dictated that a prison would be approved by the session's end.

Although Rogers's February 15 ruling meant that legislators would have to face the construction issue, it also provided increased leverage for those who advocated expanding community corrections programs and reforming sentencing guidelines. In both the House and Senate, lawmakers linked the passage of Senate Bills 49 (community corrections) and 50 (creation of a sentencing commission). In the House this linkage became explicit in mid-March; leaders appointed a bipartisan task force and delayed consideration of a bill that would commit $6 million for the initial stages of designing a new prison in El Dorado.

As the session wore on, communications among the key actors – the governor, DOC Secretary Endell, and legislators – became worse and worse. The Democrats' leader on prison and corrections questions, Rep. Kathleen Sebelius, whose support was crucial, argued that the DOC operated in secrecy and without any consistent overall plan. Upon learning of a new twist in the debate over where to place mentally ill prisoners, she observed, "There's something fundamentally wrong with being more than halfway through the session and reading what's going on in the newspaper."[21] She noted that plans "have changed daily," which has led to "increasing skepticism about what is actually needed."[22]

The last two weeks of March found lawmakers deadlocked over what prison plan to endorse. The joint construction committee found it difficult to agree on a specific proposal, especially given a lack of clear guidance from the administration. Finally, in late March it did approve a 512-bed facility.

Complicating the prison/corrections/sentencing set of issues was the problem of expanding facilities for mentally ill convicts. Although DOC Secretary Endell wanted the new prison to house these inmates, Governor Hayden was committed politically to placing the new facility near a state mental hospital in the western Kansas town of Larned, which was represented by freshman Sen. Jerry Moran, who had defeated a leading Democratic incumbent in the 1988 election. Hayden's commitment to Larned remained steadfast, despite the costs and staffing problems of establishing a new facility in a rural locale. Ironically, Hayden's commitment did not help him gain Senator Moran's vote on two key issues – Washburn, early in the session, or funding the water plan, at its very end (see p. 148).

Uncertainty continued to dominate prison policymaking; this was highlighted in a stunning ad hoc proposal made in late March by two Republicans, Rep. Clyde Graeber and Sen. Ed Reilly, which would address the Rogers order with a $12 million renovation of three existing prisons, including one (Lansing) in their Leavenworth districts. Virtually all actors agreed that this plan would not gain the judge's approval, but in an April Fool's Day vote, the

House endorsed this unrealistically inexpensive option as a direct attack on Endell and an indirect slap at the governor. Moreover, the House vote demonstrated its great reluctance to spend substantial funds on prisons. With the end of the session in sight, the House had favored a plan that would not, in all probability, address the judge's concerns. Hayden press secretary Kathy Peterson used the now-familiar loaded gun metaphor to summarize the situation; she noted that "the House action leaves Kansas looking down the double gun barrels of turning some prisoners loose . . . or the appointment of a special master who could order us to build a new prison right away."[23]

If the House as a whole was acting emotionally and perhaps irresponsibly on prison construction, its committees were making progress that would lead to the ultimate resolution of the broad issue of corrections. The House Judiciary Committee passed an expanded community corrections program, and sentencing reform remained in the pipeline. Democrats, who had voted overwhelmingly, if cynically, for the Graeber proposal, could exert influence by demonstrating that without their support, no new acceptable prison proposal would be adopted. Led by Representative Sebelius, they had long championed many of the reforms that were now on the table. In the Senate, Sen. Wint Winter, Jr., playing his complementary roles as Judiciary Committee chair and acting Ways and Means chair, could provide formal linkage between the community corrections and sentencing proposals and prison construction.

As the legislature adjourned in early April, the Senate had endorsed a $73 million, 768-bed prison. Judiciary Committee Chair Winter scheduled a day-long session with prison professionals to rehash the issue one more time the day before the conference committee was to take up the prison issue in late April. Using the advice of the corrections professionals and heeding the state architect's revised cost estimates on the House's renovation option ($42 million), Winter sought to focus debate on the Senate bill, which reflected the apparent Hayden/DOC priorities.

The difficult politics of prisons became a little less convoluted with Roger Endell's April announcement that he was resigning as DOC secretary, effective May 1. In the waning days of the session he could lobby for his construction proposal as a disinterested professional who was doing the right thing to comply with the judge's order. This reduced a good deal of the tension between the legislature and the administration, especially when coupled with the state architect's costly estimate of the Graeber proposal, which summarily removed the House-passed alternative from serious consideration.

The sequence of endgame politics on prisons initially resembled the resolution of the highway issue. The Senate had coalesced around a substantial proposal, which roughly reflected the governor's priorities. The House came to support a less costly program, as it would include funding for a 512-bed facility in the wrap-up session's omnibus appropriations bill (although it had not authorized anything beyond the modest renovation of the Graeber bill). In addition, both House and Senate recognized the need for a 256-bed structure to house mentally ill inmates. Ordinarily, when such differences exist, a compromise position can be reached relatively easily. But little came easily in the 1989 House.

On April 27 the Senate approved the 768/256 bed plan, 34–5, sending the bill to the House, which rejected it 94–24. Minority Leader Marvin Barkis observed that while there was support for a "modest prison building plan. . . . *We've got plenty of time*, we certainly don't need to stampede it out of here the first day [of the veto session]."[24] The next day the House amended the catch-all omnibus appropriations bill to include the 512-bed facility. Funding would come from the state budget, not through bonding, which was central to the Senate proposal. This commitment to funding was crucial. Rep. David Miller observed that "without the floor amendment on the omnibus bill, the House had no credible position."[25]

In the last days of the session, Democrats and rebel Republicans once again combined to stymie the House leadership and the governor. Democrats generally desired to build the fewest number of beds possible. Rebel Republicans supported a new facility, but wanted to eliminate, or more realistically, minimize, the amount of borrowing. Both forces, and especially the rebels, fervently desired to adopt some proposal other than the governor's, for their own political reasons. On the highway bill, these groups had not been able to form a coalition to enter into real negotiations with those who advocated a large highway plan; with prisons, however, the situation was different. The opposing sides (House versus Senate; GOP/Senate/Governor versus House Democrats/rebel Republicans) were roughly equal, and all involved had to make educated guesses as to what Judge Rogers would accept.

Endell continued to lobby the senators, concluding that the 768 figure could well be central to the judge's assessment of the legislature's final bill. With the highway example of wearing down the House, the Senate and House leaders continued to stand firm on size and bonding issues.[26] But the House Democrat–rebel Republican alliance held together in rejecting conference committee results. Finally, in a most unusual move, Senate President Burke and House Speaker Braden agreed to appoint four additional conferees to the prison conference committee. Central here was the May 1 inclusion of the Democratic whip, Rep. Donna Whiteman, and the chief prison spokesman among the Republican rebels, Rep. David Miller. Only with these additions were the House majority's wishes adequately represented within the conference. In contrast to highways, where neither Democrats nor rebels held unified positions, on prisons they could play their own effective endgame that would force a move from the House leadership.

Subsequently, a group of legislative leaders—Senate President Burke, Minority Leader Johnston, Representative Whiteman, and Speaker Braden—met with Judge Rogers to try to pin down what legislative actions would meet his standards. Although no explicit figure was agreed upon, given the judge's formal respect for the legislature's independence, the leadership did gain a reasonably good understanding of what he would accept.

The conference committee met from late Monday afternoon on May 1 through early Tuesday morning, when an agreement was finally reached. Bonding would be reduced, the prison's size was tentatively set at 640 beds, and a 256-bed facility for mentally ill prisoners would be constructed. By Tuesday morning both houses had overwhelmingly passed the compromise measure, and all sides saw themselves as winners. No sites were designated in the legislation, although all expectations were that El Dorado and Larned would receive the two facilities. Most importantly, Judge Rogers reacted positively to the outcome, noting that "the Legislature does a lot of writhing, twisting and turning. In the end, they usually do the right thing."[27] Especially, one would conclude, when they have a loaded gun pointed at their heads.

CAMPAIGN FINANCE REFORM: AN ENTREPRENEURIAL EXCEPTION

When the 1989 session of the Kansas legislature began, few observers expected a substantial campaign reform measure to receive serious consideration. There were some modest indications of interest, mostly within the press. The *Wichita Eagle-Beacon* ran an extensively researched series of articles on campaign finance issues written by a University of Kansas journalism professor on leave. The *Eagle-Beacon* committed substantial resources to this reportage, which it followed with a lengthy editorial that strongly advocated beefing up the state's underfunded Public Disclosure Commission. Indeed, within the ranks of the state's media, the Wichita paper was exceptional in its attempts to affect the debate, set the agenda, and influence decisions on several key issues. The *Eagle-Beacon* could take substantial credit for placing campaign finance on the state's policy agenda.

In addition, several other editorials, mostly from small-city dailies, called for additional reforms including better reporting practices—especially for the governor, limitations on PAC spending, and an end to the practice of allowing legislators to convert campaign funds into personal income. This latter concern had also become an issue in Congress, and as the 1988/89 Kansas legislative cycle proceeded, the call for changes in Washington (during Speaker Jim Wright's decline and fall) intensified concerns in Topeka.

Still, the state's legislative agenda was full, and neither the House nor the

Senate harbored much strong support for campaign finance reform. In fact, the prevailing attitude within the legislature lay somewhere between indifference and outright hostility. To push this issue onto the agenda and through the legislative process, an entrepreneur was needed. Stepping into the breach was not just a rank-and-file legislator, but a party leader, one who could command attention for the policy and, more importantly, help move it through the obstacle course of bill passage.

When Republican Rep. Robert H. Miller won the majority leader's position in December 1988, he brought his long-term support for campaign reform with him. He had never taken PAC money, nor did he accept lobbyists' social invitations. As an activist, Miller sought a leadership position in large part because of its agenda-setting possibilities, noting that leaders "determine what issues are going to be put on the agenda, which are going to be put off and maybe go away."[28] Campaign finance would reach the Kansas legislative agenda in 1989 because Miller could place it there.

At the start of the legislative session, Miller put together a working group on campaign finance, and in February he and a bipartisan set of House members introduced a major package of reforms. Miller perceived a window of opportunity for these measures, in that "the rapidly escalating cost of campaigns, the dominance of PAC money in campaign coffers and the negative news accounts about the use of this money, give support to reform this session, before we get into another campaign year."[29]

The House Elections Committee, despite some members' intense hostility toward both Miller and his ideas, reported out a modified version of the reform package, which the sponsors hailed as proposing sweeping changes in the 1974 state law, which had been written in the wake of Watergate. Key provisions would require candidates for local offices to file campaign reports, prohibit personal use of money from campaign accounts that have been closed, require annual disclosure of campaign accounts, and lower from $750 to $500 the amount that a PAC could contribute to a candidate in each election. The House overwhelmingly passed an amended version of the reform measure, which incorporated (on a 62–61 vote) a Republican amendment that disallowed separate contributions from any group and all its subsidiaries (for example, the National Education Association and its local affiliates) that exceeded the limits for one unit. Given the somewhat unusual alliance between regular and rebel Republicans, this interjected a partisan note into a bipartisan piece of legislation. On balance, however, the measure continued to be viewed as a bipartisan set of significant changes.

The state press accorded Miller a good deal of credit for the success of the campaign finance legislation in the House, as both editorial writers and reporters featured the majority leader in their discussions of the issue's progress. Miller had succeeded in moving the issue onto the agenda and had helped forge a working coalition in the House. Senate approval, however, was anything but assured.

The Senate took no action until near the end of the session, when it passed (22-14) an extensively rewritten campaign finance bill that deleted many House provisions and added items that prompted considerable partisan wrangling. The key player in the Senate was Wichita Republican Sen. Eric Yost, whose goals were to eliminate the ability of officeholders to convert campaign funds to personal use and to retain the House prohibition on multi-tiered organizations (especially the Democratic-leaning Kansas National Education Association). The Senate deleted all new reporting requirements in action taken on Friday, April 28, 1989. Most observers and legislators expected the session to adjourn by Sunday, April 30. With the House and Senate versions of this bill so far apart and many other key issues, including highways and prisons, still in need of resolution, the chances for passage of the campaign finance reform seemed slim.

Nevertheless, a conference committee did meet in the waning days of the session, which was extended until Tuesday, May 2, by issues other than campaign finance. Miller did not take a formal role in the conference, but one of his original cosponsors was a conferee, as was Yost on the Senate side. The campaign reform conference committee operated in sharp contrast to those on highways and prisons, the glamour issues of the session, whose conferences were well attended and highly publicized. The campaign reform conferences were held, like those on many other relatively minor issues, in small leadership conference rooms, with one or two staff members assisting the six legislators. Ordinarily, no spectators or journalists were present. The conferees did much of the writing, as they all worked against the deadline of the session's imminent adjournment.

The end result was a bill that combined much of what was passed by each house and ultimately won approval in the legislature's waning hours. Although Yost could legitimately take some credit for passing the bill, without Miller the legislation never would have seen the light of day. Two rebel Republicans (Reps. King and Shallenberger) sat on the conference and worked to produce a legislative product. The Democrats, while generally supportive of campaign reform, were leery of the Republican-dominated process — and especially any limitation on multi-tiered contributions.

All in all, there was no pressing reason for passing a campaign finance bill; the reform issue was not a major concern for most Kansans in 1988/89. No major scandals had come to light, nor had campaign costs risen out of sight. Yet there were specific problems: Governor Hayden had promised to open the books of his campaign and then reneged, which prompted some editorial jabs; former Lt. Gov. Dave Owen had allegedly channeled campaign funds illegally to the 1986 Hayden campaign; and Gov. John Carlin had raised and spent $300,000 in campaign funds in 1983/86, even though he was ineligible to run for reelection. Political action committee donations had risen sharply between 1978 and 1988, but Kansas elections remained relatively clean and reasonably inexpensive (averaging about $7,000 in the House and $20,000 in the Senate for 1988).

In many ways, the legislature was premature in passing its 1989 reforms. The problems were not well articulated, nor were the solutions well developed. Rather, the presence of an entrepreneur and a set of favorable political conditions allowed for passage. Without adequately developed alternatives, however, the legislative crafting was weak. The conference committee met on the run in the last couple days of the session, with inadequate staff assistance and lots of political motivations. State Common Cause Chair Lynn Hellebust, a long-time advocate of campaign reform, stated flatly that "this is the sloppiest piece of legislation I've seen in a long time."[30] Senator Yost, while acknowledging the effects of the last-minute compromising, waxed more philosophical: "But that happens. One problem you have in the Legislature is that you are absolutely swamped with work towards the end, and the staff is absolutely swamped and it's very hard to get it right. Half the bills we pass every year are cleanup for the bills we passed before."[31]

Given the legislature's propensity for delay, its decision to endorse a campaign reform package was surprising. An interim committee and a year's further sharpening of alternatives would surely have made for more thoughtful institutional reform. Even Miller's role as an entrepreneur does not account for the bill's final passage. Rather, the conference committee and the legislature as a whole responded to the state's editorialists, who continually called for campaign reform. Ironically, the legislators believed the editorial writers lacked any appreciation for the nuances of campaign reform, simply seeking reassurance that reforms were being implemented.[32] As Yost put it, "There were very few of us that felt a need to pass something. . . . This was a rare instance in which the editorial writers agreed with me. All that it does is make it look like we placated them."[33] In fact, the appearance and the reality were not far apart. The editorial voices had carried the day and had obtained, in the end, a set of ill-considered, half-baked, and essentially symbolic reforms.

FUNDING THE WATER PLAN: PERSISTENCE (FINALLY) PAYS OFF

Water. Its availability. Its quality. Its cost. Of all the issues facing Kansas policymakers in 1988/89, those surrounding water were as politically intractable as any. Since the 1950s the state had attempted to construct a coherent, adequately funded water plan that would produce a consistent set of policies balancing the state's agricultural, industrial, and consumer interests. All significant groups and key state officials agreed that a coherent water plan was essential for the state, and House Energy and Natural Resources Committee Chair Dennis Spaniol noted that "virtually every candidate in the state voiced support for the state water plan."[34] More importantly, the governor was a strong advocate of the plan, as he had been during his fourteen years in the state legislature. For all this backing, the water plan was finally funded in the last hour of the last day of the 1989 legislative session, only after Sen. Gus Bogina, recovering from a heart attack and bypass surgery, was whisked to the Senate chamber after a dramatic high-speed drive from Johnson County.

The politics of water policy brought together the three central elements of political time: the long-term trend of increased water usage in a state where water resources were marginal; the reapportionment cycle that would diminish rural representation in the next legislature; and the deadline of the 1989 session's final days, when a supportive governor might well forge short-term alliances to produce a significant change in Kansas policy. Water policy also contrasted sharply with the endgame politics of campaign reform. In this arena, the problem was explicit (the need to implement an existing plan), and the solutions were straightforward (a detailed plan and a series of funding alternatives). There was a clear window of opportunity in 1988/89. Only the politics of water — caught up in the state's traditional urban-rural divisions — might have prevented a successful "coupling" of problem with policy.[35]

The Water Plan

In 1984, after decades of wrangling, the legislature passed Gov. John Carlin's proposal for broad state water policies, which required "continuous, comprehensive, and coordinated" planning by the Kansas Water Office.[36] In practice, the so-called water plan comprised a series of related plans that were regularly updated and revised. These dealt with agriculture, the environment, conservation, urban needs, recreation, and a host of other issues. With the 1984 adoption of the water plan, Kansas had adopted the mechanisms to care for its most precious natural resource, but the legislature had never come close to providing adequate funding to implement the policy. The chief obstacle remained the classic question: "Who will pay?"

Simply put, agricultural and rural interests wanted the funds to come from the state's general fund. As Howard Tice, executive director of the Kansas Wheatgrowers' Association, stated in asserting that farmers would pay their fair share: "Everyone now agrees that water is, and should be, the number one issue in the state. . . . We agree that protecting our most vital resource is the proper function of state government. State government is funded by taxpayers, who benefit from the government's services."[37]

Relying on the prospect of general fund monies, however, meant that the water plan had gone largely unfunded. In 1988/89, Governor Hayden and an interim legislative committee both favored relying substantially on dedicated funding sources rather than general fund revenues; such a strategy would place a major part of the burden on heavy water users, especially within the agricultural community. The legislature's 1988 special interim committee, chaired by Representative Spaniol, recommended a set of proposals that emphasized surcharges on farm fertilizers and pesticides, along with additional charges for all water usage across the state. Spaniol observed that "this is a package deal. If we remove the surcharges from farm fertilizers and chemicals, we'll lose urban votes. . . . If we remove the surcharge from monthly water bills, we'll lose rural votes."[38]

Although the 1988 legislature had provided $4.5 million in funding, the water plan remained woefully short of monies. The governor argued that most financing should come from newly available lottery funds earmarked for economic development. But Hayden's proposal was defeated, and the water plan was funded from general revenues. Given its relatively rosy financial picture in 1988/89, the state could have allocated considerably more general fund revenues for water policy, but this level of support could not be guaranteed in future years. As water official Clark Duffy noted,

> We're still in the position of having to fight for the money every year. When water is a visible issue . . . and there's enough money to go around, the system works great. But when there's [not] . . . nothing gets done. . . . The next big step is to dedicate a certain amount of money each year to take on priority projects. We did that this year, but . . . only on an ad hoc basis and there's no way to know what's in store for next year.[39]

In 1988, the water issue remained highly visible, and advocates sought to use this prominence to provide long-term support for a coherent policy.

The Politics of Drought

With the state's dustbowl roots and 100-degree summer days, Kansans' concerns with water make sense. When drought strikes, these concerns become all-consuming as the weather offers discomfiting reminders of how tenuous life on the prairie can be, even in an age of reservoir systems, irrigation, and air-conditioning.

From June 1988 through March 1989, the state suffered a serious drought, which moved the water issue higher and higher on the state's policy agenda. As with the funding question, state water officials emphasized the long-term nature of the problem. In June 1988, Water Office head Joe Harkins described the worsening drought as a part of a trend; he stated: "This has all the indications of a multiyear problem that actually started last year and is just reaching us now."[40] The drought continued through the fall and into the winter. By February planning had begun for prospective shortages in the spring, with more than twenty Kansas counties registering "severe conditions" on a key drought index. The Water Office's Duffy noted that "right now we're preparing for the worst. We're going to assume the worst."[41]

By March the drought alert was in full swing, as Governor Hayden toured the most seriously affected areas; reporters wrote poignant stories of failed wheat crops and the prospect of selling off livestock.[42] If legislators needed any further evidence that the drought was real, it came midsession in the form of a March dust storm that silhouetted the "skyscrapers" of Topeka against a brown-gray background. If March could produce a dust storm, what would July bring? More important for the legislature, however, was the daily attention that the drought brought to water policy. Even if funding the water plan could not insure more moisture, it could demonstrate that the state was responding to the problem. Indeed, the "water plan" label, with its broad reach, may have been more important politically than any of the specific provisions aimed at reducing runoff of agricultural chemicals, preserving wetlands, and cleaning up pollution, as well as ensuring steady water flows for both rural and urban areas.[43]

Money for Water

One of Mike Hayden's priorities—both long-term and for the 1989 legislature —was funding the water plan. In October Representative Spaniol's interim legislative committee proposed $15 million in earmarked funds and surcharges; in December the Water Authority requested $19 million and argued for permanent funding sources. Hayden's January budget message endorsed $16.6 million in spending to implement the plan: $6 million from the general fund, $3 million from the lottery, $1.2 million from existing fees and federal funds, and $6.2 million from new sources outlined in the interim committee's report. The blend of general fund revenues and new user fees, which would fall largely on agricultural interests, was not universally popular, but the idea of sharing the burden would serve as a hardy vehicle for the long trip through the legislative process. Especially potent was the notion of providing a long-term solution to funding the plan. As the *Wichita Eagle-Beacon* editorialized, "Funding the water plan consistently loses out to education and social welfare programs on a year-to-year basis, . . . [while] a user-fee funding proposal . . . would establish a self-perpetuating fund for Kansas water needs now and in years to come."[44]

Still, rural interests were unhappy that so much of the burden (more than $5 million) would come from the agricultural sector. As the bill was debated on the House floor in February, rural legislators tried unsuccessfully to reduce the reliance on users' fees; then, in a stunning move, rural Democratic lawmaker Don Rezac proposed increasing the funding level from $12 million to $18 million. He had concluded that "the fees were going to remain intact; and I was afraid if we didn't do something to make sure the general fund money was there, it would get taken out and we would end up with a water plan that was two-thirds funded."[45]

With a broad base of support, a funding mechanism, and a bulging state treasury, the water plan appeared to be well on its way toward funding when it passed the House on February 22. The Senate, however, would prove a more difficult test, even as the unusual spring drought worsened. The bill would bog down in the Senate Energy and Natural Resources Committee, where the state's farm organizations' "solid wall of opposition" found a sympathizer in the committee chair, Sen. Ross Doyen, a veteran rural legislator and former Senate president who had stated in late March that he did not plan to press the committee for a vote.[46]

So the water plan funding bill sat in the Senate committee with virtually all sides in agreement on the legislation's object and with agricultural interests vehemently opposed to the additional burdens imposed upon them. Nevertheless, rural interests and legislators were faced with a time-based strategic dilemma. They might well defeat the funding bill in 1989, and given the composition of the Senate, they could possibly prevail through 1992. After that, however, both chambers would have gone through reapportionment and the agriculture sector would be substantially weakened. More importantly, such intransigence would delay effective implementation of the water plan until at least 1993, while the state was in the midst of a serious drought in 1989.

Just before the legislature initially adjourned in early April, two separate agents moved to break the impasse. First, at the suggestion of Joe Harkins, the conservation-minded governor, who had pushed for the water plan since entering the legislature in 1972, endorsed a compromise position that would reduce the agriculture sector's costs. Increasing the chances for success was the conversion of the second key agent in this process: the Kansas Farm Bureau. As long as rural interests remained united in their opposition to bearing additional costs, they had an excellent chance of blocking the funding bill. By early April, however, the Kansas Farm Bureau had broken with its allies. Not only did the Farm Bureau endorse the governor's compromise position, but its "lobbyists worked hard—along with the environmental groups—at great personal risk to the Bureau's president,"[47] who was also a member of the Kansas Water Authority. More generally, the Farm Bureau had long supported the broad concepts embodied in the water plan, although it had aggressively worked to minimize the cost to the agricultural community.[48]

In the face of the governor's commitment and the Farm Bureau's change of position, opponents mounted an active, effective grass-roots campaign during the April 8–26 recess, and Senate action remained doubtful when the legislators returned to Topeka for the wrap-up session. Chairman Doyen would countenance no new agricultural charges at all, and on April 28 the Senate committee defeated an $18 million funding proposal that would have imposed new fees on water usage, pesticides, and fertilizers. House Natural Resources chair Spaniol concluded that he had "just about come to the conclusion that the Senate does not want a water plan."[49]

Still, with the governor, the House, and the state's largest farm group committed to funding the plan, there was hope—in part, ironically, because there was almost no time. By Sunday, April 30, the highway bill had passed, and the session was rapidly coming to an end. But the prison issue remained to be resolved, which gave the water plan advocates a chance to use their leverage. First, Speaker Braden pulled the funding bill out of Spaniol's Natural Resources Committee and gave it to the leadership-dominated Calendar and Printing Committee. The funding measure was added to a federally mandated piece of storage tank legislation, which the Senate had previously passed. This was a risky maneuver, in that failure of the amended bill would mean higher insurance costs and increased liabilities for small service stations throughout the state.[50] But the governor and the legislative leaders felt confident that they could find a Senate majority for the bill if they could just get it to the floor.

With no Senate floor debate on the funding issue, the amended bill went directly to a conference committee, which favorably reported out an initial version for consideration on Monday, May 1. The Senate remained hostile, however, and defeated the conference report 25-14. The conference committee reduced its demands upon the agricultural community and reported out a $16 million funding package on Tuesday morning, May 2, the day the legislature would adjourn. All that remained was for each chamber to pass the conference report. Governor Hayden and former Governor Carlin (also a long-time water plan supporter) worked the phones diligently to round up support. The top leaders were not, however, the only players to exert pressure in this endgame. A core of Wichita-area legislators decided to link their votes on the water plan to a bill that would provide legal standing to a citizen's utility rate board (CURB). As Wichita-area Democratic Sen. Jim Francisco argued, "We thought if stuck together, we could cut a deal to get the House to move on the CURB bill and the Senate on the water plan."[51]

By May 2 the legislature was running on empty; trying to hold these two bills together was difficult, yet water plan funding advocates had to jump through this final hoop. A deal was struck to run the measures simultaneously, and the linkage held. Adjournment was in sight, as long as the Senate would pass the funding package. But the Senate balked. The leadership and the governor's top environmental aide, John Strickler, thought they had twenty-one votes, the necessary constitutional majority; Sen. Jerry Moran (R-Hays) had second thoughts, noting that although he supported the water plan, "I am just not for this bill. [The Senate leaders and the governor] would have had a lot more than 21 votes if they had allowed discussion, compromise, and amendment."[52] Perhaps, but much of the sting had already been removed from the funding plan. Rural Sen. Jim Allen (R-Ottawa) pragmatically switched his vote to support the bill, observing that after reapportionment agricultural interests would be worse off. "We're going to have to take the best possible deal we can."[53] Nevertheless, the Senate was left with a 20–19 tally, one short of a 21-vote constitutional majority. After a series of frantic phone calls and aborted conversations, Senate President Bud Burke announced a call of the Senate, which required all senators to remain on the floor while the one absent member — Sen. Gus Bogina, who had undergone heart bypass surgery four weeks earlier — was driven to the capitol.

Alerted that his vote might be necessary, Bogina was eagerly waiting in his Johnson County office, sixty miles from Topeka. An hour and fifteen minutes after the call of the Senate was instituted, Senator Bogina, clearly ecstatic to be back in the midst of the legislative fray, made his dramatic entrance onto the Senate floor. Shaking hands and basking in the moment, Bogina related his hair-raising trip to Topeka. Chauffeured by a state trooper at speeds up to 120 mph, Bogina recounted with childlike enthusiasm that he had "never had [such] a ride. . . . I loved the siren and the red light."[54]

Almost incidentally, Bogina cast the twenty-first favorable vote, and the funding bill passed. Of the $16 million in the package, only $2.9 million would come from agriculture-related sources, while municipal and industrial water use fees provided $5.8 million and state general fund and economic development monies totaled $8 million. Considering that 87 percent of all state water usage was agricultural, the rural interests fared well, even if their historic expectations of getting their own way were not met.

Within minutes, both chambers had adjourned, although the House did pass one more measure — a $6 million tax cut in the form of eliminating the alternate minimum tax. One rebel Republican legislator made a brief move to filibuster the chamber, as Rep. Kerry Patrick had done a year earlier, but he backed off. The Speaker brought the gavel down. The last endgame had been played. The 1989 legislature was history.

10

Time after Time

After the historic 1989 legislative session, everyone declared victory. With good reason. So much had been accomplished that the governor, regular Republicans, rural and urban forces, Democrats, and the legislature's guerrilla band of rebel Republicans could all claim great satisfaction with the session's results. Indeed, the near-euphoric short-term assessment was that the public had been well served as the legislative logjam broke apart in the final few days of the 1989 session. For example, the *Wichita Eagle-Beacon* opined hyperbolically that "perhaps at no time in state history was more done to ensure a better future for Kansas than during the seven-day wrapup session" that had ended two days earlier.[1] Credit was spread around among virtually all legislative factions, as well as the governor. The *Kansas City Times* viewed the session as a "blockbuster," in which

> major, complex issues were resolved, some of them after it appeared highly unlikely, even to sponsors, that a consensus could ever be reached. It was hardly a political love-in; a dozen or so conservative dissidents in the House kept the tension level high. In the end, a winning accommodation was reached on an agenda that will upgrade the state.[2]

Other editorial voices raised substantive objections — to the size of the tax increases, the emphases of the highway program, the session's wrangling — but the general tenor was strongly upbeat, especially when Kansas was compared to neighboring states. David Awbrey of the *Eagle-Beacon* noted that "while Kansas was deciding to build highways, keep its water clean and enhance its universities, Missouri was talking about closing a college, Arkansas was rejecting more money for school teachers and Louisiana was facing budget cuts that could cripple state operations."[3] More pointed than

149

many of the editorial assessments were those of the key participants, nearly all of whom saw themselves as winners. Still, these rosy short-term judgments were sure to pale over time. Given the diverse long-term interests of these politicians, the 1989 session would prove to have nurtured as many thorns as blossoms.

STRATEGIC POLITICIANS: AS TIME GOES BY

Despite their perceptions and claims, the three warring factions of Kansas politics — regular Republicans, rebel Republicans, and Democrats — could not all emerge as long-term winners in the wake of the 1989 legislature's decisions. Elections in 1990 and 1992 would sort some things out, and the politicians' careers would rise or fall in coming years, as individuals made choices based in part on the context created by the watershed decisions of 1989. Within two years Mike Hayden would be unemployed, lobbying for a job in the U.S. Department of Interior; rebel spokesman Rep. David Miller would be back in Eudora, Kansas, running his insurance agency; Rep. Marvin Barkis would be Speaker of the House (only to be upset in the 1992 elections); and the state's treasurer, Joan Finney, a nonplayer in the policymaking of 1988/89, would be sitting in the governor's office.

Mike Hayden and the Regular Republicans: A Marathon Victory

When we get up and read the newspapers, the sausage is going to look pretty good.
— Majority Leader Robert H. Miller, May 2, 1989[4]

Both as a policy activist and a strategic politician, Gov. Mike Hayden could scarcely have been more pleased with the legislative sausage of the 1988/89 political year. One day after the legislature adjourned, he was brimming with confidence: "If leadership is the issue in the next campaign, Mike Hayden will be the next governor."[5] He could claim achievements, if not total victory, on five of six key issues — the windfall, highways, prisons, tort reform, and higher education funding. As a persistent policy entrepreneur, he had also gained permanent funding for the state water plan. By his count, only the death penalty was a defeat, and he continued to believe that this issue would work to his advantage in the 1990 campaign. From a political point of view, Hayden's successes had increased the risks for Democratic U.S. Congressman Jim Slattery, who was deciding whether to enter the 1990 gubernatorial race. Hayden looked a lot less vulnerable in May than in February, and Slattery would delay his decision on whether to challenge the sitting governor.

Not only did the results of the 1989 session slow Slattery's move to become a candidate, they also changed Hayden's fund-raising calculus for 1990 (one more key consideration for strategic politicians). With tort reform off the agenda, no candidates would profit greatly from soliciting the medical and legal communities. Rather, the greatest single potential source of funds for Hayden would be highway-related interests, who would reap a bonanza over the coming decade as the state spent its $2.65 billion dedicated to roads. Hayden brushed off suggestions that his holding a $1,000 per couple fund-raiser near Fredonia, where he would sign the highway bill, implied any relationship at all between the program and support for his reelection. Although Hayden would receive substantial support from contractors and others who would benefit from the highway program, these interests did not dominate his reelection funding efforts. Instead, his campaign attracted support from a wide array of interests ($2.1 million altogether, up from $1.4 million in 1986).

Still, in May 1989 the focus of attention was the legislative record, which Hayden could legitimately view with confidence. The legislature had passed a raft of historic legislation, all on his watch. Senate President Burke observed that, although the governor was not continuously involved in the session's policymaking, "every time there was a kink in the hose, he was there to straighten it out."

The legislative leaders could also bask in the glow of a productive session. Burke's decision to cut out substantial minority participation looked very sound; on key issues — highways, prisons — the unified Senate dominated the shaping of alternatives. Braden, the often-ineffective Speaker, was happy to have survived the session. Although he won the title of "boss" in one editorial, he knew better. No one "bossed" the House in 1989, least of all the Speaker. Shortly after adjournment, Braden wearily concluded: "It's been interesting, and . . . the end product has been great for Kansas. But I'm glad the marathon is over."

Even in this moment of triumph, clouds gathered on the horizon for the governor and the Republican regulars. In particular, three political problems appeared especially worrisome: (1) the unresolved issue of property taxes; (2) modest ending balances for FY 1990 and increased spending requirements for programs adopted in 1989; and (3) Governor Hayden's public support, which stood at lower levels in various polls than might be expected after a truly historic legislative session.

Property Taxes: The Costs of Delay

> *Reappraisal is a politician's nightmare. If your taxes go up, you're mad. If they don't, you deserve it.*
>
> —Mike Hayden, May 2, 1989

Throughout the 1988/89 legislative cycle, numerous homeowners, small business operators, and realtors protested the coming impact of classification and reappraisal. Nevertheless, the governor and legislative leaders of all stripes sought to defer serious consideration of the issues of tax rates, ultimate liabilities, and shifts in the state's tax burden, with its growing reliance on local property taxes. Despite the vocal opposition of rebel Republicans and some Democrats, solid majorities in both houses (as well as the governor) simply did not want to open the Pandora's box of property taxes by tinkering with the still-to-be implemented scheme of reappraisal and classification; the first wave of new tax bills would not be distributed until November and December 1989. However clear the implications might be for real estate and small business interests as well as some homeowners, the impact of the process would not be full-blown until property tax bills arrived around December 1, with half the total due December 20.[6]

Thus, while appeals of property values needed to be made in March 1989, when new appraisals arrived, the impact of changes in rates and classifications would not be completely apparent until nine months later. The legislature had appropriated a modest $10 million for a short-term "circuit-breaker" program that would address only those low-to-middle income individuals whose taxes increased by more than 50 percent. Mike Hayden and the Republican legislative leaders, long-time advocates of the reappraisal and classification process, had made the apparently sensible short-term decision to let the issue mature while they attacked other high-priority issues.

Combined with the spending down of the state's balances (see below), the decision to delay turned out to be politically unwise. Hayden found himself fighting a vicious primary election in 1990 against Nestor Weigand, former head of the national realtors' association, who chose rebel Rep. David Miller as his running mate. Although he won the primary by a very narrow margin, the governor lost the general election to State Treasurer Joan Finney, whose fluky, low-turnout upset victory in the primary over former Gov. John Carlin (the initial reappraisal and classification architect in 1985/86) provided the Democrats with a candidate who could campaign strongly on the property tax issue.

In short, Governor Hayden had acted as a strategic politician would be expected to act in 1988/89. He knew he had to produce a strong legislative record that reflected his own vision of progress for the state. Especially with victories on highways and water plan funding, he accomplished that goal. At the same time he had apparently ingratiated himself with various other interests, including those in Johnson County, who had demanded and received income tax cuts. More important, Hayden had kept his toughest potential adversary, Congressman Jim Slattery, out of the governor's race. And he had begun to raise a formidable campaign war chest from a broad range of individuals and interests. All in all, the governor had played his role with acumen. Yet it was not enough.

There are great limits to any individual's ability to maneuver strategically, and Hayden operated within those limits. He made a choice to defer consideration of property tax issues. If he had faced former governor Carlin, property tax increases might well have been of little significance, since both candidates carried property-tax baggage. In Joan Finney, however, a conservative populist with no track record on the most important issue of the 1990 campaign, Hayden found himself at a fatal disadvantage.[7] The governor's 1989 accomplishments, however real and substantial, simply were not perceived as enough to outweigh the property tax issue and Hayden's lack of personal popularity.[8]

Commitments to Spend:
Republicans as the Party of Government

> *The one disappointment [in the 1989 legislative results] is the level of overspending. We can afford it this year, but . . . these programs have to be funded every year. They're ongoing costs. We're hopeful that the economy will let us support these programs at the level we've established.*
> —Mike Hayden, May 2, 1989

The 1989 legislature went on a spending spree. When the final obligations were sorted out, the state's FY 1990 total budget stood at $4.76 billion, compared to $4.29 billion for 1989. Not only that, but the state had added continuing commitments on highways, the water plan, and social and children's programs, while cutting income taxes and terminating the alternate minimum tax. Aside from Hayden, four key Republican legislative leaders—Speaker Braden, House Appropriations chair Bunten, Senate President Burke, and Senate Ways and Means chair Bogina[9]—had raised frequent warnings about the overall levels of state spending, as had Budget Director O'Keefe and Legislative Research Director Richard Ryan in a series of widely distributed memos.

In many instances, Hayden had little capacity to act strategically in deciding whether to agree to substantial new spending commitments. A veto of social spending would have earned him the animosity of Democrats whose support he needed for the highway program, which in turn was more expensive than he might have wished. Earlier in the session, the legislature had dictated the terms of the windfall's return. In addition, Hayden had been a major advocate of water plan funding for years; it would have been unthinkable for him not to grasp the opportunity to resolve this long-term problem. In short, Hayden and many of his Republican allies in the legislature represented the "party of government," which frequently combined with Democrats to increase state spending.

Despite the warnings of Representative Bunten, the cautionary notes of Legislative Research's Ryan, and the scolding caucus speeches of Speaker Braden, legislative Republicans and the governor chose to expand fiscal commitments and spend down the state's balances — from $325 million in June 1989 to a projected $175 million remainder in June 1990. Although such a balance was not a paltry amount, it would leave much less room to maneuver than Hayden had enjoyed in 1988/89. In addition, the Democrats had added to spending at virtually every opportunity (see below), often because they believed in the programs at hand, but just as frequently with the goal of reducing the state's general fund balance.

Post-Session Surveys: The Limits of Achievement

Mike Hayden is vulnerable on his handling of issues — particularly those surrounding taxation. The electorate believes Hayden has failed on other important issues; he is perceived to lack the right qualifications for the office of Governor; and most voters simply see the need for change in Topeka.
— Executive summary from Penn-Schoen poll
commissioned by Congressman Jim Slattery, June 1989

Without question, the acme of Mike Hayden's public standing as governor came in the immediate wake of the 1989 legislative session. He had won victories on key issues and had received considerable positive media coverage for these successes. In late May and early June 1989, the two leading Kansas Democrats, Reps. Dan Glickman and Jim Slattery, hired major survey research firms to sample Kansas public opinion. Governor Hayden did not have access to these polling results, but as an inveterate poll-watcher he had his own data to reflect upon. The Hickman-Maslin survey for Glickman and the Penn-Schoen survey for Slattery reached very similar conclusions that were, in all probability, roughly equivalent to the governor's results.

All in all, the findings were mixed for Glickman and Slattery, as well as for the governor. Among statewide Republican elected officials, Hayden (53 percent favorable rating) was viewed much less positively than either Sen. Robert Dole (71 percent) or Sen. Nancy Kassebaum (82 percent); he had higher negatives by far than any other Republican, even after his legislative successes. Indeed, the only statewide figure with (marginally) higher negatives than Hayden was former Gov. John Carlin, the Democrats' most likely candidate if Slattery did not run.[10] An even 50 percent of likely voters thought Hayden should be returned to office, and in a head-to-head race with Hayden, Glickman trailed only by a 49 percent to 41 percent margin.[11] Slattery trailed the governor by a greater margin, largely because he was less well known throughout the state than his congressional colleague.

Hayden was viewed most negatively when it came to his handling of the reappraisal and classification issue; only 9 percent in the Hickman-Maslin survey thought that "someone else" would have done *worse* than the governor on these property tax issues.[12] Likewise, the Penn-Schoen results indicated that property taxes were Hayden's "worst category" of issues, with 59 percent rating the governor *poor* (and 25 percent fair).[13]

In sum, the survey results pointed to a wounded governor whose 1989 successes had not overcome substantial negatives. As a well-defined veteran politician, Hayden's strategic options were limited; even in his moment of triumph his negatives remained high, and his room to maneuver in the coming year had been severely restricted. He could raise substantial campaign funds, but they would be of little assistance if he could not effectively address the property tax issue. And it was that issue that dissident Republicans and Democrats would emphasize in the 1990 primary and general election campaigns, respectively.

Democratic Majority Building

Looking back on the 1989 session, Minority Leader Marvin Barkis did not focus on specific policies or the overall legislative record. Rather, he emphasized two political results: an "unbelievable" redistricting map and great success "in spending down the governor's resources" prior to the 1990 election. This is not to say that Barkis and his fellow top Democrats in the House lacked strong and specific policy preferences. But even in league with the rebel Republicans, their minority status greatly hindered their capacity to set the agenda or to define policy alternatives.

As both strategic politicians and policy activists the Democrats believed nothing was more important than capturing the levers of government. From this perspective, they judged the 1989 session highly successful. They saw the reapportionment results as offering them a reasonable chance to capture the House in 1990, and they consistently sought to limit the governor's ability to commit new funds in 1990, which would make him more vulnerable to a Democratic challenge. On both counts their analysis proved correct. The Democrats' victories in winning control of the governorship and the House in 1990 began with their actions in the 1989 legislative session. Nevertheless, Democrats acknowledged that Hayden benefited in the immediate aftermath of the 1989 session. Rep. Kathleen Sebelius (D-Topeka) noted that the Democrats had frequently provided Hayden with the margin of victory (highways, the windfall). She observed: "An important question is 'How much does what we did help the governor?' There's a short-term glow of Mike Hayden being back in the saddle."[14]

In particular, the Democrats worried that they had given up too much on two fundamental long-term issues: (1) the changes in the tax burden that shifted the emphasis from the more progressive income tax to a regressive sales tax and a property tax structure that was viewed as inequitable; and (2) a highway program that might well claim inordinate amounts of resources in the years to come.

On neither the tax mix nor the highway program did Democrats come away with their policy preferences, yet they did position themselves to campaign effectively in the future on both highway spending and tax issues, broadly defined.[15] There is always tension between the desire for policy results and a craving for viable campaign issues, since electoral strategies speculate on anticipated actions rather than the best results possible in the present. Minority Leader Barkis reflected: "As a political leader, I think the [taxes and fees of the highway program are] the best thing that could ever happen to Kansas Democrats. . . . as a person interested in policy, it's one of the worst things . . . because we put all our money into one area."[16]

The politics-policy highway tradeoffs were straightforward, if open to interpretation, but the changes in the mix of Kansas taxes were relatively subtle, more a result of a series of decisions than a single up-or-down vote. Key policy decisions (on a tax mix) were made on political grounds as the session progressed. Politics dictated the return of the windfall, while the governor embraced a sales tax increase for highways in light of surveys that showed it as "the least onerous tax."[17] Various fees were also increased, while the alternative minimum tax was repealed. The *Wichita Eagle-Beacon* placed the tax shift in a strategic context, reasoning that the "return of the windfall"

could haunt the 1990 Legislature, which may find that it has little money to meet the expected demands for property tax relief from reappraisal. Funneling $69 million in income tax cuts into the pockets of mostly middle-class and wealthy taxpayers will raise questions of fairness if, as many people predict, higher property taxes threaten to wipe out many small businesses.[18]

Understanding the nature of political-policy tradeoffs is essential for strategic politicians. All major actors could make the basic calculations here as the game progressed, but Democrats, in part because they were in the minority, could focus clearly on both politics and policy simultaneously. They had no responsibility for passing a program. Still, the mix of motives took its toll. Rep. Joan Wagnon, a key tax committee member, saw the tax burden shift as "the worst result" of the 1989 session. "The biggest abomination," she noted, "was the adoption of federal deductibility, where $8 million went to about 1,000 taxpayers." In addition, she pointed out that Wichita State University economist Glen Fisher's studies show that we're underrelying on the income tax and overrelying on the sales tax. And now we've increased sales tax reliance and decreased the income tax share. And do we raid the general fund for highways? Yes. The question then becomes "Do we do it progressively or regressively?" Politically, [the income tax cuts] weren't stupid, but philosophically . . .[19]

At the same time, as strategic politicians, minority Democrats could advocate (social programs) or accept (highways) spending that would reduce ending balances. Just as they had sought to put Republicans on the record with a series of embarrassing votes in 1987/88, they consistently worked to lower the general fund balance throughout 1989. This strategy often meant choosing to cooperate with one Republican House faction or the other. On procedures, process, and prisons they frequently joined the rebels; on numerous substantive decisions they provided enough votes to endorse major spending initiatives (social issues, higher education, and the water plan, among others). And sometimes (as with highways), they lost on substance but claimed political gains in terms of reducing the governor's fiscal flexibility. As a minority party they could, to an extent, have their cake and eat it too. In providing the decisive sixteen votes in support of the highway package in the House, certain Democrats could take credit at home for securing a substantive victory, while Minority Leader Barkis could claim that the party was not responsible for the tax and fee increases that would fund the plan.

With a mix of policy successes, a favorable reapportionment scheme, a reduced ending balance, and a handful of political issues for 1990 — most notably the property tax — Democrats could legitimately feel satisfied. More effectively than the regular Republicans, they had been able to lay out and follow coherent political and policy strategies in 1988/89. Particularly in the House, where they could benefit from their alliance with the rebels and hope to affect policy outcomes, Democrats could act simultaneously as policy advocates and strategic politicians as they sought to attain majority status.

The Rebels: Tactics, Theories, and Theatrics

[Rebel Rep.] David Miller was in charge [at the beginning of the session] and he was still in charge at the end.

— Democratic legislator[20]

From the writing of the chamber's rules to the forging of a compromise prisons bill, the dozen or so House Republican rebels profoundly affected the context of Kansas politics and policymaking in 1989. On one level these lawmakers were a highly frustrated bunch who had absorbed a long series of real and imagined slights from the Republican legislative leadership, especially Governor Hayden. They depicted themselves as conservatives who wanted to impose priorities (their own, of course) on state policies. In particular, they had harbored hopes, if not expectations, that Hayden would be an energetic conservative force in setting the state's policy agenda, a force they believed had been missing for decades. According to Rep. David Miller, these hopes were dashed by the beginning of Hayden's second year in office:

> In 1986 [the conservatives] thought that they'd gotten a conservative in Mike Hayden, though not a barebones conservative. But problems developed immediately. One week after the '87 session started, we had a budget reduction bill, to address serious problems, and everyone was on board. In the aftermath of the crisis, Hayden submitted a [1988] budget with a large increase.[21]

For all their conservative convictions and long-term frustrations, the rebels' real prowess came not in refocusing the state's policy agenda, but in acting with the tactical inspiration of guerrilla warriors reinforced by an intellectual arrogance toward the legislative leadership. "We chose our battles," noted Rep. Kerry Patrick, "where we could win, and where we could make a difference."[22] They struck at opportune moments, often with politically attractive amendments, and forged a session-long alliance with Democrats; the true north of their efforts was a consistent desire to embarrass Governor Hayden, as much as it was a well-articulated conservative philosophy.

Like the regular Republicans and the Democrats, the rebels could legitimately declare victory as the session wound down. David Miller noted especially the rules decisions, federal deductibility on income taxes, and reductions in bonding commitments for prisons. More significant, perhaps, was the palpable sense of uncertainty on the House floor whenever a potentially controversial vote was taken. Would the rebels take a position? Would they join the Democrats? In substantive terms their impact was relatively modest; the governor got much of what he wanted. But in 1991 the Democratic leadership left the 1989/90 rules intact, which may have been the longest-lived of the rebels' impacts.

The rebels took great strategic advantage of the fact that they held the balance of power in 1989/90 in a closely divided House. After the 1990 elections their leverage declined precipitously, since the majority Democrats often went fishing for support among moderate Republicans instead of conservative rebels. Career ambition moved several key members to forsake the state House. As the lieutenant governor running mate of failed gubernatorial candidate Nestor Weigand, David Miller left electoral politics.[23] Patrick, who had little in common on policy grounds with his Democratic partners of 1989/90, could not influence the Democratic House leadership in 1991/92 (although he did frequently have Governor Finney's ear). In 1992 he lost a bid for a U.S. House seat, rather than seek a new Johnson County state Senate position. And Rep. J. C. Long left the House to manage Sen. Eric Yost's unsuccessful U.S. House race.

As strategic politicians, the rebels generally acted rationally to leave a chamber that was not especially hospitable to them. Most rebels were secure in their elected positions. Patrick and Miller were popular at home, and Long noted that "being a rebel played extremely well back in the district."[24] In addition, they understood more than any other group in the legislature the potential power of the property tax issue and the governor's inability to deal with it effectively. Still, none of them benefited much from this foresight, nor could they cause the legislature to bend much in their direction. In the end, they remained political guerrillas who won a host of significant battles but not the war.

EXECUTIVES AND LEGISLATORS: A DIFFERENCE IN PERSPECTIVES?

Legislators are generally seen as adopting a short-term approach to politics and policymaking since their terms are short (especially in the lower house) and responses from constituents are often immediate. In addition, most state legislative sessions last only ninety days or less, so the end of the session is always within sight. As state legislative scholar Alan Rosenthal observes:

> Nearly everything revolves around processing legislation, and members are greatly concerned with promoting their own bills *now*. . . . The legislature is a problem-solving body, but the problem to be solved often becomes that of ensuring that a bill will be enacted rather than the original problem that gave rise to the bill's introduction.[25]

At the same time, term limit movements have attacked the growth of seniority in the states as legislative careers have lengthened. Both as policy entrepreneurs and political careerists, state legislators frequently provide a long-term context for their actions.

While the tendency is to view legislators as pursuing short-term goals, with an overlay of longer-term strategic calculation, interpretations of executive behavior are often the reverse. Presidents and governors are supposed to be able to take longer, more comprehensive views of politics and policymaking. Eight years stretch out, prospectively, before these executives (more or less for some governors); Light has demonstrated how presidents introduce substantial amounts of legislation early in their terms with the assumption that these proposals represent a four-year agenda, at the minimum.[26] In the states, Rosenthal observes that "the executive can, and often does, take a longer point of view"; one gubernatorial aide concluded: "The legislature lives in the here and now, while the governor has to look to tomorrow."[27]

Still, chief executives often operate in the close quarters of extremely limited time dimensions. A so-called honeymoon period provides an early but temporary window of opportunity. The fourth year of presidential and gubernatorial terms is almost completely given over to politics. Executives have become increasingly aware of their immediate impressions; Ronald Reagan's White House was consumed by what appeared on the evening news, and all recent presidents have had access to daily tracking polls during their terms of office. Governors are scarcely less concerned with their impressions. The capital press corps pays substantial attention to the governor's daily activities, whether the legislature is in or out of session.

Both governors and legislators must mix their short-term perspectives with more extended points of view. Also, there is the tendency to link short-range thinking to mere politics and longer time perspectives to some kind of policy vision. No such logical connection exists. Key policy decisions may result from short-term maneuvering; major political choices may be structured years before an election renders them wise or foolish. What became clear in the Kansas context of 1989 was that the individual actors were constantly juggling politics and policies along with short- and long-term perspectives on both their own careers and the future of the state.

In 1989, Governor Hayden's political time horizon was exactly the same as that of the members of the Kansas House; the primary election would be held in August 1990, with the general election to follow in November. Hayden needed to build a substantive record, hold off the conservative Republicans on his right, and dissuade Congressman Slattery from challenging him. Simultaneously, he was working to pass various pieces of legislation that he had supported for years, some for more than a decade. If a new prison wasn't built, the state could suffer for years, with an appointed master dictating corrections policy. If the water plan was not funded, when would future budgets permit it? And most importantly, when would legislators ever be more inclined to pass a large-scale highway plan?

If the governor had completely adopted the strategic politician's perspective, he would have addressed the property tax issue in one of two ways: by providing more resources in the 1989 budget or by ensuring that the state's 1990 ending balances would be higher so he would have more leeway in the election year to salve coming property tax wounds. Hayden played the roles of both strategic politician and persistent policy entrepreneur who sought to take advantage of specific, long-awaited windows of opportunity. His defeat in 1990 was scarcely preordained; in May 1989, it appeared unlikely.

To the extent that it was already in the cards, however, it was derived from his continuing pursuit of often-laudable long-term policy goals as much as from deficiencies in his actions as a strategic electoral politician.

With the reapportionment of 1989 and the election of 1990 on their agendas, Kansas legislators, especially in the House, were playing a high-stakes, short-term game in 1988/89. They were concerned, but not consumed, with their own electoral survival. And most key legislators had their own policy preferences that spanned many years; Reps. Ken Groteweil (D-Wichita) and Dennis Spaniol (R-Wichita) were no less ready than Mike Hayden to fund the water plan after years of waiting. While House Democrats engaged in a successful strategic (to the point of cynicism) game of reducing the state's ending balances, they also brought to various policy areas—taxation, mental health, corrections—coherent long-term strategic visions that they acted on in 1989.

Even the electoral cycle, which ordinarily drives legislators into short-term thinking, did not operate unambiguously in 1988/89. State senators, with their four-year terms, had far more leeway that either the governor or House members to think through policies from a long-range perspective. Yet there was little evidence of such thinking; rather, the Senate majority became, more or less, an adjunct to the Hayden reelection effort, in addition to providing a stabilizing counterweight to the chaotic House. In the end, an examination of the 1988/89 version of Kansas policymaking uncovers relatively little evidence that legislators think more as strategic politicians, preoccupied with the next election, than does an executive who faces the voters at the same time. Still, neither the governor nor legislators sacrificed their long-term policy visions simply to advance politically. As they faced the public, their political explanations were couched in terms of their policy goals, which often reflected well-defined, long-term commitments on such issues as highways, the water plan, and social services.

STRATEGIC POLITICIANS AND POLITICAL TIME

As the legislature closed up shop late on May 2, 1989, we all left the capitol, driving off in the dark to our separate corners of the prairie and beyond. Department of Corrections Secretary Roger Endell, formally out of office since the day before, watched the House finally pass a prison construction bill and wasted no time in hopping into his Porsche for the long trek back to Alaska, where his family had remained during his stormy sixteen-month tenure in Kansas. Speaker Braden announced: "I can't wait to get out of this town. But my wife will have to drive. I'm too exhausted." Final deadlines had collided with physical capacity after a week of intense politicking. No one had much reserve.

As I drove home from Topeka after four months of observing the legislative session and a year of following the process, I reflected that almost every time a problem came up, it was resolved by throwing money at it, sometimes through appropriations, sometimes by reducing taxes, sometimes by generating new revenues. That pattern was established early in the session with the windfall and continued all the way to the end, with the water plan and the elimination of the alternate minimum tax. For all the arguments between the Democrats, the Hayden Republicans, and the rebels, was there much else to the session? The Democrats went along because they got many of the items on their wish list and concurrently spent down the governor's balances. The regular Republicans advocated spending because they had the opportunity (highways) or the obligation (windfall, prisons) to make major changes in state policy. When in doubt, legislators avoided conflict by spending more money. The governor was immediately wary of this; as a veteran politician he could see the implications for 1990. Still, he did not veto any substantial appropriations.

This strategy paid short-term dividends to almost all concerned, especially the governor. He and the Republican leadership received excellent reviews immediately following the session. This combination of policy plus press coverage may well have served to keep his most dangerous opponent, Congressman Slattery, out of the 1990 gubernatorial race. But [my May 2, 1989, notes read] "all this might not keep the Democrats from running a really strong campaign against Hayden in 1990. . . . And a lot . . . of this hinges on the more or less chance remarks of the 1986 campaign as Hayden one-upped Democratic candidate Docking with his firm promise to 'return the windfall.' "

In short, politicians struggle to think and act strategically, but even in the relatively small, constrained arena of Kansas politics, seeking to act strategically and doing so effectively are two entirely different things. Once the concept of the strategic politician is extended beyond Jacobson and Kernell's arena of congressional elections, it may have only modest value in helping to understand individuals' choices, especially when both politics and policy preferences are involved.[28] Politicians will try to act strategically, but their capacities to sort out political forces will differ dramatically and even the best of them may well be more beholden to luck than to vision.

Indeed, policy activists with no electoral calculus, like Federal Judge Rogers or Department of Corrections Secretary Endell, may force an unwelcome decision, such as building a new prison, upon reluctant legislators. Alternatively, deadlines may force strategic politicians cum policy entrepreneurs, like Governor Hayden, to back an imperfect alternative (an overly generous windfall return, a too-large highway bill) rather than face a politically unacceptable defeat.

11

Reflections on Political Time

Once I'd decided to examine the relationship of time to politics and policy-making, I was surprised how frequently time-related concepts came up in the discussions, debates, and deliberations I witnessed. Advocates of specific policies argued that they were needed immediately, while opponents responded that we did not know enough to act at present and delay would be prudent. On occasion after occasion, legislators came to the well of the House to declare that this was the last time that the chamber would be able to vote on one issue or another. Their colleagues took these warnings with a grain of salt, yet the possibility always loomed that this time there might not be another opportunity.

Some issues explicitly depend on a vision of alternative futures. Advocates of tort reform painted a picture of a Kansas where health care would be inadequate in rural areas, thus hastening their decline. The health care struggle, like that over highways, was a debate over competing visions of the future of Kansas. To what extent would the agricultural, rural essence of the state continue over the next few decades? More prosaically, tort reform and medical malpractice lobbyists envisioned a two-year fight emerging over a constitutional amendment. Then, with a single unexpected Supreme Court ruling, these related issues disappeared. Relieved not to decide between physicians and lawyers, the legislators immediately moved on to other matters.

Some issues are seen as annual rituals. Water plan funding was one of these, although this changed with the 1989 package. One reporter characterized the highly emotional death penalty debate as the state's "annual tap dance." Six television cameras showed up to record the predictable, though undeniably moving, arguments pro and con on reinstituting capital punishment. Although there were some surprise votes, most senators had made decisions long before the debate began. Still, the performances went on.

State editorialists relentlessly whined that the legislature was not getting much done. Then, when the seven-day wrap-up session passed a bushel of major changes, these same voices lavished generous praise on the lawmakers, all the while wondering why they couldn't have accomplished things in a more orderly fashion.

In short, virtually all political actors talk continually in time-related terms. Tactics, long-term strategy, and happenstance merge as time and timing become the common denominators of policymaking. Consider this pair of comments made as legislative Democrats discussed how best to balance the emerging property tax issue with the return of the income tax windfall early in the session (two days before a final $100 million package was approved):

> Sen. Jim Francisco: "Time will help you [focus on property taxes]. The more people who receive their [reassessment] statements, the better off we'll be."

> Rep. Joan Wagnon: "If they run the conference [windfall] bill, and it's the last time, there will be some people who will jump. . . . [Senate Tax Committee chair] Thiessen's upcoming surgery is the driving force behind a deadline here; Hayden's already missed his February 1 deadline [to lower income tax rates]."

The Democrats' meeting broke up with no resolution. All involved understood they would have to balance their desire to address growing tax problems with the requirements that they vote up or down on conference committee reports that would reduce taxes (and future revenues) by as much as $100 million per year.

Indeed, time-based notions — however rhetorical — often contain powerful policy implications. The governor desperately wanted to pass a large tax cut bill early in the session, and legislators knew they could not easily hold back a measure that promised substantial tax relief.[1] With large balances in the state treasury (but with tax cuts reducing future revenues), the 1989 session was a one-time opportunity to pass or enhance any number of initiatives that had simmered for years. He thus sought to impose deadlines and create windows of opportunity in the context of long-term trends (as with water conservation and highway needs, for example).

Timing-based strategems have great impact on policy results, especially as deadlines approach. At the end of both the 1988 and 1989 sessions, a key issue (income tax cuts in 1988, water plan funding in 1989) was rammed through the legislature with no substantive debate in one of the two houses. Legislative leaders simply served up a conference committee report on a "take it or leave it" basis. Both times the measure passed, but the 1988 endgame produced adverse consequences that lingered through the 1989 session, in that it crystallized the antagonism of House rebels toward the Republican leadership.

Overall, considerations of time and timing are central to understanding politics and policymaking. In part, there are objective elements at work: long-term trends with clear indicators; formal cycles that structure the process; and deadlines that are built into the process or are imposed by key actors. At least as important, however, are the actors' subjective perceptions of time, which become integral to the policymaking context. Rural interests weigh the value of compromise prior to a reapportionment that will reduce their influence. The governor looks down the road to a reelection campaign and decides to sign off on large-scale highway commitments while deferring a major initiative on property tax relief. Democrats seek to spend down the state's ending balances, which will reduce the governor's room to maneuver in the future, while simultaneously helping him achieve a series of major policy victories.

Once a legislature is adjourned and the legislative cycle completed, the new cycle begins immediately. The beat of political time goes on.

POLITICAL TIME AND POLICY FORMULATION

Although the multifaceted concept of political time contains many implications for the electoral calculations of strategic politicians, it may contribute most to furthering an understanding of policy formulation. In his path-breaking work on this subject, John Kingdon stitches a patchwork of metaphors (policy soup, streams of policies, problems, and politics, windows of opportunity, policy entrepreneurs, among others) into the general fabric of agenda setting and alternative development. Kingdon relies on metaphor because he is not describing a "textbook" picture of policy formulation. Rather, he notes in his concluding pages: "Events do not proceed neatly in stages, steps, or phases. Instead, independent streams that flow through the system all at once, each with a life of its own and equal with one another, become coupled when a window opens."[2]

Policies may exist before problems are defined for them to address; well-conceived alternatives often emerge in advance of the politics that will link them to specific agenda items. Without question, there is a great deal of randomness in the shaping of public policies. Still, policy formulation occurs within given contexts and under specific limitations. Constitutional restraints, governmental revenues, partisan ratios, gubernatorial powers, and myriad other regularities determine how agendas are set, alternatives are framed, and coupling is effected.

In particular, different elements of political time provide significant organizing dimensions to policy formulation. Long-term population trends (aging, migration patterns, educational needs) affect the entire process, as do the formal rules of the game embedded in constitutional and institutional cycles, such as reapportionment and biennial organization of the legislature. Finally, over and over, deadlines force actions in settings that ordinarily encourage deferral and delay; legislative time, patience, and energy simply run out, and further delay means defeat or the imposition of unwanted policy consequences. For example, the water plan funding bill was not a total victory for any single interest or actor, but it was good enough to pass, given the alternative of no major policy change.

Within the annual cycle of the legislative process, lawmakers become accustomed to a set rhythm. Windows of opportunity may be anticipated, as experience in past sessions informs present and future behavior. For legislative leaders, the governor, and a handful of well-connected lobbyists, the possibilities for coupling solutions to problems may occur only under late-session conditions of tremendous pressure and high expectations tempered by growing physical exhaustion.[3] This pattern is repeated, year after year, and all involved come to expect the endgame politics, even though every session has its own quirks and idiosyncrasies.

The notion of political time also relates to the distinction between discretionary and required policy choices and to the activities of policy entrepreneurs.[4] Required policy decisions are often the result of statutory or constitutional deadlines: for example, reapportionment following the 1990 census was mandatory; inaction was simply not an alternative. Conversely, the states exercise great discretion in their regulation of campaign finance. Frequently, discretion is reduced through the agenda-setting process, as when Judge Richard Rogers forced the issue of prison overcrowding in 1988/89. Federal mandates also increasingly impinge on state discretion; thus, while state legislators and executives technically have discretion in forging policy alternatives, in practice their latitude is severely limited. To continue to receive federal Medicaid funds, for example, the state must play by the federal rules on cost sharing. This may mean that other discretionary programs must be cut, or taxes raised, so the state can keep its federal funding.

Policy entrepreneurs often provide some organization to the policy formulation process through their repertoire of actions. An entrepreneur may push a bill onto the agenda, or frame the policy alternatives, or lobby hard for final passage, or some combination of the three. Sen. Bill Bradley worked at all three of these tasks in his entrepreneurial role on tax reform in the 1982–86 period.[5] Conversely, Governor Hayden played a major entrepreneurial role in getting the highway issue on the state's agenda in 1986/87 and again in 1988/89, but he subsequently disappeared from the stage as alternatives were put forward in late 1988 and during the 1989 legislative session. In the end, he received credit for the highway program, but largely because it became law "on his watch," rather than through his entrepreneurial efforts.

Table 11.1 lays out the major policy decisions discussed in chapters six through nine and relates them to the dimensions of political time as well as the amount of discretion involved and the reliance on policy entrepreneurs. A majority of 1988/89 policy decisions reflected the influence of an entrepreneur, but rarely does that individual affect all major aspects of policy formulation.

The policies shown in Table 11.1 were passed in the order listed, but aside from the first four, all were finally passed or signed by the governor in the last week of the session. More important, these policies were developed simultaneously, with many key actors playing multiple roles. Of course party leaders were involved in a host of issues; that is one of their jobs. But many other legislators were equally active. Rep. David Miller, for example, was integral to the reapportionment process, but he simultaneously exerted great pressure to reduce the bonding component of the new prison financing. Miller's strong working relationship with the Democratic leadership on reapportionment encouraged Minority Leader Barkis to support his appointment to an enlarged prisons conference committee, which then quickly resolved the corrections issue.

With his Judiciary Committee chairmanship, his role as acting chair of Ways and Means, and his constituency-driven interest in higher education, Sen. Wint Winter, Jr., continually juggled a number of policies during the session. This often took its toll, as conference committee negotiations on appropriations conflicted with efforts to resolve the prisons impasse. Even early in the session, Winter was overextended. On a key January windfall vote, he waited until the end to vote no, even though the bill would pass. Reporters gathered around him, seeking an explanation for his decision. He started to write one out on a legal pad; he stopped, requested that a journalist bring over a pile of other senators' explanations. He leafed through them, asking rhetorically, "Isn't law just plagiarism, anyway?" He found one he liked, and wandered off to ask the other senator if he could sign on. Despite opposing the governor on the most important vote of the session's early days, Senator Winter was already focusing on other issues; he appeared uninterested in thinking strategically. He simply wanted to get beyond the windfall and proceed to the corrections, appropriations, tort reform, and education issues that were already consuming his attention.

In sum, both regularities (cycles and regular deadlines, among others) and multiple personal commitments structure policy formulation. Policy entrepreneurship does not occur in a vacuum; Governor Hayden could not vigorously pursue his highway package for fear that he would hurt its chance

Table 11.1. Policy Formulation in Political Time, Kansas, 1988/89

Policy	Trends	Cycles	Deadlines	Discretionary or Required	Policy Entrepreneur	Remarks
"Windfall" return	Tax receipts increase; high balances	Semiannual revenue est.; 1990 election	February 1, imposed by Governor Hayden	Discretionary	No	Response to ad hoc 1986 campaign promise
Death penalty	Consistent poll support	1990 election	None	Discretionary	Governor Hayden	
Tort reform	High insurance rates; loss of rural MDs	1990 election issue; campaign fund sources	None	Discretionary	No	Absent supreme court ruling, Hayden might have pushed issue.
Washburn entry into university system	Decline of municipal university	Budget cycle	None	Discretionary	Governor Hayden	Hayden did not display needed persistence.
Reapportionment	In-state rural/ urban shifts	State constitution mandate	Court review; filing deadline	Required	No	Done again in 1992 for both houses, Congress
Property tax/ school finance	Dated appraisals; classification/ reappraisal	Annual budget; 1990 election	Various dates to complete process, send out valuations, tax notices	Required	No	Rep. Kerry Patrick and rebels were active, not entrepreneurs

Issue	Problem		State-federal	Discretionary/Required	Actors	Comments
Highways	Deteriorating roads; decline in maintenance funds; SE Kansas needs	Maintenance cycle; 1990 election	State-federal maintenance match; 1989 revenue balances; governor's need for 1989 victory	Discretionary (perception of requirement for federal match)	Governor Hayden, early; Economic Lifelines; Representative Crowell, Senators Morris, Francisco; lobbyists Hurley-McGill	Various entrepreneurs; no single one dominates.
Prisons	Overcrowding; aged prisons; lawsuit from 1970s	None	Judge Rogers' series of prison population limits; need to act by May 1989	Required	Judge Rogers	Corrections Secretary Endell plays key temporary role
Water plan funding	Aquifer depletion; agricultural run-off; drought; rural/urban population shifts	Reapportionment	None	Discretionary	Governor Hayden, various others in supporting roles	Excellent case of endgame politics/available alternative
Campaign finance reform	Increasing costs, PAC money	1990 campaign fund reports	None	Discretionary	Rep. Robert H. Miller	Major role of editorialists as continuing irritants

of passing. Conversely, with his experience as a party leader in the legislature and with two years as governor under his belt, Hayden could be coolly instrumental in pressing for acceptance of the water plan funding proposal in the last hours of the 1989 session. The highway bill had been indisputably more important to him on political grounds, but he was unable to act as a key "coupling" force. On water plan funding he could both cater to his rural constituents and fulfill a long-term policy commitment by employing his policy and political expertise to pull together a winning coalition. Having played the legislative endgame ten times previously as chair of Ways and Means, House Speaker, and governor, Hayden was confident of his ability to take advantage of 1989's historic window of opportunity to resolve the water plan funding issue.

POLICY FORMULATION
AND POLITICAL INSTITUTIONS

In the 1980s and 1990s, the jobs faced by governors and state legislatures have grown increasingly difficult. Policy obligations, both internal to the states and thrust upon them by the federal government, have become more onerous. Budgets must be balanced, and thus politicians must allocate ever-larger amounts of fiscal pain. Policies ranging from environmental protection to health care to public education have become more complex and contentious.[6] Governing institutions have been challenged by a rising tide of initiatives and referenda, which often impose additional limitations on policymakers' leeway. At the same time, the 1980s and 1990s produced a pair of succeeding fiscal trends. Carl Van Horn notes that faced with "greater social programs and reduced tax collections" in the early 1980s, twenty-eight states increased their income taxes and thirty boosted their sales tax rates; then in 1984/85, nineteen states increased one or the other.[7] In 1986 federal tax reforms also provided for state revenue growth. Van Horn observes that "when the state treasuries bulged [in the late 1980s] most states spent the windfall instead of giving it back to the taxpayers."[8] Although Kansas appeared to act with its customary prairie prudence by returning much of the windfall, it also greatly increased spending obligations in 1989, despite clear indications that balances would shrink dramatically, even without the recession of 1990/91.

Within this context of rising expenditures and greater policy commitments, the stakes of state government grew dramatically during the 1980s. Both the executive and legislative branches have come under much greater pressure, and governors and legislatures have acted to strengthen their institutions over the past two decades.[9] Their success at becoming more professional and increasing their expertise has made policy formulation all the more contentious.

As legislators and chief executives struggle over setting the state's policy agenda, Van Horn argues they "may ignore the long-term needs of their state. Electoral expediency crowds out other important values. State officials may ensure their reelection but undermine their state's future."[10] Perhaps, but such a conclusion rests on two key assumptions: that elected officials operate effectively as strategic politicians and that this role is incompatible with long-term policy thinking.

In the Kansas environment of 1988/89, short-term, expedient considerations were scarcely lacking. Senate Democrats had forced politically motivated votes in 1988, and Senate Republicans had retaliated forcefully by reorganizing the chamber in 1989. House leaders denied advocates of federal deductibility a vote in May 1988; in January 1989 rebel Republicans essentially removed control of the chamber from the party leadership. House Democrats sought to spend down the governor's revenue balances, while the governor pushed hard for a death penalty measure that surveys showed to be popular. But even though they were embroiled in interparty, intraparty, and interinstitutional conflicts, the governor and the legislature combined to make substantial and generally responsible long-term policy decisions, including income tax reduction, increased spending on children, broad-based corrections policies, and funding the water plan. Even in a highly politicized setting such as this, the actors could act with foresight and a measure of prudence. Ending balances may have been reduced, but the state avoided the kind of fiscal crisis that confronted California, Texas, and Connecticut.

The 1988/89 year did demonstrate the cracks in a system that relies on part-time legislators to make and oversee increasingly complex, expensive policy. The late-session passage of prison and water policies represented the culmination of lengthy formulation processes; only the final political deals were hammered together on the spot. Campaign finance legislation, on the other hand, had a distinctly slap-dash quality. Adequate expertise simply was not brought to bear on this difficult, highly charged issue, and a major piece of legislation slipped through without enough deliberation. Even more problematic was the increasing difficulty of monitoring expensive state policies.

In 1991, for example, the legislature belatedly began to investigate the extensive financial reverses of the Kansas Public Employment Retirement System (KPERS). A portion of the KPERS assets, which totaled over $4 billion, had been invested in relatively risky businesses, as mid-1980s legislation initiated by Governor Carlin had mandated. The legislature began to oversee these investments only very late in the game, when losses had surpassed $500 million. A part-time legislature may be unduly limited then, in monitoring the large-scale enterprise of contemporary state government.

ALL THAT JAZZ: THE RHYTHM OF POLITICAL TIME

Policy formulation defies easy explanation — even easy description. Thus it encourages the use of metaphor as Kingdon has done to catch the essence of the thing. Legislators and journalists fall back upon their own favorite metaphors. Putting on his chef's hat, Rep. John Solbach contends that "passing legislation is like baking bread. You've got to take your time, let things rise." Reporter Martin Hawver notes that deadlines create situations in which "you're going to watch public policy being made like water gushing through a fire hose." These are useful images of certain parts of the process, but they don't capture the combination of structure and fluidity that characterizes much contemporary policymaking. Kingdon's streams/soup/window notions emphasize the changeable elements, but the repeating elements in the process receive less attention.[11]

Nor does Kingdon's focus on policy entrepreneurs adequately weigh the simultaneous calculations of these same individuals as strategic politicians. The policy-politics tension consistently affects decisions, both in the present and in the participants' views of the future, which are simultaneously murky and very real.

This exploration has entertained various theatrical metaphors, such as divisions into acts and the casting process, but these images are also, in the end, too restrictive, too static. Although there is considerable room for interpretation in the theater, the fact remains that the actors do follow a script. Nuances surely change from production to production, even from night to night, but the essence remains, anchored in the text.

While rooted in language and persuasions, policy formulation has no single text; it has some set structure, especially in those formalities that surround the legislative process. One state senator likened the legislative pace to that of a National Basketball Association contest, in which all the important actions take place in the last five minutes. But that excludes the blowouts, when Michael Jordan has found his place on the bench by the middle of the third quarter, or when a major tax cut is passed in the first few weeks of the legislative session.

Ruminating about policy formulation, I am most reminded of an improvisational jazz group that plays together night after night. The performances are loosely structured, often around an old standard, yet all of the players have room to innovate and improvise, both in solos and as a unit. The end product is always unique, yet it progresses along well-established patterns of riffs and harmonies. New members join a group and its sound changes. Its musical products are less formal than laws, but just as well articulated. The jazz group, like the legislature, learns from its past performances. The governor may seek to lead this band, but the syncopated rhythm of a Duke

Ellington has given way to the more improvisational touches of contemporary executives who are encouraged to reinvent government.

Still, no set of metaphors adequately conveys the complexity of policy formulation. Long-term trends continue to emerge, often teased into relevance by social scientists, think tanks, and editorial writers; electoral, budgetary, and legislative cycles overlap to make strategic politicians' calculations increasingly difficult, especially in hard times; and policymakers must continually confront contexts set by their peers, outside forces, or a "crisis," real or perceived. For every problem addressed, a handful of new ones arise. Both in setting deadlines and reacting to them the key actors will, year in, year out, seek to accomplish their mixed policy and political goals. Whoever the nominal leader may be, the members of the policy jazz band will pick up their instruments and improvise a new tune, all the while relying on the old chords and years of playing together to make the music fresh once more.

Notes

PREFACE

1. John Kingdon, *Agendas, Alternatives, and Public Policies* (Boston: Little, Brown, 1984); and Gary Jacobson and Samuel Kernell, *Strategy and Choice in Congressional Elections* (New Haven, Conn.: Yale University Press, 1981).

CHAPTER 1. INTRODUCTION:
THE BEGINNING OF POLITICAL TIME

1. This account of the Patrick filibuster is drawn from press reports and personal interviews.

2. Kerry Patrick interview, February 24, 1991.

3. Ramona Jones, "Turtle Bill Inches toward Passage," *Wichita Eagle-Beacon*, April 2, 1986.

4. Patrick interview.

5. Roger's April 1988 order applied only to the Lansing penitentiary; the rest of the system would be included a year later.

6. Kansas did vote for President Bush, of course, but his 56 percent–43 percent margin was unexceptional in a state that supported Reagan over Mondale, 66 percent to 33 percent, in 1984.

7. William Muir, *Legislature* (Chicago: University of Chicago Press, 1982).

8. Marvin Harder and Carolyn Rampey, *The Kansas Legislature* (Lawrence: University Press of Kansas, 1972). See, in particular, their discussion of the "capital community," pp. 3-9.

9. V. O. Key uses the term "friends and neighbors" politics in *Southern Politics* (New York: Knopf, 1949). My usage is more general here, but it does convey a similar kind of informality and shared context.

10. Karl Kurtz, "Understanding the Diversity of American State Legislatures," *Extension of Remarks*, June 1992, 1-5.

CHAPTER 2. THE NATURE OF POLITICAL TIME

1. Stephen Skowronek, "Presidential Leadership in Political Time," in Michael Nelson, ed., *The Presidency and the Political System* (Washington, D.C.: CQ Press, 1984), pp. 87-132; and Eric Uslaner, "A Contextual Model of Coalition Formation in Congress: The Dimensions of Party and 'Political Time'," *American Behavioral Scientist* 7 (March/April 1975): 513-529.

2. The contrast between Jimmy Carter in 1980 and Ronald Reagan in 1981 is noteworthy. More generally, see Paul Light, *The President's Agenda* (Baltimore, Md.: Johns Hopkins University Press, 1982).

3. See Richard E. Neustadt and Ernest R. May, *Thinking in Time* (New York: Free Press, 1986); and T. Alexander Smith, *Time and Public Policy* (Knoxville: University of Tennessee Press, 1988).

4. Bruce I. Oppenheimer, "Changing Time Constraints on Congress: Historical Perspectives on the Use of Cloture," in Lawrence Dodd and Bruce I. Oppenheimer, eds., *Congress Reconsidered*, 3d ed. (Washington, D.C.: CQ Press, 1985), pp. 393-413.

5. See Kenneth A. Shepsle and Barry R. Weingast, "The Institutional Foundations of Committee Power," *American Political Science Review* 81 (March 1987): 85-104; and Stephen S. Smith, "An Essay on Sequence, Position, Goals, and Committee Power," *Legislative Studies Quarterly* 13 (May 1988): 151-176.

6. See Lawrence C. Dodd, "A Theory of Congressional Cycles: Solving the Problem of Change," in *Congress and Policy Change*, Gerald Wright et al., eds. (New York: Agathon Press, 1986), pp. 3-44. Richard F. Fenno, Jr., *The Making of a Senator: Dan Quayle, The Presidential Odyssey of John Glenn*, and *The Emergence of a Senate Leader: Pete Domenici and the Reagan Budget*, all from CQ Press (Washington, D.C.: 1989, 1990, and 1991, respectively).

7. Paul Light, *The President's Agenda* (Baltimore, Md.: Johns Hopkins University Press, 1982).

8. Bert Rockman, *The Leadership Question* (New York: Praeger, 1984).

9. For one example among many, see James Anderson, *Public Policymaking* (Boston: Houghton Mifflin, 1990), pp. 35-36.

10. Gary C. Jacobson and Samuel Kernell, *Strategy and Choice in Congressional Elections* (New Haven, Conn.: Yale University Press, 1981); John W. Kingdon, *Agendas, Alternatives, and Public Policies* (Boston: Little, Brown, 1984).

11. Jacobson and Kernell, *Strategy and Choice*, p. 86.

12. Ibid.

13. Kingdon, *Agenda*, p. 173ff.

14. See, among many others, Daniel J. Levinson, *The Seasons of a Man's Life* (New York: Ballantine, 1978).

15. In particular, Uslaner, "A Contextual Model of Coalition Formation," pp. 513-529.

16. Light, *President's Agenda*; Rockman, *Leadership Question*.

17. See Hubert H. Humphrey, *The Education of a Public Man* (New York: Doubleday, 1976), Prologue.

18. I am grateful to John Hanna for making this point.

19. Theodore Lowi, *The End of Liberalism* (New York: Norton, 1979); Clive Thomas and Ronald I. Hrebenar, "Nationalization of Interest Groups and Lobbying in the States," in Allan Cigler and Burdett Loomis, eds., *Interest Group Politics*, 3d ed. (Washington, D.C.: CQ Press, 1991), pp. 63-80.

20. Kingdon, *Agendas*, p. 115ff.

21. In the context of policy development, this interpretation reflects that of Arthur Schlesinger, Jr., *The Cycles of American History* (Boston: Houghton Mifflin, 1986), p. 36; Rockman, *Leadership Question*, 104. For recent thinking, see Walter Dean Burnham, "The Politics of Repudiation," *American Prospect* (Winter 1993): 22–33.

22. Neustadt and May, *Thinking in Time*, p. 251.

23. Deborah Stone, "Causal Stories and the Formation of Policy Agendas," *Political Science Quarterly* 104, 2 (Summer 1989): 281–300.

24. Schlesinger, *The Cycles of American History*, p. 27. Also, see his evaluation circa 1992 in the *New Yorker*, November 16, 1992.

25. Skowronek, "Presidential Leadership in Political Time," p. 88.

26. Rockman, *Leadership Question*, p. 90.

27. Light, *President's Agenda*; Rockman, *Leadership Question*, 116–120.

28. Richard Neustadt, *Presidential Power: The Politics of Leadership from FDR to Carter* (New York: Wiley, 1980), p. 149.

29. Fenno, *Making of a Senator*; *Presidential Odyssey of John Glenn*; and *Emergence of a Senate Leader*.

30. Jacobson and Kernell, more generally, Sen. Alphonse D'Amato (R-N.Y.) and Rep. Stephen Solarz (D-N.Y.) have demonstrated their ability to think in six- and ten-year cycles, respectively, as D'Amato raised money throughout his term of office, while Solarz has faced redistricting crises in 1981 and 1991 armed with tremendous amounts of funds that are designed to deflect the destruction of his district until the 1992 lines were drawn. Solarz's district disappeared, and he spent $2 million fruitlessly seeking election in a heavily Hispanic district.

31. Kingdon, *Agendas*, p. 190.

32. Jack Walker, "Setting the Agenda for the U.S. Senate," *British Journal of Political Science* 7 (1977): 432–456.

33. Richard F. Fenno, Jr., *The Power of the Purse* (Boston: Little, Brown, 1966); Aaron Wildavsky, *The Politics of the Budgetary Process* (Boston: Little, Brown, 1964).

34. Aaron Wildavsky, *The New Politics of the Budgetary Process* (Boston: Little, Brown, 1988), among others.

35. See Daniel P. Franklin, *Making Ends Meet* (Washington, D.C.: CQ Press, 1992), chapters 3 and 4, for a discussion of the 1990 budget summit.

36. Paul Light, *Artful Work* (New York: Random House, 1985).

37. Anthony Downs, "Up and Down with Ecology: The 'Issue-Attention' Cycle," *Public Interest* 28 (September 1972): 38–50.

38. George E. Connor and Bruce I. Oppenheimer, "The Changing Uses of Time in Congress: The Decline of Deliberation," paper presented at the Carl Albert Center Conference "Back to the Future," Norman, Okla., April 2–3, 1990, p. 3.

39. Timothy Conlan, Margaret Wrightson, and David Beam, *Taxing Choices: The Politics of Tax Reform* (Washington, D.C.: CQ Press, 1990), p. 213ff.

40. See Joseph Cooper and David W. Brady, "Toward a Diachronic Analysis of Congress," *American Political Science Review* 95 (December 1981): 988–1006.

41. See D. B. Hardeman and Don Bacon, *Rayburn* (Lanham, Md.: Madison Books, 1987), chapter 23.

42. See Skowronek, "Presidential Leadership in Political Time," p. 100ff; and James Sundquist, *Politics and Policy: The Eisenhower, Kennedy, and Johnson Years* (Washington, D.C.: Brookings, 1968).

43. The Kansas legislature is neither highly professional (like California's) nor committed to amateur status (like Wyoming's). Rather, like most state legislatures, it

reflects a "semi-pro" approach: aside from some homemakers, a few retirees, and some individuals willing to live on a pittance, Kansas legislators work simultaneously at two full-time occupations. In its semi-professional approach and its limited term, the Kansas legislature is typical of many other state legislatures. See Karl Kurtz, "Understanding the Diversity of American State Legislatures," *Extension of Remarks* (legislative studies newsletter) (June 1992), 1–5.

44. See, for example, Alan Rosenthal, *Legislative Life* (New York: Harper and Row, 1981), p. 144.

45. "The 1990 Census Figures: Highlights for Kansas," Institute for Public Policy and Business Research, University of Kansas, p. 1.

46. Allan Cigler and Burdett Loomis, "Kansas: Two-Party Competition in a One-Party State," in Maureen Moakley, ed., *Party Realignment in the States* (Columbus: Ohio State University Press, 1992), pp. 163–178.

47. The decisions of so-called strategic politicians to run for higher office are complicated and tied directly to questions of timing. See Jacobson and Kernell, *Strategy and Choice*; and Linda Fowler and Robert McClure, *Political Ambition* (New Haven, Conn.: Yale University Press, 1989).

48. See Kingdon, *Agendas*, pp. 89–94.

CHAPTER 3. CASTING THE DRAMA: MARCH–NOVEMBER 1988

1. Indeed, turnout dropped in 1988, and George Bush won only 56 percent of the state's vote.

2. Martin Hawver, "Dole Absence Could Benefit State GOP," *Topeka Capital-Journal*, August 21, 1988.

3. Ibid.

4. See Barbara G. Salmore and Stephen A. Salmore, *Candidates, Parties, and Campaigns*, 2d ed. (Washington, D.C.: CQ Press, 1989); and Burdett A. Loomis, *The New American Politician* (New York: Basic, 1988), chapter 8.

5. "Hochhauser Files to Oppose Knopp," *Manhattan Mercury*, June 10, 1988.

6. Wagnon interview, June 15, 1989.

7. Roger Myers, "State Races Shaping up As Referendum on Hayden," *Topeka Capital-Journal*, July 3, 1988.

8. For a more extensive discussion of this issue, see Chapter 6.

9. Hayden interview, August 22, 1989.

10. Indeed, Hayden was often most effective in mobilizing Republicans when he absented himself from the public debate; this irony was especially noteworthy in his efforts on behalf of the huge highway bill during the 1989 legislative session.

11. Dale Goter, "Distance Increases within GOP Ranks," *Parsons Sun*, October 13, 1988.

12. *Emporia Gazette*, June 9, 1988.

13. Jim Sullinger, "Democrats Gain Seats in Kansas," *Kansas City Star*, November 9, 1988.

14. Lori Lindenberger, "Vote Cuts Legislative Majority," *Wichita Eagle-Beacon*, November 10, 1988.

15. Sullinger, "Democrats Gain Seats in Kansas."

16. For a much fuller discussion of the Republican rebels, see Chapter 5.

17. Rep. Bob Ott, who probably would have challenged Knopp for the majority leader position, lost his seat, largely because of his vote on the pension issue and

local opposition to his cosponsorship of a bill that overturned Kansas' 96-year "prevailing wage" law.

18. Morgan Chilson, "Hochhauser's Win a Surprise to Many," *Manhattan Mercury*, November 9, 1988.

19. Gary Jacobson and Samuel Kernell, *Strategy and Choice in Congressional Elections* (New Haven, Conn.: Yale University Press, 1981).

20. Robert Dalleck, *Lone Star Rising* (New York: Oxford University Press, 1991), p. 207. He quotes Walter Jenkins, who called Johnson at 7 A.M. with the news. "He was immediately interested in that. I mean immediately."

21. See Linda Fowler and Robert McClure, *Political Ambition* (New Haven, Conn.: Yale University Press, 1989).

22. Personal interview. Miller's wife, Linda, was an effective sounding board. With a Ph.D. in economics and a long list of political activities and concerns, she could offer counsel from both personal and professional perspectives. She had also served on the governor's task force on children, which had just made its policy recommendations for the 1989 session (see Chapter 7).

23. Roger Myers, "GOP Legislators Vying for Leadership Posts," *Topeka Capital-Journal*, November 20, 1988.

24. In addition, the friendly, accessible Heinemann is an inveterate shutterbug, forever snapping photos on the House floor. This probably did not add to his stature as a potential leader, although another camera addict, former Senate Majority Leader Howard Baker, did not seem diminished by practicing this hobby throughout his career.

25. Quoted in Roger Myers, "Kerr Reported Looking at No. 2 Senate Post," *Topeka Capital-Journal*, December 3, 1988.

26. The leadership included Eric Yost, a young, ambitious Wichita senator, who won a contested race for Senate vice-president. At least one reporter observed that Yost helped smooth relations between Burke and Kerr, whose personal and political ties were not strong. At the same time, neither Burke nor Kerr trusted Yost completely.

27. Burke interview, January 21, 1992.

28. Hayden and his staff always played up other candidates, such as Wichita's Tom Docking, the 1986 nominee, but most independent observers saw Slattery as the strongest potential candidate.

CHAPTER 4. SETTING THE STATE'S POLICY AGENDA

1. See William Muir, *Legislature* (Chicago: University of Chicago Press, 1982); Frank Smallwood, *Free and Independent* (Brattleboro, Vt.: Stephen Greene Press, 1976); JeDon Emenhiser, ed., *The Dragon on the Hill* (Salt Lake City: University of Utah Press, 1970); Mike BeVier, *Politics Backstage* (Philadelphia: Temple University Press, 1979).

2. Jack L. Walker, "The Diffusion of Innovations among the American States," *American Political Science Review* 63 (September 1969): 880–899; Virginia Gray, "Innovation in the States: A Diffusion Study," *American Political Science Review* 67 (December 1973): 1174–1185.

3. Roger W. Cobb and Charles D. Elder, *Participation in America*, 2d ed. (Baltimore, Md.: Johns Hopkins University Press), pp. 85–86.

4. Barbara Nelson, *Making an Issue of Child Abuse* (Chicago: University of Chicago Press, 1984).

5. Robert Eyestone, *From Social Issues to Public Policy* (New York: John Wiley, 1978).

6. John Kingdon, *Agendas, Alternatives, and Public Policies* (Boston: Little, Brown, 1984), chapters 2, 3.

7. In odd-numbered years there is no formal limit to the number of days in a session; in even-numbered years, a ninety-day limit exists, but the legislature can vote to extend the session. In practice, the legislature meets for about ninety days in both odd- and even-numbered years, takes a ten to twenty day break, and returns for a week-long wrapup (or veto) session.

8. Michael Cohen, James March, and Johan Olson, "A Garbage Can Model of Organization of Choice," *Administrative Science Quarterly* 17 (March 1972): 1–25; Kingdon, *Agendas*, p. 20.

9. Kingdon, *Agendas*, p. 211.

10. Jack Walker, "Setting the Agenda for the U.S. Senate," *British Journal of Political Science* 7 (1977): 432–445.

11. Alan Rosenthal, "The Legislative Institution," in Carl E. Van Horn, ed., *The State of the States*, 2d ed. (Washington, D.C.: CQ Press, 1992), p. 136ff.

12. Despite some unavoidable ambiguity, I will use the term "agenda" to reflect the major policy items that most policy actors see as most important — roughly the issues listed in Table 4.6.

13. For extensive details, see chapter 8.

14. For details, see Richard W. Ryan and Darwin Daicoff, "Estimating Revenues of the State General Fund in Kansas," (Topeka, Kans.: Capitol Complex Center, 1983).

15. Kingdon, *Agendas*, pp. 182–184.

16. Personal interview, Lew Ferguson, Associated Press bureau chief, September 9, 1988.

17. Information here is drawn from Ryan and Daicoff, "Estimating Revenues."

18. O'Keefe interview, November 26, 1988.

19. O'Keefe interview. A, B, and C budget levels relate to spending proposals based on differing revenue levels.

20. Quoted in Lori Lindenberger, "Hayden Spells Out Agenda," *Wichita Eagle-Beacon*, January 9, 1989.

21. Chapter 9 will consider in detail both funding for the water plan and the decision to build a new maximum security prison.

22. See Cobb and Elder, for example.

23. Kingdon, *Agendas*, p. 124.

24. Ibid., chapters 2, 3.

25. This research contains no systematic analysis of television coverage of the 1989 legislative session because television was simply not a major factor, either in news coverage or editorial comment. No stations came close to offering regular television coverage, even though Topeka is the state's third largest television market (after Wichita and suburban Kansas City). And since television did not dedicate much time, interest, or resources to the legisative process, legislators and other policymakers responded in kind.

26. Aggregate preferences in public opinion are difficult to summarize; operationalizing a "public agenda" is extremely problematic. Unless the results of a survey can be built into a meaningful index measuring issue importance, firm conclusions cannot be drawn about which issues are the most important to the public. This does not mean that the poll data are worthless; the data identify general trends and divergence between elite and public agendas.

CHAPTER 5. RULES OF THE GAME

1. Speakers in Oklahoma, Connecticut, and North Carolina were overthrown in the late 1980s. For more general information see Alan Rosenthal, "The Legislative Institution," in Carl Van Horn, ed., *The State of the States*, 2d ed. (Washington, D.C.: CQ Press, 1992).

2. Floor debate, January 9, 1989.

3. Quoted in John Marshall, "Leadership Promise in the Legislature," *Parsons Sun*, December 28, 1988.

4. Martin Hawver, "Senate Starts Year with Bitter Fight over New Rules," *Topeka Capital-Journal*, January 10, 1989.

5. From 1989 to 1992, only one roll call vote was taken on an amendment (to a 1992 abortion bill, which split both parties). In divisions of the chamber senators stand to be counted when the "yeas" and "nays" are requested, respectively.

6. Johnston interview, December 13, 1991.

7. The dissident Republicans came to be labeled the rebels, a term that the AP's John Hanna attributes to *Topeka Capital-Journal* reporter Roger Myers. Early on, the rebels referred to themselves as "reformers," and the terms "guerillas," "mavericks," and "cowboys" gained some currency. In the end, "rebels" seemed to convey the essence of their behavior as they continued to keep fellow Republicans Braden and Hayden in their sights.

8. For a detailed examination of this issue, see Chapter 6.

9. Long interview, December 1, 1989.

10. Ibid.

11. The press was ready to make Vancrum's background on pari-mutuel gambling a real issue, if he had been appointed State and Federal Affairs chair.

12. David Miller interview, June 22, 1989.

13. Barkis interview, July 7, 1989.

14. Also, to put a committee-rejected bill on the House calendar or advance a bill on the debate calendar.

15. Long interview, December 1, 1989.

16. Diane Silver, "GOP Dealt Setback in House," *Wichita Eagle-Beacon*, January 11, 1989.

17. Associated Press release, January 12, 1989.

18. Personal interview with anonymous staff member.

19. Many observers concluded that committee positions were not attacked because of the Republican rank-and-file's very negative reaction to the leadership's stripping Rep. Elizabeth Baker's vice-chairmanship in the previous legislature.

20. It is unclear who Braden is counting here; of the original ten, four were chairs, three were vice-chairs.

21. Braden interview, March 3, 1991.

22. Roger Myers, "Logan Letter Criticizes GOP Rebels," *Topeka Capital-Journal*, January 17, 1989.

23. Student quoted in Martin Hawver, "Hayden Says Republicans Didn't Do Job," *Topeka Capital-Journal*, February 21, 1989.

24. Quoted in ibid.

25. Miller interview, June 22, 1989.

26. Lori Linenberger, "GOP Fight Stalemates Committee," *Wichita Eagle-Beacon*, February 23, 1989.

27. Miller would run as the lieutenant governor nominee on a ticket that came close to defeating Governor Hayden in the 1990 primary.

28. Maag interview, November 14, 1989.
29. McGill and Hurley interviews, October 16, 1990.
30. Long interview, February 24, 1991.
31. Hayden interview, August 22, 1989.
32. Maag interview, November 14, 1989.
33. Barkis interview, July 7, 1989.

CHAPTER 6. DEATH AND TAXES: THE GOVERNOR'S AGENDA

1. John Kingdon, *Agendas, Alternatives, and Public Policies* (Boston: Little, Brown, 1984), p. 99ff.
2. Deborah Stone, *Policy Paradox and Political Reason* (Glenview, Ill.: Scott Foresman-Little, Brown, 1988), p. 116.
3. *Merriam-Webster Dictionary* (New York: Pocket Books, 1975), p. 801.
4. Jerry Heaster, "Bigger Than Expected Windfall Makes for More Hot Air," *Kansas City Star*, June 5, 1988.
5. *Topeka Capital-Journal*, November 12, 1988.
6. Stone, *Policy Paradox*, pp. 133-134.
7. Richard Ryan, direcctor of legislative research and veteran of 36 years of revenue estimates, concluded that the $135 million figure was surely low and that "it might be a lot low." Quoted in Diane Silver, "Economic Argument Fuels 'Windfall' Fire," *Wichita Eagle-Beacon*, November 20, 1988.
8. John Hanna, "Size of Windfall to Be Debated First," *Emporia Gazette,* November 15, 1988.
9. *McPherson Sentinel*, November 21, 1988. In McPherson, in the center of the state, sentiments in support of the windfall's return were scarcely as rabid as those in Johnson County.
10. Kingdon, *Agendas*, p. 174.
11. Lori Linenberger, "Hayden Ups Funding But Asks for Tax Cuts," *Wichita Eagle-Beacon*, January 10, 1989. The governor sought rates of 3.9 percent and 4.9 percent, respectively, for married taxpayers below and above $35,000. For single taxpayers the rates would be 4.45 percent and 5.85 percent for those above and below $27,500, respectively. The cuts averaged about .25 percent.
12. Lori Linenberger, "Windfall Proposal Advances to Final Vote in Senate," *Wichita Eagle-Beacon*, January 21, 1989.
13. John Petterson, "Tax Windfall Plan Moves to Senate," *Kansas City Times*, January 23, 1989.
14. "Hayden Sets Legislator Trap," *Wichita Eagle-Beacon* editorial, January 31, 1989.
15. Associated Press story in *Parsons Sun*, February 1, 1989.
16. Quoted in Roger Myers, "House Targets Half of Windfall Return for State School Aid," *Topeka Capital-Journal*, February 1, 1989.
17. Jim Sullinger, "House Passes Bill to Return $53.1 Million of Windfall," *Kansas City Star*, February 1, 1989.
18. Quoted in Roger Myers, "Hayden Takes Stand on Windfall," *Topeka Capital-Journal*, February 2, 1989.
19. Quoted in Martin Hawver, "Conference Panel Meets," *Topeka Capital-Journal*, February 3, 1989.
20. For extended considerations of conference committees—in the U.S. Congress—

see Lawrence Longley and Walter Oleszek, *Bicameral Politics* (New Haven, Conn.: Yale University Press, 1989), and David Vogler, *The Third House* (Evanston, Ill.: Northwestern University Press, 1971).

21. If all six members of a conference committee could not reach agreement, the conference could return to work with the requirement that only four signatures — two from each house — be obtained to send the legislation to the floors.

22. Patrick interview, February 24, 1992.

23. Quoted in Martin Hawver, "Windfall Plan Forwarded Again," *Topeka Capital-Journal*, February 15, 1989.

24. Ibid.

25. Quoted in Lori Linenberger, "Governor Hayden Taxes Credit for Tax Cut," *Wichita Eagle-Beacon*, February 16, 1989.

26. One further result of the windfall decision and other 1989 legislation was to greatly alter the allocation of tax burdens in Kansas (see Chapter 10).

27. From a *Topeka Capital-Journal* survey taken October 31–November 3, 1988.

28. Hayden's press secretary, Kathy Peterson, quoted in "Hayden to Present Death Penalty Again," *Topeka Capital-Journal*, November 29, 1988.

29. Murder committed during a felony, regardless of premeditation.

30. Hurst Lavina, "Hayden to Renew Death Penalty in Fight in Legislature," *Wichita Eagle-Beacon*, December 26, 1988.

31. "Governing Gaffe," *Hutchinson News*, January 19, 1989.

32. Alissa Rubin, "Senate Panel OKs Bill," *Wichita Eagle-Beacon*, January 31, 1989.

33. This ultimately became law, passing the Senate 39–1.

34. Lynn Byczynski, "Kansas Senate Rejects Capital Punishment," *Kansas City Times*, February 2, 1989.

35. Ibid.

36. Quoted in ibid.

CHAPTER 7. DOGS THAT DON'T BARK,
THOSE THAT WON'T HUNT

1. See Daniel Franklin's work on federal-level budgeting, where difficulties are enormous, *Making Ends Meet* (Washington, D.C.: CQ Press, 1993).

2. Although the MOE was funded in 1989, it was ignored in 1990 and 1991; by 1992 the term was no longer used, save sarcastically.

3. *Topeka Capital-Journal*, September 27, 1988.

4. Dennis Darrow, "Washburn President Says University Must Go into State System," *Hutchinson News*, October 28, 1988. President Duggan, an effective and energetic spokesperson for Washburn, died December 1. His death did hurt Washburn's cause, but few saw it as determining Washburn's fate.

5. Tim Carpenter, "House Panel Pares University Funding," *Lawrence Journal-World*, March 15, 1989.

6. Lynn Byczynski, "College Lobbying Blitz On," *Kansas City Times*, March 20, 1989.

7. "Strange Logic," *Emporia Gazette* editorial," March 22, 1989.

8. "Does Bribery Work?", *Hutchinson News* editorial, March 22, 1989.

9. Dale Goter, "Lawmakers Fatten Pensions," *Garden City Telegram*, July 8, 1988.

10. Diane Silver, "Increased Pensions Revisited," *Wichita Eagle-Beacon*, December 12, 1988.

11. Diane Silver, "Pension Measures Languish," *Wichita Eagle-Beacon*, March 13, 1989.

12. "House Leaders Get Pension Topic on Agenda," *Hutchinson News*, March 27, 1989.

13. To be fair, some legislators, as well as the governor, chose not to enter the program with its enhanced benefits, but they remained in the minority. The pension issue stayed on the agenda, and the full legislature, in anticipation of the 1992 elections, did rescind the enhancements.

14. Tom Laing, quoted in "Hayden Creates Commission to Study Youth, Family Issues," *Wichita Eagle-Beacon*, May 24, 1988.

15. Lori Linenberger, "Care for Children Targeted," *Wichita Eagle-Beacon*, May 25, 1988.

16. Bonnie Dunham, "Child Care Top Concern of Governor's Commission," *Lawrence Journal-World*, September 18, 1988.

17. Barclay interview, November 11, 1989.

18. Ibid.

19. See E. E. Schattschneider, *The Semisovereign People* (New York: Holt, Rinehart, and Winston, 1960).

20. "Bogina to Have Heart Surgery," *Topeka Capital-Journal*, April 4, 1989.

21. Personal interview, anonymity guaranteed.

22. See, among others, John Kingdon, *Agendas, Alternatives, and Public Policies* (Boston: Little, Brown, 1984); Murray Edelman, *Political Language* (New York: Academic Press, 1978); Roger W. Cobb and Charles D. Elder, *Participation in American Politics*, 2d ed. (Baltimore, Md.: Johns Hopkins University Press, 1983); Anthony Downs, "Up and Down with Ecology—The Issue-Attention Cycle," *Public Interest* 28 (Summer 1972): 38–50.

23. Lynn Byczynski, "Medical Suit Limit Tossed Out," *Kansas City Times*, June 4, 1988.

24. Ibid.

25. Martin Hawver, "Hayden Calls for Malpractice Summit," *Topeka Capital-Journal*, July 23, 1988.

26. "More on malpractice," *Garden City Telegram* editorial, October 21, 1988.

27. Kleila Carlson, "Malpractice Issue May Die of Neglect This Session," *Hutchinson News*, January 25, 1989.

28. See, generally, Allan J. Cigler and Dwight C. Kiel, "The Changing Nature of Interest Group Politics in Kansas" (Topeka, Kans.: Capitol Complex Center, 1988).

29. Dan Hess, "Hayden Backs Vote on Lawsuit Limits," *Salina Journal*, March 22, 1989.

30. Quoted in "Lawyers Disagree with Malpractice Award Caps," *Salina Journal*, March 26, 1989.

31. Alissa Rubin, "Court Upholds Limit on Damages," *Wichita Eagle-Beacon*, March 31, 1989.

32. Lynn Byczynski, "Kansas Court Allows Caps on Jury Awards," *Kansas City Times*, March 31, 1989.

33. The census side of reapportionment will not be explored in detail. Not only was the state's position on the 1988 census upheld, but the 1992 federal census, according to the amendment adopted in 1988, was "corrected" to reflect permanent resident populations prior to redistricting calculations in 1992.

34. Barkis interview, July 7, 1989.

35. Roger Myers, "Reapportionment Unresolved," *Topeka Capital-Journal*, March 13, 1989.

36. Paul Light employs the term "gang" in discussing informal private groups that come together to hammer out difficult policy decisions. See his *Artful Work* (New York: Random House, 1985), p. 185ff.

37. Classification categories and taxation rates under the new scheme were: residential (12 percent rate); commercial, individual personal property, and utilities (30 percent rate); commercial personal property (20 percent rate). In addition, one-fourth of all state properties would be reappraised every year on a rolling basis. Alissa Rubin, "Leaders Uneasy over Classification Change," *Wichita Eagle-Beacon*, October 30, 1988.

38. Diane Silver, "Lively Debate Likely on School Financing," *Wichita Eagle-Beacon*, January 3, 1989.

39. Alissa Rubin, "Leader Uneasy over Classification Changes," *Wichita Eagle-Beacon*, October 30, 1988.

40. Cece Todd, "Funding Would Help Lower Property Taxes," *Pittsburg Morning Sun*, November 11, 1988.

41. Alan Stolfus, "KNEA Pushes Change in School Funding," *Salina Journal*, January 4, 1989.

42. Karen McClain France, "Classification Could Backfire," *Topeka Capital-Journal*, January 8, 1989.

43. Quoted in Roger Myers, "Demos Seek to Ease Property Tax Hikes for the Poor," *Topeka Capital-Journal*, February 1, 1989.

44. Quoted in David Toplikar, "Legislators Brace for Reappraisal Outcry," *Lawrence Journal-World*, February 7, 1989.

45. *Wichita Eagle-Beacon*, "Avoid Haste on Classification," March 12, 1989, editorial.

46. *Kansas City Times* editorial, "No Reversing Reappraisal," March 13, 1989.

47. Alissa Rubin, "Ire Marks Hearing on Taxes," *Wichita Eagle-Beacon*, March 22, 1989.

48. Ibid.

49. Quoted in Martin Hawver, "Reappraisal 'Winners' Oppose Delay in Property Classification," *Topeka Capital-Journal*, March 23, 1989.

50. John Marshall, "Government by Arrangement," *Parsons Sun*, March 22, 1989.

51. By this point in the session, one Democratic member of the House had switched party affiliation and begun to caucus with the Republicans, thus reducing the Democratic membership from its initial fifty-eight.

52. Quotations from floor debate, March 28, 1989. These issues would become linked three years later when the 1992 legislature passed (1) a school finance bill that sharply cut property taxes across the state; (2) slightly increased corporate taxes as part of the funding package; and, on the same day, (3) endorsed a constitutional amendment that would modify the classification levels for various categories of real estate.

53. Lew Ferguson, "School Funds to Final Vote," *Pittsburg Morning Sun*, March 30, 1989.

54. This figure would have been $14 million if two-year averaging had not been adopted.

55. Diane Silver, "Safety Net for Schools Gets First OK," *Wichita Eagle-Beacon*, March 30, 1989. Braden offered a version of the governor's plan to the House; it was defeated 100–21. Although an extreme example, the defeat of the governor's plan demonstrates the continuing inability of the governor and his chief legislative leaders to control results on the House floor.

56. Michael Horak, "Senate Panel Cuts Property Tax Relief Fund," *Lawrence Journal-World*, April 25, 1989.

CHAPTER 8. ENDGAME I: HIGHWAYS

1. John Kingdon, *Agendas, Alternatives, and Public Policies* (Boston: Little, Brown, 1984), p. 1.

2. Hayden interview, August 22, 1989.

3. John Marshall, "K-61 Symbolic of Road Dreams Going Nowhere," *Salina Journal*, September 25, 1988.

4. In 1986, Hayden also chaired a Public Agenda Commission that endorsed substantial highway spending. His first secretary of administration, Ed Flentje, served as the commission's staff director and generally favored the highway program as well.

5. Flentje interview, July 12, 1989. Various observers saw Flentje as pushing the special session idea in the wake of the January conference, but both he and the governor argue that it was the latter's call.

6. See Jack Walker, "Setting the Agenda in the U.S. Senate," *British Journal of Political Science* 7 (October 1977): 423-445.

7. *Garden City Telegram* editorial, "Highway Cavalry," December 15, 1988.

8. Kingdon, *Agendas*, pp. 134-138.

9. Flentje interview.

10. Interview with Chris Beal, administrative assistant to House Majority Leader Robert H. Miller, June 6, 1989.

11. Kingdon, *Agendas*, p. 184ff.

12. Burdett Loomis, "Groups and the Grassroots," in Allan J. Cigler and Burdett A. Loomis, eds., *Interest Group Politics* (Washington, D.C.: CQ Press, 1983), pp. 169-190.

13. Interview with Department of Transportation analyst Deb Miller, October 24, 1989.

14. Lew Ferguson, "Highway Promotion Organization to Propose No Specific Program," *Topeka Capital-Journal*, October 10, 1988.

15. Martin Hawver, "Lawmakers Urged Not to Squabble on Road Plan," *Topeka Capital-Journal*, August 23, 1988.

16. "A Noble Search," *Hutchinson News*, October 27, 1988.

17. *The Kansas Highway System*, Central Research Corporation, Wichita, Kans., December 1988, p. 4.

18. "Action Will Drain Highway Fund by 1991," *Hutchinson News*, July 1, 1988.

19. Lew Ferguson, "Strategy behind Fight for Highways," *Wichita Eagle-Beacon*, May 7, 1989. Ferguson, the AP bureau chief in Topeka and a veteran statehouse reporter, gave the lion's share of credit to Senators Morris and Francisco and Representative Crowell. My conclusion is that they were important, but not all important.

20. The actual cost of the proposal remained open to interpretation. The AP's John Hanna used a $2.13 million figure, while Roger Myers of the *Topeka Capital-Journal* referred to a $2.34 million plan. The *Wichita Eagle-Beacon* rounded it off at $2 million. All of these had some basis in reality, but given length of the program and questions about revenue and matching funds, no one figure seems clearly correct.

21. Quoted in "Edwards Defends Road Figures," *Parsons Sun,* February 26-27, 1989.

22. Quoted in ibid. Spaniol eventually did request the Legislative Post-Audit Committee to meet and seek a report on the DOT figures. The report noted that DOT numbers had been consistent, given relatively modest changes in economic assumptions. Spaniol, as a dissident Republican, may have also been motivated to force a meeting of the Post-Audit Committee (which had not met), in part because of the

leadership's unwillingness to have rebel Rep. David Miller elected as its chair (see Chapter 5).

23. All quotes from Pat Hurley and Pete McGill come from personal interviews, October 16, 1990, unless otherwise noted.

24. Roger Myers, "Highway Panel Stuck in Neutral," *Topeka Capital-Journal*, March 1, 1989.

25. Al Polczinski and Lori Linenberger, "Hayden Still Hopeful on Road Plan," *Wichita Eagle-Beacon*, March 2, 1989.

26. Lew Ferguson, "Hayden Puts Highway Plan at Distance," *Topeka Capital-Journal*, March 2, 1989.

27. Except where noted, the following discussion derives from personal observations at the Republican caucus on the morning of the initial highway debate. At about 8:30 A.M. on most legislative days both House parties hold open caucuses, which provide the only forum for the entire party to hash out the issues of the day. The discussions are reasonably frank, given the presence of the press. Closing the meetings would seem a reasonable action, but experience has taught the leaders that the leaked contents of the caucuses can cause more problems than allowing the press to attend. In the years since 1989, Republicans have sometimes closed their meetings, especially when divisive issues were discussed.

28. The rebel Republicans consistently opposed bonding during this session, both for roads and prisons. The quality of debate on bonding questions in both chambers was often simplistic; the alleged expense of bonding was the main objection of these conservatives. Much of their fire was concentrated on the governor; embarrassing him seemed a more important goal than obtaining specific policy ends.

29. Martin Hawver, "Highway Plan Forwarded to Senate," *Topeka Capital-Journal*, March 18, 1989.

30. Roger Myers, "House Approves Road Work Plan," *Topeka Capital-Journal*, March 17, 1989.

31. Martin Hawver, "State Highway Bill Starts at $2.8 Billion," *Topeka Capital-Journal*, March 25, 1989.

32. Deb Miller interview, September 24, 1989.

33. "Roads to Future," *Wichita Eagle-Beacon* editorial, April 27, 1989.

34. Quoted in Lori Linenberger, "House-Senate Clash on Roads Shapes Up," *Wichita Eagle-Beacon*, March 28, 1989.

35. Personal interview, anonymity guaranteed.

36. Historically, the legislature came together to override gubernatorial vetoes — hence the term "veto session." By 1989, however, this session was regularly used to pass new legislation, and many participants had begun to label it the "wrap-up session."

37. Although the salami metaphor came to mind during the proceedings, I could find no reference to such a tactic. However, on February 3, 1993, the *New York Times* reported that Israeli Prime Minister Rabin explained his compromise on exiled Palestinians in this way: "These are not salami tactics — it's a package deal."

38. On conference committees in the U.S. Congress, see Lawrence Longley and Walter Oleszek, *Bicameral Politics: Conference Committees in Congress* (New Haven, Conn.: Yale University Press, 1989); and David Vogler, *The Third House: Conference Committees in the U.S. Congress* (Evanston, Ill.: Northwestern University Press, 1970).

39. Lori Linenberger, "Senate OKs Bill on Roads," *Wichita Eagle-Beacon*, April 28, 1989.

40. "Take the Honors," May 17, 1989.

41. In an interview on October 24, 1989, DOT analyst Deb Miller noted, in particular, an Iowa study that found few economic development benefits. Such evidence was generally ignored by highway proponents, who expressed their unwavering belief in the economic development potential.

42. Deb Miller interview.

43. Despite some protestations, the fact is that the spending was truly substantial. The $2.65 billion cost amounted to approximately $1,000 per capita, over eight years.

44. Jim Maag interview, November 14, 1989.

45. My thanks to Tom Sloan for bringing this interpretation to my attention.

46. Maag interview, November 14, 1989.

47. On the Senate side, Hayden aide David Mills, a former legislator, proved a consistently effective liaison; the governor had no equivalent presence in the House, which was a much more difficult environment in any event.

CHAPTER 9. ENDGAMES II: PREPARATION AND EXHAUSTION

1. The following quotations are from personal interviews with Braden, Burke, and Hayden.

2. See Aaron Wildavsky, *The Politics of the Budgetary Process* (Boston: Little, Brown, 1964); Richard F. Fenno, Jr., *The Power of the Purse* (Little, Brown, 1966); and Ira Sharkansky, *Routines of Politics* (Chicago: Rand McNally, 1970), for various examples of these legislative bargaining strategies.

3. Maag interview, November 14, 1989.

4. See John Kingdon, *Agendas, Alternatives, and Public Policies* (Boston: Little, Brown, 1984).

5. Vickie L. Walton and Randell Beck, "Prison Package May Finally Put Kansas On the Right Road," *Kansas City Star*, May 5, 1988.

6. Ibid.

7. "The Reluctant Bridegroom," *Emporia Gazette* editorial, May 5, 1988.

8. Walton and Beck, "Prison package."

9. John Petterson, "Firm Hired to Provide Prison Facilities," *Kansas City Times*, May 18, 1988.

10. See Paul Schulman, *Large-Scale Policy-Making* (New York: Elsevier, 1980).

11. John Hanna, "Task Force Endorses Expansion of Local Corrections Program," *Topeka Capital-Journal*, August 10, 1988.

12. John Hanna, "State Must Move Quickly to Comply With Court Order, Prison Chief Says," *Topeka Capital-Journal*, July 19, 1988.

13. These issues were not new; many had been raised by a special corrections committee in 1987/88, chaired by Senate President Robert Talkington.

14. "Hayden to Push Prisons," *Wichita Eagle-Beacon*, August 31, 1988.

15. Ibid.

16. John Hanna, "Testimony Ends in Suit By Inmates," *Topeka Capital-Journal*, October 27, 1988.

17. Kingdon, *Agendas*, p. 88ff.

18. "Progress on Prisons," *Wichita Eagle-Beacon* editorial, November 21, 1988.

19. Diane Silver, "Judge Orders Prison Depopulation," *Wichita Eagle-Beacon*, February 16, 1989.

20. Lynn Byczynski, "Kansas' Choice: Build Prisons or Free Inmates," *Kansas City Times*, February 16, 1989.

21. Lori Linenberger, "Larned Inmate Proposal Questioned," *Wichita Eagle-Beacon*, March 15, 1989.

22. John Hanna, "$18 Million Added to Expected Prison Building Plan," *Topeka Capital-Journal,* March 15, 1989.

23. Roger Myers, "House Rejects Proposal to Construct Big Prison," *Topeka Capital-Journal*, April 2, 1989.

24. Alissa Rubin, "Prison Bill Rejected by House," *Wichita Eagle-Beacon*, April 27, 1989.

25. David Miller interview, June 22, 1989.

26. In addition, the Senate continued to reject a "prevailing wage" construction standard, which added one more bone of contention to the conference proceedings.

27. Phil Jurik, "Judge Likes Plan for New Prison," *Kansas City Star*, May 23, 1989.

28. Robert H. Miller interview, July 12, 1989.

29. Lori Linenberger, "Ethics Concerns Overflow in Bills," *Wichita Eagle-Beacon*, February 9, 1989.

30. Jim Sullinger, "State's Campaign Reform Efforts Criticized," *Kansas City Star*, May 17, 1989.

31. Diane Silver, "Finance Reports Snag on Details," *Wichita Eagle-Beacon*, May 24, 1989.

32. See Murray Edelman, *The Symbolic Uses of Politics* (Urbana: University of Illinois Press, 1964).

33. Eric Yost interview, June 5, 1991.

34. Lynn Byczynski, "Kansas Legislators Say Action Urgent," *Kansas City Times*, Janaury 31, 1989.

35. See Kingdon, *Agendas*, p. 181ff.

36. *Report on Kansas Legislative Interim Studies* (Topeka, Kans.: Legislative Research Department, December 1988), p. 171.

37. Letter to the editor, *Wichita Eagle-Beacon*, March 3, 1989.

38. Roger Myers, "Water Plan Calls for Hike in Taxes, Fees," *Topeka Capital-Journal*, October 29, 1988.

39. Dave Ranney, "Water Projects Get Some Money, But Not As Much As Needed," *Hutchinson News*, May 19, 1988.

40. Roger Myers, "State Water Official Warns of Long-term Shortage," *Topeka Capital-Journal*, June 26, 1988.

41. "Drought Advisers Plan for Shortage of Water in Spring," *Salina Journal*, January 17, 1989.

42. Sharon Montague, "Hayden Views Effects of Drought," *Salina Journal,* March 14, 1989.

43. See, generally, Murray Edelman, *Political Language* (New York: Academic Press, 1978).

44. "Water Cleanup is State's Job," *Wichita Eagle-Beacon* editorial, February 14, 1989.

45. Alissa Rubin, "House to Pay for Water Plan from User Fees, General Fund," *Wichita Eagle-Beacon*, February 21, 1989. Ironically, the House approved by design a proposal very close to one it had endorsed by accident three days earlier when Republican Rep. Susan Roenbaugh offered an amendment that added $6 million in general revenue funds while cutting various user fees. At that point the House did not understand what it was voting on, and subsequently reversed the decision. The Rezac amendment kept the fees but added the $6 million in general revenues.

46. Matt Truell, "Farm Groups Present Solid Wall against Water Plan Funding Bill," *Topeka Capital-Journal*, March 22, 1989; Lynn Byczynski, "Water Tax Plan Stalled in Senate Committee," *Kansas City Times*, March 25, 1989.

47. Interview with Joe Harkins, September 17, 1991.

48. In particular, the Farm Bureau had angered many legislators with its February 1989 newsletter, which bluntly and selfishly challenged the plan's costs to the agricultural community. Most legislators saw the Farm Bureau as having exercised inordinate power over the years, and its seeming unwillingness to budge was viewed with hostility in many quarters.

49. "Panel's Action May Kill Water Project Funds," *Lawrence Journal-World*, April 28, 1989.

50. Alissa Rubin, "Legislators Try to Save Water Bill," *Wichita Eagle-Beacon*, April 4, 1989.

51. Alissa Rubin, "Financing OKd for Water Plan," *Wichita Eagle Beacon*, May 3, 1989.

52. Ibid. Senator Moran's action demonstrated both his own ingratitude and the governor's political weakness. Hayden had acceded to Moran's choice of Larned as the site for the new prison facilities for the mentally ill. Nevertheless, Hayden could not persuade Moran to provide the twenty-first vote, even though the senator generally supported the water plan and the agricultural interests in his district would experience only a modest hike in fees.

53. "Ailing Senator's 120-mph Ride Got Him to the Vote on Time," *Lawrence Journal-World*, May 3, 1989.

54. Ibid.

CHAPTER 10. TIME AFTER TIME

1. *Wichita Eagle-Beacon* editorial, "A Superb Session," May 4, 1989.

2. *Kansas City Times* editorial, "A Good Kansas Session," May 4, 1989.

3. David Awbrey, "Kansas Catharsis," *Wichita Eagle-Beacon*, May 7, 1989.

4. All quotes in this section not footnoted come from public comments at the end of the legislative session personally recorded by the author.

5. Lew Ferguson, "Hayden Believes Re-election in '90 All But in the Bag," *Garden City Telegraph*, May 6, 1989.

6. Much of the information in this section is derived from Alissa Rubin's extensive report, "Your Property Taxes," in the *Wichita Eagle-Beacon*, December 18, 1988.

7. The legislature did not pass any substantial property tax relief measures in 1990, thus exacerbating Hayden's problems.

8. Many local analysts attributed Hayden's defeat to a personal style that did not allow for much adaptation. To the extent this was true, it demonstrates further limits to the idea of acting as a flexible "strategic politician."

9. Labeled the "Killer B's" by capitol wags.

10. Confidential Tabular Report, May 1989, Kansas Poll, Public Opinion Research, p. xii.

11. Ibid., p. xiv.

12. Ibid., p. xviii.

13. Penn-Schoen poll, June 1989, executive summary, p. 15, emphasis in original.

14. Sebelius interview, June 15, 1989.

15. A minority of legislative Democrats did strongly support the highway package. Those from Southeast Kansas and a few other pockets had strong local and regional reasons for doing so.

16. John Petterson, "GOP, Democrats See Gain in Session," *Kansas City Times*, May 4, 1989.

17. Mike Hayden interview, August 22, 1989.

18. "A Superb Session," *Wichita Eagle-Beacon*, May 4, 1989.

19. Wagnon interview, June 15, 1989.

20. Personal interview, anonymity guaranteed.

21. David Miller interview, June 22, 1989.

22. Patrick interview, February 24, 1991.

23. Miller did not leave politics, however. By 1992/93 he had helped organize religious right and antiabortion forces in a strong effort to win control of the Kansas Republican party and to recruit conservative candidates for the legislature.

24. Long interview, February 24, 1991.

25. Alan Rosenthal, *Governors and Legislatures* (Washington, D.C.: CQ Press, 1990), pp. 53–54.

26. Paul Light, *The President's Agenda* (Baltimore, Md.: Johns Hopkins University Press, 1982).

27. Rosenthal, *Governors and Legislatures*, p. 54.

28. This limitation may simply encourage students of political actors to take seriously the multidimensional perspectives on goals, incentives, and motivations as put forward by Richard Fenno, Glenn Parker, and Douglas Arnold, among others.

CHAPTER 11. REFLECTIONS ON POLITICAL TIME

1. Governor Hayden and others frequently argued that the income tax cuts would be worth only about $65 annually to Kansas residents, but this average figure masked the major impact a reduction would have on high-income taxpayers, who resided disproportionately in Johnson County.

2. John Kingdon, *Agendas, Alternatives, and Public Policies* (Boston: Little, Brown, 1984), p. 215.

3. This may be especially true in states that have little history of calling special sessions. In Kansas, despite two recent such sessions, it is not usually a case of "it ain't over till it's over." Rather, when the regular session concludes, traditionally there's no going back into special session.

4. On entrepreneurs, see Kingdon, *Agendas*, p. 188ff. On discretionary policy, see Jack Walker, "Setting the Agenda in the U.S. Senate," *British Journal of Political Science* 7 (1977): 432–445.

5. Jeffery Birnbaum and Alan Murray, *Showdown at Gucci Gulch* (New York: Random House, 1987); see also Timothy J. Conlan, Margaret T. Wrightson, and David R. Beam, *Taxing Choices* (Washington, D.C.: CQ Press, 1990).

6. See, in general, Carl E. Van Horn, ed., *The State of the States*, 2d ed. (Washington, D.C.: CQ Press, 1992).

7. Van Horn, "The New Storm over the States," in Van Horn, ed., *The State of the States,* p. 217.

8. Ibid..

9. Larry Sabato, *Good-Bye to Good-time Charlie* (Washington, D.C.: CQ Press, 1983), 2d ed.; Alan Rosenthal, *Governors and Legislatures* (Washington, D.C.: CQ Press, 1990).

10. Van Horn, "The New Storm over the States," p. 222.

11. Kingdon does discuss "randomness and pattern" (pp. 216–217) but does not emphasize repetition or the power of long-term trends and deadlines. Rather, he notes various criteria that limit randomness within each of his streams and what may encourage or impede coupling of the streams.

Index